Steely Eyed Killers of the Deep

A collection of Sea Stories,
Memories, Musings, and More
Written by Crew Members of
USS NAUTILUS (SSN-571)

Copyright © 2013 by Tommy Robinson
First Edition – November 2013

ISBN
978-1-4602-3325-2 (Paperback)
978-1-4602-3326-9 (eBook)

All rights reserved.

No part of this publication may be reproduced in any form, or by any means, electronic or mechanical, including photocopying, recording, or any information browsing, storage, or retrieval system, without permission in writing from the publisher.

Produced by:

FriesenPress
Suite 300 – 852 Fort Street
Victoria, BC, Canada V8W 1H8

www.friesenpress.com

Distributed to the trade by The Ingram Book Company

Table of Contents

Foreward vii

Preface ix

1 - CDR Eugene "Dennis" Wilkinson *and* Plank Owners 1

2 - CDR William R. "Bill" Anderson *and* PANOPO'S 43

3 - CDR Lando Zech, Jr. *and* Lando's Commandos 77

4 - CDR Jeffrey "Jeff" C. Metzel, Jr. *and* Crew 105

5 - CDR Francis "Frank" Fogarty, USN *and* Crew 111

6 - CDR Norman "Earl" E. Griggs, USN *and* Crew 149

7 - CDR David "Duke" S. Cockfield, USN *and* Crew 159

8 - CDR Alex Anckonie, III, USN *and* Crew 177

9 - CDR Richard "Dick" A. Riddell *and* Decommissioning Crew 193

10 - Flotsam & Jetsam *or* Miscellaneous Submarine Stuff . . 209

11 - Eulogies and Tributes 231

12 - Nautilus Time Line 253

Tommy Robinson

Cover painting courtesy of *Nautilus* crew member and artist Lieutenant Commander Frank Bonaquisti, Jr., USN, Ret.

Commanding officer photographs courtesy of archivist Wendy Gully, Naval Submarine Library and Museum, Groton, CT.

Steely Eyed Killers of the Deep

In memory of our shipmate extraordinaire,
Commander Alfred "Al" Charette, USN, Ret.,
a pioneering submariner and
a driving force in writing this book.

"Inside every old sailor is a very young sailor wondering what the hell happened! Also, it has been proven by poll after poll, some at the Gallup, that old sailors have been known to remember, in greater and greater detail, as times goes on, circumstances about events that may NEVER have happened!

I just can't wait to read, hear and witness more stories than anyone can believe ever happened to just one submarine crew. The First & Finest Submarine crew! Can you all imagine what stories must be bouncing off the walls of Davy Jones Locker where all our shipmates on eternal patrol reside?"

Al

Foreward

Did you know that submarine sailors are professionals at telling sea stories?

This is primarily because of the closed environment that we live in. The people tank, about 300 feet long and about 25 feet in diameter, is our home away from home, beneath the sea. Being cramped in a tube with 100 other awful smelling sailors whose odors combine with other chemicals in that closed environment has special effects on us.

It is the amine, battery acid, carbon dioxide, carbon monoxide, cooking oils, diesel fumes, freon, grease, hydraulic oil, hydrogen, ozone, salt water, venting sanitary tank inboard, sweat and other equally nostril burning odors that tend to get into our blood streams, maybe by osmosis, and affects our aging brains.

After a few drinks, these effects tend to increase geometrically and because of radiation on nuclear submarines, these effects also increase exponentially. In any case, we submarine sailors, find this phenomenon as enhancing our ability to remember more, in greater detail, sometimes in color, about events of the past, which are our sea stories.

Some of these stories take on a life of their own. This is NOT lying, stretching the truth, or even embellishment. It is simply increasing the quality of the story and there is nothing better than a quality sea story!

We believe these stories to be true and even more so with each telling. It will be a fun time when we all gather together and try to extract the real truth from the real sea story.

Jules Verne said, *"What one man can imagine, another can achieve."*

I say, *"What one submarine sailor can imagine and tell in great detail, another submarine sailor can corroborate, expand and improve on, in much greater detail."*

Alfred "Al" Charette - Who claims to be the biggest wart of all.

Preface

Submarine sailors are notorious for seeking diversion from daily submarine routine. Sometimes the diversion is in the form of a simple joke or it can be a much more elaborate scheme. We have been known to do just about anything for a good laugh ... even at the expense of a fellow shipmate. All in good fun, of course.

This book contains a loose collection of Sea Stories and Memories written by crew members of USS *Nautilus* (SSN-571). They are arranged, as best possible, in chronological order from her commissioning in 1954 to her decommissioning in 1980.

Be aware, these articles were written by submariners for submariners and some may contain "salty" language. Some are funny while others focus on more serious events. Of course, many years have passed since these events occurred so a few cobwebs had to be swept aside in order to remember and pen "the way it was – warts and all." These stories are a true reflection of the author's experiences.

We hope that things we did both officially and unofficially, the escapades of the "Big N's" crew members are captured in these pages.

The original instigators and force behind this project are:

Al Charette, John Yuill, Barry Danforth, Reds Knouse, David Ross, George Clancy, Gordy Roberts, Gary Brown, Mike Harmody, Wayne Hock, Chris Pauli, and Joe Degnan

The stories were collected and compiled by:
Tommy Robinson

1 - CDR Eugene "Dennis" Wilkinson *and* Plank Owners

September 1954 – June 1957

1954 – Aggravate

When a navy ship goes into commission, it is assigned a voice call. The voice call comes out of a book and cannot be a call that has already been assigned. My voice call on *Volador* was Pokeweed. We made Pokeweed a known name in the Western Pacific with the anti-submarine forces, but it wasn't as grand as my voice call on *Wahoo*, which was Old Ace. When I got to *Nautilus*, the voice call assigned was Club Moss and I hated it. I didn't want to keep referring to myself as Club Moss, so I decided what the hell, I would get it changed before we even went into commission.

My officers and I looked through the book at all the voice calls that weren't assigned. Lieutenant Carr, whose wife's name was Molly, really wanted me to put in for Molly Moe, but I didn't do that. The call that I liked and that seemed best for *Nautilus* was Aggravate. I wrote a letter to the CNO, as voice calls were under his office, and requested that my voice call be changed from Club Moss to Aggravate. The letter went up the chain of command and struck a nerve when it reached the Commander in Chief Atlantic Fleet. I don't know what his voice call was, but it obviously annoyed him because in his forwarding endorsement he wrote, *"Forwarded, recommended, and what's more I don't like my voice call either and I want it changed!"*

So before *Nautilus* was built, we got our voice call changed, and over the years Aggravate proved to be a good call. We probably aggravated quite a few ships that we were in contact with while operating against the evaluation forces. At least we tried our hardest to.

Eugene "Dennis" Wilkinson, '53 – '57

1954 – AWOL for Launching

One day in Idaho Falls, Idaho there was a party. Can you believe that? Otto Wepler attended the party and partied too much. The next morning he overslept and missed the bus to the site. He was driving himself there and fell asleep at the wheel. Otto ran into a ditch and took out a power pole along with power to the site. The site went down and Otto ended up in a body cast in the local hospital.

As a result, he missed the launching of *Nautilus*. Several other crew members also missed the launching for other reasons. A group from

Idaho were snowed in at Chicago's O'Hare Airport and Lieutenant Ken Carr was snowed in, somewhere in Virginia.

Alfred "Al" Charette, '57 - '61

1954 – Unexpected Overnight Liberty

Some of the men who were training at the Idaho site, including myself, received an unexpected overnight liberty in Chicago the night before *Nautilus* was launched. We wore civilian clothing and we were flown from Idaho to Chicago, Illinois in a fancy passenger plane, under control of the the Chicago area Admiral. We were treated as guests of honor on the plane by the enlisted Stewards until they learned that we were all enlisted men too and not nuclear physicists. They still treated us well. However, on the remaining flight to Chicago, we had to get our own coffee and snacks from the galley. Our plane was grounded in Chicago due to bad weather. We were all granted overnight liberty in Chicago and that was the closest we got to the Connecticut launching. The next morning we watched the *Nautilus* launching ceremonies on television.

After the launching we were loaded into an old DC-8 airplane and flown back to Idaho. On the return flight no one offered to serve us coffee. I have to admit that this was the furthest I have ever travelled for an over night liberty.

William "Bill" O'Halloran, '54 - '55

1954 – Plank Owners and Asbestos

I left the USS *Sea Cat* (SS-399) for detached duty with the Atomic Energy Commission (AEC) to train for *Nautilus* in 1953. I first trained at Bettis Field in Pittsburgh, Pennsylvania followed by training at the National Reactor Training Station (NRTS) later called S1W in Idaho. It was at these training facilities that I met Leroy Engles, Ed Davis and Al Lewis along with a group of other fine men. Al Lewis, Ed Daisey, Bob Moran and myself rented a place together in Blackfoot, Idaho.

In May 1954 I reported for duty to *Nautilus*, which was still under construction, and I served on board until Thanksgiving Day 1955. I noted both Leroy and Al had an asbestosis condition and now wonder how many other Plank Owners have had that problem. Me? They say, *"It's probably summer asthma?"* During construction, beyond being placed in "service," and up to commissioning we crew members literally waded in a sea of shredded and torn sheets of asbestos strewn throughout the Reactor Compartment and Engine Room. Some asbestos was tracked throughout the boat. What a mess!

James "Jim" Herwig, '54 – '55

1954 – The Early Days

In May 1952 I was ordered from USS *Cusk* (SSG-348) to Pittsburgh, Pennsylvania for the first atomic submarine, USS *Nautilus* (SSN-571). It was required that my wife Marilyn and I both be third generation Americans and cleared by the FBI. We had a good laugh at being ordered to Pittsburgh. The previous year while driving through Pittsburgh on Route 30 en route to gyro-compass school in Washington, DC we were halted at a stop light during several light changes and the smoke from the steel mills was very thick and dirty. We said we were sure glad there was no Navy in Pittsburgh. One year later we were there!

There were 28 enlisted men and two officers in our class. Five Plank Owners came from *Cusk*. We attended school in an old farmhouse at the Betties Field Airport that had been converted into a nuclear design and manufacturing facility by Westinghouse Atomic Power Division. We went six days and two nights a week to Duquesne University to study and steam generators and turbines. We also had lots of homework. In order to help our studies, six of us rotated apartments. The wives and kids would visit, vacating an apartment, so the men could have peace and quiet and help each other study. This was very hard on our families but we continued from June 1952 to March 1953 at which time we were transferred to the *Nautilus* prototype in Arco, Idaho.

Many of us lived in Idaho Falls and travelled by bus 54 miles each way to the site. During special test periods we stayed on site in Quonset huts. We continued academic training, kept regular submarine qualifying notebooks, and drew system schematics along with gaining actual experience operating the first power-producing reactor.

In October 1952 the Canadians melted down a reactor inside an airtight building at Chalk River, Ontario. They requested help to decontaminate the area. They did not have enough nuclear cleared or trained people. So, in February 1953, us *Nautilus* NUCs [nuclear trained] went to help. We also received training in actual high level decontamination. The quarterly dose then was 3,900 millirem per quarter. It's now reduced to 1,500 per year. Most of us received over 3,000 for the week that we were there. I received 4,100 millirem, most of it in about 45 seconds, while working a cutting machine on top of the reactor.

I was promoted to Electrician's Mate 1st/class, assigned to the Reactor Control gang, and then sent to the Bailey Meters Plant in Cleveland, Ohio to learn the pneumatic control system which was part of the automatic reactor rod controls. The pneumatic control system also controlled the hot well levels of the reactor coolant pumps and the ships service and main propulsion turbines. In January 1954, while still in Idaho, the Navy flew most of us back East to participate in the launching of *Nautilus*, but adverse weather grounded us in Chicago where we watched it on television.

The leading Chief Electronics Technician was promoted to Ensign which created a vacancy for a Reactor Operator (RO) so I commenced training to be an RO. I was the seventh man in the Navy to qualify as RO and ninth to qualify in nuclear submarines. We made history in Idaho when we did a full power simulated run to London, England using the water brake as a submarine screw. It, in fact, was the first power producing reactor.

In 1954 I transferred to *Nautilus,* in her final stages of construction, and assisted in the final testing of all systems; mechanical, electrical, pneumatics, rod control, etc. The boat was commissioned in September 1954 and we finally went to sea in January 1955. I was advanced to Chief Electrician's Mate in February and in November 1955 I transferred to the Navy's first Nuclear Power School at Groton, Connecticut. I helped establish the school by developing lesson plans and instructing.

Irwin "Bruce" Pierson, '54 - '55

1954 – A New Order of Atomic Sailors

The commissioning crew was known as:	
The Atom	– Commanding Officer
The Nucleus	– Wardroom
Protons	– Chief Petty Officers
Neutrons	– Petty Officers
Electrons	– Seaman and Fireman

Excerpt from the Commissioning Brochure

1954 – Executive Officer Memo #3

Lieutenant Dean Axene's Executive Officer Memo #3 dated November 9, 1954 established the policy for qualification in nuclear submarines. All Plank Owners were submarine qualified (in diesel submarines) when selected for the commissioning crew. New non-qualified crew members were assigned later. The following Plank Owners were designated as compartment instructors:

Compartment – Instructor

Torpedo Room and Fwd Crew's Quarters – Fields, G.W., Daisey, E.J.
Crew's Quarters, Galley and Mess Decks, Battery Tank – Baird, J.L.
Officer's Quarters – Baird, J.L.
Attack Center, Sonar Room, ECM Bay, Periscope Center – O'Brien, F., Armstrong, J.W.
Control Room, Radio Room, Radar Room – Welper, O.H.
Amidships Auxiliary Machinery Space – Welper, O.H.
Reactor Compartment – Mixon, R.I., Foster, R.V., Hughes, R.C., Graham, O.A., Ringer, R.G.
Engine Room, Maneuvering Room – McNamara, L.V., Gates, G.H., Morrissey, J.H., Reece, T.C.
Stern Room and Aft Auxiliary Machinery Space – McGovern, J.P.
Topside and Bridge – Watkins, P.G.

When the crew of *Nautilus* was selected there was an equal rate assortment in the crew; one Chief, one First Class, one Second Class, one Third Class Petty Officer and it was pretty much the same in other ratings. However, when *Nautilus* went to sea the first time, the numbers were more like; 20 Chiefs, 30 First Class, 20 Second Class, 25 Third Class Petty Officers. The remaining were Fireman/Seaman and most of the Third Class Petty Officers were Mess Cooks at one time or other.

Torpedoman's Mate 1st/class George W. Fields was the first enlisted crew member to be qualified in nuclear submarines and Electronic's Technician 1st/class Edward M. "Mike" Lovejoy was the first enlisted to qualify as Reactor Operator.

Thomas "Tom" Brames, '54 – '56

When I reported on board, March 16, 1957, we were certainly top heavy. There were 17 Chiefs and I was number 67 of the First Class Petty Officers. Of course at the time we were heavily involved in training and crew turnover. Crew members were being relieved rather quickly.

Alfred "Al" Charette, '57—'60

1954 – *Nautilus* and the Ship's Patch

I served on board *Nautilus* with an exceptional crew of officers and enlisted men who were as concerned with their shipmates' careers as they were their own, and the camaraderie they displayed, directly influenced my decision to make the Navy a career. *Nautilus* was nothing like the two diesel boats that I had previously served aboard. The boat was unique, and a true fighting machine. *Nautilus* had all the creature comforts the crew needed. We had a washing machine, a Crews Mess that could be transformed into a movie theater, a coin-operated soda machine, a jukebox, private fiberglass bunks with individual ventilation and bunk lights.

I enjoyed drawing cartoons and tried to document life aboard *Nautilus*. When Walt Disney Studios sent *Nautilus* their concept of what the ship's patch should look like, it was a version of the craft depicted in the movie, "Twenty Thousand Leagues Under the Sea." The crew thought that a different version would be more appropriate and asked me to provide a drawing representing our *Nautilus*. I drew my version and my artwork was sent to Walt Disney Studios. They embellished my drawing and it is now recognized as the official ship's patch. I'm extremely proud to have served on board *Nautilus* and enjoy taking friends through the boat. *Nautilus* will always have a place in my heart.

William "Bill" Engdall, '53 – '56

1954 – Liberty with JJK

My absolute best remembrance while on *Nautilus* is John J. Krawczyk. He was a remarkable man in so many ways. Not only did he take great pictures on board *Nautilus*, but also at all ship's social events, sports activities, and locations like Idaho Falls, Pittsburgh, New York, and every other place he or the boat visited.

After the launching, he, my wife Marilyn and I drove to New York City for a little R and R [Rest and Relaxation]. He somehow arranged to get to the very top of the building across the street from Saint Patrick's Cathedral in order to take a stunning picture of the front view and street at the Cathedral. Then he told us to wait for him at a small restaurant while he drove to the Brooklyn side of the East River, just to take a picture of the United Nations building. That little diversion took him nearly three hours; but he got a great picture.

John was just a fantastic person; quite, gentle, friendly and very aware of what *Nautilus* meant; much more than most of us. John was the last Plank Owner to leave *Nautilus* and he was presented with a bronze plaque engraved with all of the original crew members names. John was, indeed, Mr. *Nautilus!*

Thomas "Tom" Brames, '54 – '65

1954 – Lola

That wasn't her real name, only a nickname. She wasn't born with that moniker, but acquired it shortly after she fledged into the U.S. Submarine Fleet with her commissioning on September 30, 1954. Her real name was USS *Nautilus* (SSN-571), the world's first atomic powered ship – the "Atom" sub. I say atomic because that's the term that was used way back on January 21, 1954 when, as the brainchild of then Captain Hyman G. Rickover, she was launched down the ways of the Electric Boat Company. in Groton, Connecticut. Eventually the term atomic was replaced by nuclear to describe the type of power plant that drove this new kind of ship.

Being the new "Queen" of the submarine navy, she was lavished upon befitting any real live royalty. Her every whim was met, almost without question. However, the U.S. Navy had budgets to adhere to at every level of command and the submarine fleet was no exception. However, whatever *Nautilus* wanted or needed, she got, sometimes at the expense of other submarine's budgets. All of a sudden, along came this new-fangled boat with all its "hoop-la" and publicity, getting anything she wanted. That was not well received among the other submarines attached to the Sub Base in New London (Groton, CT), who sometimes had to exhort many means to gain equipment for their boats. Soon, *Nautilus* became known around the submarine fleet (at least around the Sub Base in New London) as, "Lola," after the song in which the lyrics claim, "Whatever Lola wants, Lola gets." It was a somewhat derogatory term, but to *Nautilus*, it mattered not. It could have been rumored that crew members were known to hum the tune while filling out supply requests. Who knows?

As in all of life, times change and things never stay as they once were. That was also true of *Nautilus*. As the years progressed after 1960, she matured into the submarine fleet and her assignments changed from the headline grabbing kind into more standard type of submarine operations. Also, as newer and more advanced nuclear subs came off the ways, they grabbed the headlines and notoriety. Slowly but surely, *Nautilus'* fame and fortune began to fade into memory as she aged. She was no longer known as "Lola," the submarine that got anything she asked for, but became just another submarine in the fleet that had needs like every other boat. After more than twenty-five years of service she had became an "old lady" whose parts, as they wore out, became increasingly difficult to replace. On March 3, 1980, she was decommissioned in Mare Island Naval Shipyard, her future, if any, to be determined.

Eventually, in 1982, she was designated a National Historic Landmark and on July 3, 1985, after an extensive conversion as a museum ship, she triumphantly returned to Groton, the place of her birth where she became the showcase of the Submarine Force Library and Museum. As such she will forever remain, "The First and Finest" of the nuclear submarine fleet. But in the hearts and minds of her early crew, she will continue to be fondly remembered as "Lola."

John "JC" Yuill, '57 – '60

Steely Eyed Killers of the Deep

1954 – E Street Motel

When those of us in Pittsburgh, were transferred to Idaho Falls, most of us stayed at the "E Street Motel." Probably a two star residence, but it was a great place for nightly parties in one room or another. It spawned lots of great memories. Ah yes, winter time, sailors in civvies [civilian clothes], loads of extra money to spend, friendly bars, and "other kinds of friendlies."

Being newly married my activities were somewhat different. HOWEVER, Idaho was a gambling state when we were there and slot machines were EVERYWHERE, in restaurants, grocery stores, gas stations, barber shops, etc. When I gave a clerk a ten dollar bill for a two dollar purchase I got back eight SILVER DOLLARS, there was hardly an exception anywhere. When Marilyn and I left Idaho Falls to fly to the east coast for the launching, we CASHED IN EVERY ONE OF THOSE SILVER DOLLARS; a little over 800 of them ... damn, damn, damn!

Thomas "Tom" Brames, '54 – '56

1954 – Ray Binn's Story

When *Nautilus* called for crew members I applied. I was amazed to get orders to a hanger at Bettis Field, Pennsylvania. The directions to the site were lacking. Our Yeoman said go to Pittsburgh, call a number for further directions, and wear civilian clothes. I finally made it to the old Bettis Airport, late at night, and was directed to a Quonset hut. Fortunately the guys already there knew where to go the next day. We met in the Dravosburg Volunteer Fire Department. We were in the fourth group to report and what a collection of Navy ratings we where!

Class convened in the Fire House and the auxiliary ladies prepared our lunch. Westinghouse engineers and local college professors taught us. "Doggie" Rayl, "Ski" Sarisky, Shelley Cole and me decided to stay in the Quonset hut. It was cheap living and we could walk to class. We ate well, "Doggie" and "Ski" had cars, and we helped each other with our studies.

I went home on leave and found it difficult to explain that I was going to submarine training in Idaho. People thought I had become addled. I took the train to Blackfoot, Idaho, a very small town, and stayed at The Grand Hotel which was built at the turn of the century. It had all the comforts a submarine sailor needs; the roof didn't leak, it had a communal head [toilet] for the whole floor, and it was located down town. We hung out at Snowballs, a combination restaurant, pool hall and bar, and we had bus service to the site. For extended operations we stayed on site in Quonset huts. I missed the bus two days in a row and was restricted to the site for two weeks. I learned reliability is a virtue! With no radio or television on site, I worked diligently on qualification.

After two months of training in Idaho, inter-laced with good liberty, I reported to *Nautilus* at Electric Boat (EB) shipyard. They put us engineering type single John's up in a work barge. That was okay except for weekends when they secured steam and we had no heat. Eventually another living barge from the reserve fleet was dragged up river which greatly improved our living conditions. My finances also improved. I was promoted to Engineman's Mate 2nd/class. The year of training and testing gave me hands-on experience and I gained additional knowledge from the senior guys that I was privileged to work alongside.

Two testing and operating events really stand out. I witnessed and documented the complete disassembly of the main coolant pumps due to a failure at the prototype in Idaho. I also witnessed a steam leak in the crossover line between the steam drums which John Morrissey calmly isolated which prevented severe injuries. The leak also lead to cutting out all steam piping down to the high pressure drains and installing an improved system.

Nautilus was commissioned, got "Underway on Nuclear Power," and did a high speed run to Puerto Rico. Then we ran up and down the east coast demonstrating *Nautilus'* considerable capabilities for senior Navy Officers, Congressmen, VIPs, and any other folks who may have doubted Admiral Rickover's nuclear vision. In December we entered EB for an upkeep. I was advanced to Engineman's Mate 1st/class and then with a complete lack of rationality I took a discharge from the Navy and fell directly into the depths of a recession but that's a whole different story.

Raymond "Ray" Binns, '54 – '55

1954 – the nautilus [Blue Book]

Bill Endall was the genius behind the various sketches and humorous captions in "the nautilus" a blue cruise book. The blue book is a pictorial and historical chronology of events between 1951 and 1957 of the "World's First Nuclear Powered Vessel," USS *Nautilus* (SSN-571). Of course, John Krawczyk also had a vision for the book long before it took shape and became reality. He wanted to chronicle every event and every crew member. Bill's artwork and John's photos made the book GREAT! We have nearly worn out the book over the years and continue to laugh remembering those events. I was fortunate to get autographs of nearly all of the men in that book; they signed their names below their pictures. Most were obtained at the ceremony making *Nautilus* "An Historic Landmark."

Thomas "Tom" Brames, '54 – '56

1955 – Plank Owner

During the first months of *Nautilus'* sea trials, a forward portion of the sail and section of the teak wood deck was torn away when we conducted a high speed submerged run. Little was made of the incident by most of the crew except Cook George Denny. George was an outstanding cook, great friend, a person with "unique and talented contacts at EB." He arranged, through a shipyard worker, to have those broken pieces of teak wood fashioned into a dozen small planks with an equal number of chrome-plated brass plates engraved and mounted on the wood. I don't know who else received a plank from George, but I was given one that I treasure deeply.

Although the tradition of "plank-ownership" dates back hundreds of years, it is today, mostly represented by a piece of paper stating such ownership. I can truly state, without an argument, that I am indeed a Plank Owner of *Nautilus*. Although my life after the Navy took many twists and turns, I find that I view myself much like a U.S. Marine does; "Once a marine, always a marine." In my case, "Once a *Nautilus* sailor, always a *Nautilus* sailor." It's as much a part of me as my bones.

Thomas "Tom" Brames, '54 – '56

1955 – Near Drowning

Captain Wilkinson surfaced *Nautilus* and announced the only swim call I ever remember while I was on the boat.

Tommy Robinson

I became incapacitated in the water and Ed Davis saved me from drowning. No one said a word that I recall. Swim call was cancelled and down we went - Dive! Dive!

Ed should have received a Life Saving Medal for his action but again no one said a word. I'm sorry that I did not speak up!

The Navy sent me back to Idaho where sage brush and the mountains got into my blood but the sea and salt water will never leave me alone.

James "Jim" Herwig, '54 – '55

1955 – Reporting for Duty

I reported for duty on November 17, 1955 as listed on my qualification card. Yes, I still have my qualification card. There's a lot of great memories just looking at the signatures: P.J. Boyle, Larry Harjgehausen, George Fields, Jim Brissette, Jim Armstrong, A.P. "Line Locker" Lewis, Bill Miller, Bobby Ringer, George Daisey, Ed Carlson, John Nicholson, Al Wood, Ken Carr, Ray Engle (Division Officer), and E.P. Wilkinson (Commanding Officer).

I graduated from sub school with Bill Brown, class #125, on November 10, 1955. I still have the class photo. I honestly can't recall if Denny Breese was one class ahead of me or one class behind. But, as I recall, Denny reported to *Nautilus* after Bill Brown and I did. I have to admit that after almost 57 years there area few things I can't accurately recall.

When I reported on board, I was assigned a bunking space on the work bench in a small work barge tied up forward of *Nautilus* at pier Charlie. There was a small bunk room but it was occupied by Petty Officers with no room for an apprentice non-qual [yet to be submarine qualified]. The bunks were taken by Ed Davis, Tom Deane, Jimmy Youngblood, Bob Simonini, "Bump" Hadley and a few others who were very intolerant of us non-quals. My blankets were nothing more than foul weather jackets that were strewn about. It was a cold tough holiday period, but character building as they say.

William "Bill" Gaines, '55 – '61

1955 – Spaghetti and Meatballs

Frequently a meal was prepared of spaghetti and meatballs plus salad, bread, etc. On one such occasion someone forgot to put grated Parmesan cheese on the tables. Someone went into the galley and came back with a small bowl of what looked exactly like the cheese. Several of us put some "cheese" on our food and started to eat it. Suddenly, someone yelled out, *"This ain't no f..k'in cheese."* But by that time several of us had already swallowed healthy portions. Very soon thereafter, I started to feel lousy, bolted to the head and deposited what was inside my stomach, into the toilet bowl. I suppose the word "stupid" comes very close to how I felt, but I was also thankful to whoever yelled the warning.

Thomas "Tom" Brames, '54 – '56

1955 – Early Qualification

A few weeks after the launching of USS *Nautilus* (SSN-571) a request was sent to the fleet requesting an Electrician's Mate 3rd/class already qualified in submarines and an Electrician's Mate 3rd/class just graduating from submarine school to volunteer for duty on *Nautilus*. The volunteer had to have a least two years remaining on their current enlistment. I extended my enlistment another year in order to be eligible. At this time I was serving on USS *Spikefish* (SS-404) as an Interior Communications Electrician's Mate 3rd/class. The reason for the request was to try and determine how long to make submarine school for nuclear powered submarines. The rest of the crew members went through training at the Westinghouse Atomic Power Division in Pittsburgh, Pennsylvania and the National Reactor Training Station in Arco, Idaho.

In order to qualify on a submarine you are required to make drawings of every system in each compartment and have them excepted by an enlisted man [qualification petty officer] then an officer. You are also required to understand every piece of equipment in each compartment and be able to operate it. You must be able to stand watch in each compartment. You have to demonstrate the above to an enlisted man and an officer then you must request the Executive Officer (XO) to walk you through the boat to be quizzed by him. When you satisfactorily pass his oral examination he will sign you off, certifying you as having "qualified" in nuclear powered submarines.

We were at sea when I completed all of the requirements and I ask Mr. Axene, the XO, to walk me through the boat. He said he had some paper work to do and he would take me when he was finished. When he finished I was on watch and could not go. During my watch someone else asked the XO for a walk through the boat. After my watch the XO then took me through and I became the third enlisted man to qualify in nuclear powered submarines. The first to qualify was Torpedoman's Mate 1st/class George W. Fields.

I have always been honored and proud to have had the chance to serve my country in the military, especially in the submarine service and on USS *Nautilus* (SSN-571).

Elmer Dering, '54 - '56

1955 – "Underway on Nuclear Power"

I have read in several places, that the historic message, "Underway on Nuclear Power," was sent to USS *Fulton* (AS-11). However, I have always heard it was sent to USS *Skylark* (ASR-20). I recently read in the blue cruise book that message was indeed sent to the *Skylark*. I have never understood, why it was sent by flashing light, as opposed to radio? Maybe Admiral Carr knows?

Alfred "Al" Charette, '57 - '61

The message was sent to *Skylark* by flashing light. As I remember, Ned Dietrich drafted the message and sent it up to the Bridge for Captain Wilkinson to release. Captain Wilkinson looked it over and commented, *"The CNO told us to get underway at 1100. We don't need to tell him we carried out his order on time."* He crossed out the time, then handed the message to "Doggie" Rayl to send by flashing light to *Skylark* for relay to the Chief of Naval Operations (CNO) [By radio].

Kenneth "Ken" Carr, '54 - '60

1955 – The Steam Leak Journal

The Steam Leak Journal [boats newsletter] was published at various times, depending on what tid-bits of information were uncovered, or when some major national or world event seemed to warrant it. There were about ten copies of each journal and all were on onion skin paper; then posted on a bulletin board or bulkhead, plus several copies for the Crews Mess and Wardroom.

Chief Radioman Lou Telles was the genius behind the paper's creation. Al Ferris was the designer and John Hendrickson and I were typists and general "snoops" along with anyone else that had a nosy trait. Here are a few excerpts from the Steam Leak Journal dated 14 July 1955:

National & World

New York – Catherine Kreitzer wins 32 grand on 64 G "TV" program!
London – Britain to explode "H" bomb!
Milwaukee – "Zooming Home Run!!" Stan "The Man's" biggest thrill in 12 "All Star" appearances!!
London – Hanged by the ... NECK ... Ruth Ellis!!
Washington – Oveta Culp Hobby resigns as Secretary of Health, Education and Welfare!
New York – Brooklyn Boy, Polio Vaccinated ... Dies!

Onboard Social

... What "Radcat" locally known as the "Big Bird" reports that he Can and Has taken it in his Stride?
... What Department is "delinquent" in Title "B" Cards and in what pile of deferred work are they lying under?? Those "Fast Neutrons" not acting fast enough, hey ... Mr. Cobean??
... All hands desperately await Miller's repeat performance of cooking some of that "delicious turkey gravy," most famously known in the Crews Mess as "chicken-a-la-king." Simonini hasn't quit blinking since he ate some of that stuff.
... R.R. Dunn recently reported the loss of one of his prize "wire" baskets to the COB. The basket marked "OUTGOING" evidently did just that. The market value of this basket was not the important thing to Bob. The basket was one of numbers he'd cached away for over a year and had become mighty attached to it. The Chiefs were very cooperative. The next day Dunn found 7 wire baskets in his bunk.
... Heard on the 7-MC: *"Control, Bridge Testing 7MC."* Control's response, *"Loud and Clear, Bridge."* Shortly after ward, on the 21MC from the Maneuvering Room, *"That last word came to you thru the courtesy of the "E" Div, Control."* Guess who the EOW was???
... A radio message just received from the Laundry Workers Local of Groton (LWLG) is a full fledged protest against "20 Horse-team

Borax" McFall. It seems like the youngster of yesteryear is taking laundry in the Stern Room at below union wages.
... Paid Advertisement. McFall's "Make Um Ding How White" – 12 hour laundry service. Deposit scorched dungarees, dirty laundry, etc., in bunk #83. Free delivery up until "Baker Baker" time.
... Flash!!! Denny's slow running detergent didn't run so slow the other day! What's the dope Denny??
... More about Denny. Visit Denny's Training Camp. Specializing in weight lifting building of "bulging biceps." Boxing instructions by the great "Punchy" Curran. (Note: Free autographs by punch). Conveniently located in the basement of the troop's recreation hall. Jack Baird, Promoter; Bill Miller, Dietician; Doc Resner, Masseur.

Thomas "Tom" Brames, '54 – '56

1956 – McGaraghan's Sea

McGaraghan's Sea was an open body tank of water that surrounded the Reactor Compartment portion of the *Nautilus* hull at the prototype engineering plant in Arco, Idaho. It was named after the Civil Engineer that designed it, Jack J. McGaraghan. There was also a radioactive spent fuel cooling pool near by.

Rumors abounded that someone had jumped into McGaraghan's Sea. But Bob Fuchs and Alexander Demitropoulos had jumped into the spent fuel pool and not the Sea.

They both became contaminated. They were washed down, cleaned and decontaminated. Afterwards they taken to Idaho Falls, accompanied by a health physics gent, where they had a hairdresser continue the cleaning effort, concentrating on their ears and noses.

Machinist's Mate 1st/class Robert E. Fuchs, and Engineman's Mate 1st/class Alexander Demitropoulos were in the fifth Naval Training Group. In 1957, during the first core change, Alex slept in the middle inboard bunk in the ten man bunk room in the Crews Mess, right under me.

Alfred "Al" Charette, '57 – '61

1957/1960 – My Navy Days

"Join the Navy and see the world." That's what all the enlistment posters said back in the 1950s. I hadn't really thought much about that but I had been totally and absolutely consumed with what was beneath the surface of the sea since I was a lad of four. I devoured any and all books and magazines on the subject, which in those days, were few and far between. I sent for U.S. Divers catalogues and endlessly pored over the photos of the various equipment that was then available, day dreaming about exploring across the ocean bottoms. I even built several crude home made devices that didn't work and, in retrospect, probably saved my life. I spent endless hours sketching ideas of self powered subs that I someday hoped to build. So when I graduated from Sunset High School in Dallas, Texas in January of 1956, I informed my parents that I would like to join the Navy. They offered no strong objections though I'm sure my mother would have preferred otherwise. I signed up in Dallas and in October, 1956 and my father put me on a train to San Diego, California, where, during Boot Camp, I applied for submarine school. I was selected and before I knew it I was on my way to New London, Connecticut for Submarine School.

Submarine school was great fun for me. I had already studied some of the technical parts of diving, while skin diving in the local lakes around Dallas, so I felt very much at ease in the pressure tank and the escape training tower. I did well in the classroom and thoroughly enjoyed my excursions to sea in USS *Croaker* (SS-246) and USS *Sea Robin* (SS-407), though to my dismay, I quickly discovered that I seemed to be prone to sea sickness. I vowed not let to let that be a deterrent, a vow quickly broken every time we ran on the surface and I was below decks. Consequently, I spent a lot of time with a #10 food can tied around my neck until the Pharmacist Mate finally gave me a supply of Dramamine.

I graduated Enlisted Submarine School in Class 141 on March 27, 1957 standing at #8 in my class of 44 with a grade point average (GPA) of 3.8. I was one of four selected for the burgeoning nuclear power program. Two of us were to go to Nuclear Power School and two were to be assigned to USS *Nautilus* (SSN-571). I chose the boat. Suddenly I ended up on the very first nuclear submarine, indeed ship, in the history of mankind. I couldn't believe it.

I reported aboard April 8, 1957, a green and very nervous kid of 19. I was amazed at the boat itself; so much different than the USS *Becuna* (SS-319) class diesel boat I had studied in submarine school. However, I was suddenly in awe of the men that surrounded me, my new shipmates.

Tommy Robinson

These men were my heroes, the ones I'd read so much about for so long; the "smokeboat" sailors that had helped win the war in the Pacific during WW-II. I had absorbed so much of their history while roaming on the security watches at sub school; reading all the wartime accounts and losing myself in all the great paintings and photos that lined the walls of those buildings. I almost felt unworthy to be a part of such a crew.

I came aboard rated as a Fireman, destined for the Engineroom spaces, but changed my designation to Seaman which placed me in the Deck gang in port under the watchful eye of Gunner's Mate 1st/class A. J. Callahan, the leader of the Deck gang. There I learned the fine art of chipping and scraping paint topside. When asked what I did in the Navy by an unknowing civilian, I would reply that I was an "Oxidation Technician."

Over time I became more relaxed as I began the long process of qualifying and standing watches. While underway at sea, I first stood Helmsman and Planesman watches where I learned to steer the boat at the helm, alternating as a Bridge Lookout with the other two Planesman. When submerged I would rotate seats at the bow and stern planes maintaining depth control. The planes were external "wing-like" surface control devices that allowed the boat to ascend or go deeper in the ocean. I'm still amazed that until very recently, the Navy would take a 19 year old kid and let him drive a multi-million dollar submarine both on the surface and while submerged.

My first trip in *Nautilus* was a shakedown cruise in late April 1957 [C.O. - Eugene P. "Dennis" Wilkinson] after the boat's first overhaul and reactor core change. It was to the isle of Bermuda, officially to make sure that all systems in the boat were functioning properly. The crew, on the other hand, viewed the trip differently as I soon to found out. Bermuda was a port where liquor could be purchased and brought aboard undeclared. So, in the eyes of the crew this was a "liquor run." Since I was not yet 21, the legal drinking age, I could not obtain any of these highly sought-after commodities for myself which put me in a very popular position with the older hands who promptly solicited "my share" of the booze for themselves.

My first serious cruise was to the west coast of the United States under Captain Wilkinson where he "showed off" the boat to the Pacific Fleet and to the civilian population. While in Seattle, Washington, Captain Wilkinson was relieved as Commanding Officer by Commander William R. Anderson.

Steely Eyed Killers of the Deep

After the return trip to Electric Boat (EB) in Groton, Connecticut, we began refitting the boat which included many strange pieces of equipment in preparation for our next cruise. That trip began at 0800 on August 19, 1957 when we got underway ostensibly for an operation in the Arctic waters with the diesel submarine USS *Trigger* (SS-564) [C.O. - Les Kelly]. In fact, it was to be an under ice excursion to gather information and determine just how operational submarines could be under the Arctic ice pact. All the work installing upside down fathometers and other gear throughout the summer now made some sense. *Trigger* was there as a life guard if anything went wrong under the ice. What they could have actually done to help us if such a situation arose remains speculative at very best. *Trigger* made several short trips under the ice and then it was our turn. We proceeded further and further northward until we were within 180 nautical miles of the North Pole. Then we had a 440 volt electrical failure which knocked out the gyro compass so we slowly reversed course, at least we hoped. No gyro compass had ever been to that latitude and it acted very erratically and therefore could not be completely trusted. On the way back to rendezvous with *Trigger*, we decided to surface in a polynya, an open body of water in the ice pack. I was getting much more than I bargained for when I signed up, but it was all good. I was only 20 years old after all.

By 1958 I had become a Quartermaster striker, an apprentice in Navigation Department, under the tutelage of Chief Quartermaster Lyle "Doggie" Rayl, a Pearl Harbor survivor. He also sent the famous message, "Underway on nuclear power" by flashing light to the submarine rescue vessel USS *Skylark* (ASR-20) on January 17, 1955. Under his watchful eye and those of Quartermaster 1st/class Ron Kloch, and Quartermaster 2nd/class Rich Williamson, I gained the experience to confidently stand underway watches alone. I had also completed my submarine qualification while alongside the pier at Mare Island Naval Shipyard near Vallejo, California on May 17, 1958 (The 164th person to do so in *Nautilus*). I received my silver dolphins pin and was ceremoniously tossed off the boat into the swift running muddy waters of Mare Island Strait; alas, a ritual no longer observed.

Previously during that year and unbeknownst to the crew, a second Polar trip dubbed "Operation Sunshine," had been planned. Another attempt to gain the North Pole. The plan was top secret and known to only a few in the government. We departed our visit at Seattle, Washington on June 9, 1958 and stood out into the Pacific on what was to become an historic voyage.

Tommy Robinson

My favorite duty was to surface the boat when I stood Quartermaster watchs. When the order to surface was given, my first action was to sound the "surfacing alarm," three blasts on the klaxon, a horn with an Ooogaa sound much like the old Model "T" Fords had back in the day. That was a treat in itself. Next I would precede a few steps away from the chart desk to the lower bridge trunk ladder, ascend a few rungs and wait for the command, *"Open the lower hatch."* That done I would race up the twenty foot trunk ladder to the upper hatch and await the command, *"Crack the hatch."* I would then gently crank the hatch wheel allowing a violent rush of air past me as the pressure in the boat was lowered. When the altimeter indicated the pressure in the boat was atmospheric, the Conning Officer would order, *"All the way,"* whereupon I would spin the wheel for all it was worth, throw open the hatch, leap onto the dripping wet Bridge, do a quick look around for any close contacts, then report on the 21-MC to the Control Room and Attack Center that all was clear. For a few brief moments I was alone on the Bridge, and as the sea drained away from the sail and with decks awash in white foam, I was – I just can't describe the feeling. All I know is that nothing else in my entire life ever made me feel quite like that – and I wasn't even 22 years old.

During my three years, six months, and five days in that wonderful submarine, I survived several close calls and many exiting moments. There were the many anxious moments under the Arctic ice, a fire in the Engine Room in the Pacific, a serious flooding casualty on April 23, 1959, my 21st birthday, occasional bouts of sea sickness, hours of monotonous watches while steaming underway as well as many frozen and lonely hours as Topside watch in port, hours spent on the sonar plotting party during war games "attacking" friendly and sometimes not so friendly ships. There were seemingly endless days of mess cooking (think kitchen duty) and great fun and uncountable laughs at the usual terrible movies in the Crews Mess while underway. I visited places in the world that I will never see again. Best of all I was surrounded by some of the finest men that ever drew a breath, my shipmates. That's the finest privilege of all for, they shaped my life in ways that neither they nor I ever imagined.

John "JC" Yuill, '57 – '60

Steely Eyed Killers of the Deep

1957 – Day Late and A Dollar Short

I was so excited! It was 1000 (10 AM), March 27, 1957, I was just shy of my 19th birthday, and I had graduated with Class 141, Submarine School, New London, Connecticut. (The sub base is actually across the Thames River in Groton?) I finished pretty well too, #8 in my class of 44 with a grade point average of 3.68. The best and most amazing part, I was assigned to USS *Nautilus* (SSN-571), the first "Atomic" sub, as it was then called, and the world's first nuclear powered ship. Before reporting on board, I departed, on March 29th, for a ten day leave to see my family in Bellaire, Texas.

I had a wonderful time with my parents and two brothers, Charlie and Richard, but all too soon it was time to head back to New London. I read through my orders and decided that I needed to head back on April 7th. Dad drove me to Dallas where we said goodbye at Love Field Airport. I boarded one of the now famous Lockheed Constellations for my flight back to the East Coast. Jet aircraft were just starting to replace "prop jobs" in the field of commercial aviation. I now consider myself very lucky to have flown on perhaps one of the most beautiful airplanes ever designed.

By today's standards, that flight would have been almost intolerable in its number of stops. We made five including the final landing. The first at Shreveport, Louisiana then on to Jackson, Mississippi, Atlanta, Georgia, Washington DC, finally landing at Newark, New Jersey. The time-frame, was "wheels up" in Dallas at 0800 (8 AM) and "touch down" in Newark at 1800 (6 PM), actually not too bad considering all the stops along the way.

After visiting my cousin in Irvington, New Jersey for the evening, I took a bus to New York City and caught the New Haven Railroad train out of Grand Central at 0040 (12:40AM), bound for New London. It was now April the 8th. The train screeched to a stop in New London at 0330 (3:30 AM). I grabbed my sea bag from a "locker club" located across the street and above a pool hall then took a cab to Electric Boat (EB), where *Nautilus* was completing her first reactor core refueling. I passed through the guard shack and descended down the long, steep hill, through the "wind tunnel" between two buildings, and found the barge where *Nautilus'* crew was billeted. I found a rack (bunk) and climbed in for some shut-eye. It had been a long day.

The next morning after quarters the Chief of the Boat (COB), "Dutch" Larch, a big gruff sounding, (to my young and tender ears) Chief

23

Torpedoman pulled me aside and said, *"Come with me."* He took me to the Wardroom where he introduced me to the Executive Officer (XO) or second in command, one Lieutenant Warren "Bus" Cobean. I began to sweat as he informed me that I was a day late in returning from leave. I should have returned the previous day, April 7th. I had, in my inexperience, misread and misunderstood the return date. I had visions of breaking up rocks at the Portsmouth Naval Prison for the rest of my enlistment. Apparently the XO realized how completely "green" I was, considered my extreme youth and let it slide with no punishment. I can tell you this however, from that time forward my eyes scoured the words off the paper that any orders were written on and thereafter I always arrived before the assigned time.

John "JC" Yuill, '57 – '60

1957 – First Impressions – Not Necessarily Last

First impressions: Good or bad? Of course, that depends greatly on the subject of the first impression. First impressions of a foul tasting bit of food are immediate and well deserved. First impressions of a just opened gift package are not always apparent, based on the contents of the box and whether or not they are liked by the recipient. Upon meeting people for the first time, those initial impressions can be misleading. A case in point:

I had always enjoyed a great deal of leeway while growing up and was able to go many places and do many things on my own even at a tender age. However, I was a very green young sailor the day I reported on board USS *Nautilus* SSN-571, April 8, 1957. I found it a daunting and humbling experience. Suddenly I found myself surrounded by men of real substance and experience. Submariners who sailed in the service of their country during WW-II and were knowlegble about the real world; experiences I hadn't been exposed to before.

Very early on, only the second or third day on board and late at night, I was pondering this sudden realization. I was standing by my rack in the lower starboard bunk room, when this guy came stumbling down the ladder, shoved his way past me and stood there glaring at me. Suddenly, without any provocation, he yelled at me, *"What are you lookin' at?"* He looked menacingly towards me and I felt sure he was going to "duke me out." I was at a total loss for words. I just looked at him in total disbelief. I had done nothing to him. In fact, I had not even met or spoken to him, yet.

Suddenly, an unknown shipmate and old hand, heard the confrontation and poked his head around the corner of the compartment and told the guy to *"Lay off the kid."* He then motioned for me to leave the compartment and told me as I passed him to pay no attention to the other guy as he was like that when he got drunk. I did as he suggested and sat, rather dumbfounded, in the Crew's Mess trying to absorb this hostility towards me.

As time went along I came to see my antagonist in a different light and slowly got to know him. It was true that every time this guy went on the beach (ashore) he seemed to go looking for trouble. But when he was on board the boat and sober, I began to see another side of him, a good side. He became a real shipmate and teacher and he signed off various systems on my qualification card while underway. He was a fellow with a great sense of humor and experience in his rate. This solidified in my mind by the manner in which the rest of the crew accepted him and behaved around him. He was one of "them." They understood when he was ashore and drinking, he was a different man, but no less a shipmate and sailor. They accepted him as he was, warts and all. They knew to simply stay out of his way, or not, when he was drunk. The tales abounded about his sorties ashore and how he had been rescued by fellow shipmates from a potential incident, arrest, or just getting him back to the boat. That's how submariners are; they stand together.

He was Engineman's Mate 1st/class Alan Lewis. He picked up many nick-names along the way while in *Nautilus*, mostly for his colorful antics and sense of humor. At first he was called "Lower-level" Louie, as an Engineman, he stood his underway watches in the Lower Level Engine Room. It also happened that he always seemed to be first in the chow line whether it be breakfast, lunch, or dinner. Hence, he picked up the moniker, "Light-lunch" Louie. Finally, at muster on the after deck one morning, a sound was heard coming from one of the mooring line lockers beneath the decking where we all stood. That was the space where mooring lines are stowed while underway. Out crawled Louie, all disheveled and some-what confused. He apparently spent the night in the locker after returning from an especially productive evening of "hoisting a few." Thereafter, he was affectionately known as, "Lower-level, Light-lunch, Line-locker" Louie. That term being such a mouthful, was quickly shortened to just "Line-locker."

After I left *Nautilus* in September of 1960, I continued to occasionally hear from "Line-locker" by phone. He would call every so often, sometime "blitzed," but over time, in a decreasing degree of that state. His dear wife, Ruth had a great influence on him to finally "go on the wagon" once and for all and that changed his life. During one of our calls I related the story of our first meeting on *Nautilus*. Of course, he had absolutely no recollection of that event, but I assured him that it didn't matter as I had come to see him, even in those early days, as a true and fine person at heart and good shipmate, and since then, as a good and faithful friend. During those phone calls we talked of many things, as in the poem by Lewis Carol, "The Walrus and Carpenter," of – shoes – and ships – and sealing-wax – Of cabbages – and kings." He had a wide range of interests and knowledge and an appreciation of history. I soon learned many things about him that I never knew. He told tales of growing up in Panama where his father operated the power plant that ran the "mules"' that, in turn, gently towed all the ships through the canal. I also discovered that he was an accomplished artist with a brush.

After "A.R. went on eternal patrol in 2002, his widow, Ruth, ("Toottie" as he called her), and I continued this friendship. She sent me a box full of his memorabilia. Among them was a beautiful chrome belt buckle with a pair of submarine dolphins on it, which I proudly wear to this day. There was his personal diary of our trips under the ice in 1957 and 1958, which I copied and returned. There was also a tiny cribbage set hardly bigger than the deck of cards inside it. I also have the Easely, South Carolina newspaper story printed after his death recounting how well known and liked he was around the city.

So it was that my very first impression of "Line-locker" turned out to be misleading. Only after I got to really know the man did I then realize that there was a good deal more to him than my first impression, and consequently, he contributed greatly to my life and a friendship that I will forever cherish.

John "JC"Yuill, '57 – '60

1957 – A Cast of Characters

Everybody knows a character or two. In every walk of life and in every job or profession there are characters, you know, those few individuals who are either quirky, bizarre, or somehow just different from the rest of the population. I'm only interested here in noting the characters of the good kind, whatever their strangeness. Nicknames always seem to accompany characters. They can be complimentary or not, but they are almost always funny and often descriptive.

The armed services are full of them and I believe submarine services, particularly of the United States, Great Britain, and Australia are the apogee of such characters. I'm sure this phenomenon is largely due to the peculiar circumstances of living with 100 plus bodies packed into in a 300 foot long pipe with no privacy; working, eating, bathing, and sleeping cheek to jowl, 24/7 for months at a time, and until recently, with no contact with the outside world. These living conditions lends well to discovering every quirk or oddity in anyone, thus producing a Petri dish of characters and their nicknames.

Take for instance my late and dearest friend and shipmate, Louie. He always seemed to be the first in line at the water tight door leading into the Crews Mess. He was awaiting chow, either getting off watch or going on, and so became known as, "Light-lunch Louie." He was also an Engineman and stood his watches in the Lower Level Engine Room so he was also known as, "Lower-level Louie." Now the last part of his dubious nom-de-plume arose one morning in port at 0800 muster on the after deck of *Nautilus*. As the crew assembled suddenly Louie came crawling out of one of the deck mooring line lockers all askew. He apparently spent the night in the locker sleeping off a wonderful liberty while ashore the night before. Viola! Suddenly and forever afterwards he became "Light- lunch, Lower-level, Line-locker Louie," but that being such a mouthful, it was mercifully shortened to just "Line-locker."

Then there was a Pharmacist Mate who became known as "Major Keating of the Algerian Balloon Corps" but mostly referred to as just "Major Keating." He was a true Jekyll and Hyde character. When on board and at his duties he was mild mannered as in Clark Kent of Superman fame. Rather quiet and unassuming. Once ashore on liberty, he morphed into a clever con man who wrangled his way into any number of "high-falutin" establishments, nightclubs, fancy hotels, or just plain dives in the never ending quest for free drinks. He was a master at weaving a tale of such preposterous proportions that folks actually believed him and gladly set him up.

The most famous story about him happened in 1957 on my very first cruise to Bermuda. After several days in Bermuda posing as the dignified and interesting "Major Keating" he gravitated up the ladder of ever higher social circles. On the night before *Nautilus* was due to depart

Bermuda he arranged to have a gala thrown at one of the fanciest hotels on the island to repay the kindness of the many folks for their hospitality toward him. He invited a couple dozen of the upper crust of society asking them to please arrive about 1800 (6 PM). He also said that he had some pressing business to attend to and would be a trifle late and further ask them to please not delay because the refreshments and dinner was scheduled and he would join them later.

Well, *Nautilus* sailed at 1600 (4 PM) that day with "Major Keating" on board having assumed his true identity. Presumably the "Majors" guests arrived promptly at 1800 (6 PM), as instructed, had a festive evening and ate a hearty dinner. They no doubt were astonished to fine themselves at the end of the evening stuck with an equally hearty tab.

Another character was William McNally, Jr. He was a multi-talented fellow; a magician, hypnotist, and the master of ceremonies for most of our parties. He dressed as Santa Clause after we passed under the North Pole and admonished the Skipper for using the Garbage Disposal Unit (GDU) in his domain without permission and for disturbing him in the "off season."

One sailor, soon to become my boss, was Quartermaster 1st/class and later Chief Lyle "Doggie" Rayl. He had an illustrious career in the Navy and was a survivor of Pearl Harbor, having swum to Ford Island from the devastated battleship USS *California* (BB-44) during the attack. He then entered the submarine service and made four war patrols in USS *Cero*, (SS-225) then went on to USS *Threadfin* (SS-410), USS *Stingray* (SS-186), and USS *Angler* (SS-240). He reported on board *Nautilus* as a Plank Owner where he obtained the moniker "Doggie." He sent the famous signal, "Underway on Nuclear Power," by flashing light to the submarine rescue vessel, USS *Skylark* (ASR-20) as *Nautilus* backed away from the pier at Electric Boat Shipyard and sailed into history. No one to my knowledge knows the origin of that nick-name but he was forever known in *Nautilus* as "Doggie." When in port and liberty was "piped down" he would exit the Goat Locker [Chiefs Quarters], "screw" on his Chief's hat and announce to me that I was in charge; an ironic gesture as I was only a lowly Quartermaster Seaman Apprentice striker and usually the only one in the Navigation Department left on the boat.

There was also a "Muffy," a "Fuzzy," an "Oink," a "Rotten Ed," a "Mouse," a "Hammer," a "Horse," a "Bump," a "Slope," a "Mother," a "Mule," a "Big Daddy," a "Babalooie," and a "Zipper," so tagged as a result of a scar across his forehead obtained in an auto accident.

Some of the more obvious nick-names were "Gunner," "Dinger," and "Pappy." Gunner's Mate 1st/class Arthur "Gunner" Callahan was probably the very last Gunners Mate assigned to a United States submarine. Engineman's Mate 1st/class Robert "Dinger" Bell's "liberty" tales are legendary on the boat. There was also Torpedoman Chief Leroy "Pappy" Ingles, the first Chief of the Boat on *Nautilus* and Torpedoman Chief Linus "Dutch" Larch, the second COB on *Nautilus*. "Dutch" was another genuine WW-II hero, having served in USS *Batfish* (SS-310) for six war patrols. He was part of the Torpedo Room gang when *Batfish* sank three Japanese submarines within 75 hours.

There was also Electronics Technician Chief Ray "Chief Green" Raczek, the only other shipmate who got seasick quicker than I did. And one of our officer navigators was fondly known as "Fog Bound." It was not bestowed because of any incompetence on his part but rather because every time we got under way from Groton there would inevitably be fog so thick one could cut it with a knife.

You can see the boat contained many submariners tagged with appropriate and/or dubious nick names. Most of them were so named because they were, in fact, true characters.

John "JC" Yuill, '57 – '60

1957 – Electric Boat (EB) Yard Birds

I recall the time when "Line-locker" Louie staggered back to the boat about 0300 (3 AM) in the morning and upon entering the Crews Mess found a number of Electric Boat "yard-birds" [shipyard workers] lounging about, drinking coffee and reading *The Day*. Well, that didn't sit too well with "Line-locker," who wasn't known for his social skills when "tanked-up." He proceeded to tell the yard-birds in no uncertain terms to get the hell outta' his home. They just gave him some tired looks and dismissed him as another *Nautilus* drunk. Not seeing any action to his request, he left the compartment, only to return through the watertight door with his beautiful .357 Magnum "wheel gun," and yelled, *"I mean NOW!"* I never saw a space emptied so fast.

John "JC" Yuill, '57 – '60

Tommy Robinson

1957 – Kropp's Quals

When it was Raymond Kropp's turn to get dunked after he qualified. We were in New London at State Pier. Four of us grabbed an arm or leg to heave him over the side. Ray decided he was going to take one of us with him. He grabbed and held of one of the guy's by the hand just as he went sailing over the side. He was partially successful much to his dismay. His grip was broken before the guy lost his balance and went over too but the hand grabbing caused Ray to spin around instead of sailing out over the side. His head hit the tank top with a LOUD "thunk." By the time we retrieved him his face looked like an inflated balloon and both eyes were black.

William "Bill" O'Neill, '56 – '59

1957 – Finding Brigman

Daniel Brigman of North Carolina fame came up with the answer to the age old question, "Why is a turd tapered at one end?" His ever thoughtful reply, *"To keep your asshole from slamming shut."*

Another classic Brigman story occurred on the first west coast trip, in Washington, I believe. We were getting underway very early in the morning and Brigman was the sea detail Helmsman. No one could find him. He had returned from liberty and couldn't hit himself in the ass with either hand. He was somewhat under the weather. The boat was searched a number of times for him but no Brigman. One of the sailors eventually remembered that every time he searched the Forward Torpedo Room head one of the stalls was occupied. He went to the adjoining stall, looked over the partition, and saw Brigman sitting on the hopper fully dressed. The sailor yelled at him and Brigman woke up. Brigman explained the puke all over him by saying that while he was sitting there someone opened the door and puked on him. The sailor who found Brigman then ask him if the guy was also responsible for shitting in his underwear.

William "Bill" O'Neill, '56 – '59

1957 -- Operation Skivvies

As I remember it, on *Nautilus'* first west coast trip in May of 1957 we were to demonstrate the wonderful world of submerged unlimited endurance of nuclear power to the Pacific fleet anti-submarine warfare forces.

DuPont, Dow, or some other chemical company had just received approval for us to participate in an experiment which I will call "Operation SKIVVIES." The experiment was probably in anticipation of the extended submerged time of the forthcoming boomer [missile submarine] patrols.

Several shipmates had been hand picked by the Executive Officer, Engineer, and Chief of the Boat to be included in the experiment as the operational test group. The group was divided into three teams of five crew members.

Each team of five shipmates were provided with pairs of skivvies which had been impregnated with a chemical compound to remove and/or reduce the "fragrance" generated over a defined period of time. I don't remember the specific time periods allotted to wear the skivvies before changing into a fresh set but it was something like group 1 = 5 days; group 2 = 10 days, etc. As each participant concluded his time he was to deposit his skivvies into special plastic bags and seal them. We always wondered which lucky chemical company employee got to open the bags, do the sniff tests, and write the reports.

I will not reveal any of the few shipmates who participated but I do state amazingly that I was not one of the CHOSEN FEW. Nor have I heard of the ratio of NUC [nuclear trained] to Non-NUC participants. In those good old early days there was no antagonism between the two. As I remember we all smelled pretty much the same after a few days out.

Joseph "Joe" Degnan, '56 – '58

1957 – Portland Visit

Nautilus visited Portland, Oregon in 1957. I lived in McMinnville about 40 miles from Portland. It was during that visit that I reported aboard *Nautilus* as a 19 year old Petty Officer 3rd/class. I had just completed Nuclear Power Training in Idaho and was on leave visiting my mother in McMinnville. Normally I would have reported to the boat in Groton. But then I found out the boat was coming to Portland, just to pick me up! (I can dream can't I). My mother, Ruth, drove me to Portland. It was a day that I will long remember. I can still remember setting in the Crew's Mess and smelling the fried chicken that was being prepared for dinner. Jack Kurrus was a great shipmate. He helped me qualify and earn my silver dolphins. Jack had a great attitude and was the best looking and smartest guy in the Navy. I remember because he told me that.

Imon Pilcher, '56 – '60

1957 – The Wayward Bus to Paris

It was October of 1957. *Nautilus* had left Faslane, Scotland and crossed the English Channel into La Harve, France. I had a 72 hour liberty [no duty for 72 hours]. So along with my shipmate, Charlie Kates, we decided to run up to Paris and take in the International Auto Show. Charlie was a Petty Officer 3rd/class Cook and a fun guy to be with "on the beach." He, like me, was also very interested in foreign sports cars. Before shoving off on liberty the crew was briefed by the Executive Officer about maintaining proper decorum, etc. In regards to us sailors not speaking French, he advised that it was not a problem because most French people spoke English.

When in town, we went into a bank to exchanged fifty or sixty dollars into Francs. The notes were all in color so, unlike English money, it was easy to distinguish between denominations. Because of the exchange rate, 250 francs to 1 US dollar, our pockets were overflowing with cash. We felt rich.

We missed the 0845 (8:45 AM) train to Paris so decided to take a bus. Upon entering the bus station, we both thought it best if we "drained our crankcases" before the trip. Along a wall were two doors, one marked Men and the other Women. We entered through the door marked Men and were surprised to find ourselves in one big room with stalls on one side and urinals on the other. The only other occupant in the room was a rather large, disheveled, and disinterested woman whose apparent job was to dispense hand towels and collect a gratuity. She gestured to us but spoke no English. We quickly decided that if she didn't care then neither did we so we sidled up to the trough and completed our business.

Steely Eyed Killers of the Deep

We boarded the bus, an ancient, rattly, run down old vehicle that appeared to be leftover from WW-I. We chugged out of the station and started down the road to "Gay Paree," or so we thought. What we imagined would be a swift and uneventful trip quickly turned into a milk run, with the bus turning off the main road onto every little side road and trail along the way. We pulled into many very quaint and tiny villages all with very narrow streets that challenged the bus driver at every corner. Some of these villages still showed damage from WW-II. Many of these towns were at the very end of their road which required the bus driver to turn around and retrace his steps back to the main road. This happened far too frequently until Charlie and I began to wonder if we would spend our entire 72 hours just getting to Paris. It took six hours to go 150 miles. We arrived in Paris near 1500 (3 PM), the same time the 1300 (1 PM) train from La Harve would have arrived.

We thought it best to look for a hotel room and so began an odyssey unparalleled in the annals of seeking accommodations. Hotel after hotel made it clear to us that we were not welcome by pretending to not understand English.

At one hotel, after struggling with the proprietor who feigned to not understand us, an American couple within earshot, came over and offered their help. The couple interpreted our lament to the desk clerk. They were checking out that night and had paid for the room till the next day. They asked the management if we could stay in their paid-up room. The answer was NO. It was plain to see at that point that no one wanted uniformed American sailors as guest in their hotels.

This couple was very familiar with Paris and knew of hostels where students stayed. They offered to drive us to several. Surely now, we would find a room for the night. Our elation turned to amazement when we reached their car, a huge chauffeur driven black Cadillac limousine. We piled into the rear with our hosts and off we went. They stopped at two or three hostels but at each one the story was the same; no speak English, no room. We finally begged off from our hosts generosity and kindness and they went on their way. Who they were is still a mystery to this day. We even checked at the United Services Organization (USO) and the American Church but neither had space for us.

We were starving at this point and found a nice restaurant. We sat near a table where a couple was having those little snail thingies; escargot. They looked and smelled so good, but for the life of us, we couldn't make the disinterested waiter understand what we wanted. We were now sure that the French only spoke English when it suited them. We finally settled for two big steaks with French Fries and some dry wine.

Now with full stomachs, we wandered the Champs-Elysée's like two lost wafts out of a Dickens novel. After some hours, around 0300 (3 AM), we happened upon a U.S. Naval Ensign off a "skimmer" (a surface vessel) and a conversation ensued. Charlie, being more gregarious than I, did most of the talking. He convinced the Ensign to let us crash on his hotel floor and so we did. Morning came around all too quickly and we had to get out of his room before the staff realized we were there.

It was then time to head for the Auto Show, where we drooled over all the newest models of Ferrari, Maserati, Aston Martin, Alfa Romeo, Porsche, Mercedes Benz, BMW, Jaguar, Lotus, and the like.

We next headed for the Arc de Triomphe at the Place de Gaulle, formally the Place de l'?toile. This huge monument stands in the center of a gigantic traffic circle with eight lanes of traffic and connecting twelve avenues spreading out from the circle like spokes of a wheel. The largest arch of its kind; it was begun in 1806 and completed in 1836. It was built to commemorate the French Revolution and the Napoleonic Wars.

Now, getting to the arch seemed a challenge since it was in the center of this huge traffic circle with maniacal vehicular traffic whizzing around like a swarm of angry hornets. Being young and with yet undeveloped frontal cortex's, we decided that the only way to get there was to run for it. This seemed easier than it sounds. Once out in the middle of an endless stream of speeding vehicles coming from all directions, that mindless venture started to dawn on us, but we had no choice at that point but to "soldier on." Once at the monument, we caught our breaths and looked for a way into the monument only to find it was closed!

There were plenty of signs but we couldn't read French, and since it was closed there was no one there to ask. We scratched our heads and decided to make another mad dash for the sidewalk again. We dodged cars, trucks, and buses, mostly by standing still to let the vehicles swerve around us. Then we would sprint to the next lane, while horns honked and unintelligible verbiage and hand gestures were directed our way. We arrived at the side walk along the Champs-Elysée only to find ourselves looking into the angry eyes of a local Gendarme. He was furious and told us in no uncertain terms, in English, that we were fools and that it is forbidden to walk to the arch. He said we should have taken one of two available tunnels. Of course, dopey us, we couldn't read signs and asking anyone would have proved futile. No one it seemed, spoke English in France except, to our everlasting embarrassment, the Gendarme. We skulked away with our tails between our legs, wandering down a street which seemed to connect at the Eiffel Tower.

This magnificent steel structure is beyond description. Construction started in 1887 and was completed by only three hundred workmen in 1889 just in time for the International Exposition, a world's fair commemorating the French Revolution. The initial design was done by three men. Maurice Koechlin, Emile Nouguer, and Architect, Stephen Sauvestre, all were members of Gustave Eiffel's construction company. The tower was constructed from "Puddled Iron" and is a marvel of engineering. The tower stands 1,050 high and was the tallest structure in the world until the Chrysler building in New York City was constructed in 1930. The French at the time thought it an eyesore and predicted it would blow down in the first wind storm. The structure was only supposed to stand for twenty years then be torn down and sold for scrap. It was such a huge success that it remains open today. Charlie and I went all the way to the top and marveled at the 360 degree view of Paris. It was breathtaking. I bought a tiny statue of the tower for mom.

From that magnificent height, we came down to wander some of the many streets of Paris, marveling at the architecture and different look from American cities. Soon it was time to look for a cab to take us to the train station. Obtaining one, we once again had to converse with a "Sergeant 'I know nothing' Schultz" who feigned not to speak English. We embarrassed ourselves by making "choo-choo" sounds which the cabby surely and secretly reveled in, and off we went to the train station. We certainly weren't going to get back on that bus again.

Our train ride back to La Havre was swift and uneventful. Those trains were really something, nothing like the old rattlers that we normally took from New York City back to New London after a weekend in the Big Apple.

We rode buses, subways, and cabs and never once heard a word of English. The old 571 boat never looked so good. We were back in America where everyone spoke English.

John "JC" Yuill, '57 – '60

1957 – Personality Plus

It has long been acknowledged by seamen that their ships are thought to have "personalities," particular characteristics that are a result of the combined influence of both officers and crew. Navy ships are no exception. A submarine's personality in particular, can be more notably defined because of its small size and complement of crew. A ship's personality can vary from time-to-time depending upon the change in chemistry within the crew. I can only speak about the boats earlier years when I was fortunate enough to serve in *Nautilus* which was then blessed with a remarkable personality. Since responsibility and accountability start at the top and filter down, I believe that the leadership positions which made up that "well-oiled" submarine command during my time in *Nautilus* resulted in her particularly good personality. In my mind the three main submarine leadership positions that have the most impact on the ship are the Commanding Officer (CO), Executive Officer (XO), and the Chief of the Boat (COB).

The CO, or Skipper, is the supreme boss and has the final say and responsibility regarding the vessels war fighting readiness, safety and well being. The XO is his immediate subordinate, second in command and, among many other duties, is responsible for overseeing the overall operation of the boats various departments such as Navigation, Weapons, Supply, Communications, Electrical, and Engineering, etc.

The COB is the most senior enlisted man aboard and is the liaison between the wardroom and the enlisted crew. He is the XO's right-hand man, so to speak. Among other things, he is responsible for seeing that all ship's hands perform their daily tasks as required. He is the "go to guy" for solving many of the everyday problems on the boat at the enlisted level. The COB also monitors discipline among the enlisted hands and may dispense punishments for any minor offenses. If these three key positions are in synchronization, there is harmony and efficiency throughout the boat.

I had the great good fortune to serve under the first three skippers, Eugene Wilkinson, William Anderson, and Lando Zech. I was able to witness first hand what it was like to serve with the best of the best and experience this ships extraordinary personality.

The first skipper was the gregarious and somewhat flamboyant Captain Eugene "Dennis" Wilkinson. He loved *Nautilus* and the publicity and lime-light that shined on her. He was the perfect representative for the world's first nuclear powered ship. He never tired of meeting the press and other media to extol the virtues of his fine submarine. He was all business underway and ran the boat with flair and utter confidence.

The XO at the time I reported aboard in April 1957 was Lieutenant Warren "Bus" Cobean, the third person to hold that position. Chief Torpedoman Lynus "Dutch" Larch became the COB, relieving Leroy "Pappy" Ingles. In 1957 Commander William "Bill" Anderson took command and Lieutenant Commander Frank Adams relieved Mister Cobean as XO.

Most of my three years, six months, and five days spent in *Nautilus* were under the guidance of William Anderson as CO, Frank M. Adams as XO, and Chief "Dutch" Larch as COB. Aside from my father, these three men, among others, became the most admired and respected persons to have a positive impact on my life.

Anderson's personality, demeanor, and management style was somewhat different from that of Wilkinson. Anderson was more quiet, introspective, and soft spoken, a product of his Tennessee upbringing and honed during WW-II, where he survived eleven war patrols in three boats, USS *Tarpon* (SS-175), USS *Narwhal* (SS-167), and USS *Trutta* (SS-421). Those experiences, plus later duty in USS *Sarda* (SS-488); USS *Tang* (SS-563); and his first command, USS *Wahoo* (SS-565), no doubt, reinforced his ability to resolve any situation decisively and quickly.

With respect and confidence, he "gathered flies with honey rather than vinegar" and as such, the crew had a great affinity and admiration for him. He is probably to this day the truly most humble man I've ever known. In any situation it was never about him but always about the crew and the ship. It's my feeling that, to a large degree, it was the other way around. If we were a good crew and ship, it was because he was a good skipper.

The XO, Frank Adams, was a perfect compliment to Anderson's command style and their personalities matched perfectly. He, like Anderson, was also soft spoken and low key. They seemed to work together as one person. Those two officers exuded confidence in the crew, which was a remarkable stroke of good fortune for *Nautilus* because it made a seamless chain of command for what was to become the "mother of all tests."

"Dutch" Larch, as COB, made up the third member of this remarkable triumvirate. If the heart of a submarine is the skipper, and the soul can be found in the XO, then the pulse of the boat has to be the COB. He maintains the beat or rhythm of the boat. As such, no one did it better than "Dutch" Larch. He, along with other crew members, had seen action during WW-II. Dutch made six patrols in USS *Batfish* (SS-310), making history during his last patrol, when *Batfish* sank three Japanese submarines within 75 hours, a feat never duplicated before or since. For those feats, the boat was awarded the Presidential Unit Citation. (He would later receive another one awarded to *Nautilus*). He was a seasoned submariner and leader when he came to *Nautilus* in 1957. The crew had in those three leaders, the "real deal," and how fortunate we were for that.

Those years, 1954-1959, were without question, *Nautilus*' glory years. Once at sea, one "first" followed another as *Nautilus* showed off her "stuff," demonstrating to the Navy and the world that, unlike any other ship that had ever gone to sea, she was "cut from a different bolt of cloth." As part of showing off this "new toy," the Navy spent the early years demonstrating her wonder and prowess to naval commands and all that clambered to visit or view her. It was a time of long hours and hard work that demanded maximum effort from *Nautilus* and her crew. The boat was constantly exercised, tested, and observed, requiring the utmost from the Wardroom and the crew. It was during these times that the remarkable personality of *Nautilus* was forged and flowered. She became a reflection of those who sailed her, due exclusively, I believe, to the leadership qualities of those persons mentioned earlier. Thus, the *Nautilus* of my time developed that certain personality that set her apart from other vessels. She had it all – indeed, she had personality plus.

John "JC" Yuill, '57 – '60

1957 – The KOG and Me

Those initials refer to none other than the late Admiral Hyman Rickover, the brain child and father of the nuclear Navy which resulted in the "atomic" submarine, USS *Nautilus* (SSN-571), beginning with her "keel" laying on June 14, 1952, launching on January 21, 1954, commissioning on September 30, 1954, and "Underway on Nuclear Power" on January 17, 1955.

KOG is an acronym meaning Kindly Old Gentleman. It was a "tongue-in-cheek" reference, not always complimentary among the crew of *Nautilus*, and perhaps others as well, who had dealings with Admiral Rickover across many years of his involvement in the nuclear ship building program.

Steely Eyed Killers of the Deep

Of the many books written about Rickover, possibly the very best, was written by a close associate of his, Theodore Rockwell in his seminal recounting, *The Rickover Effect,* "How One Man Made a Difference." Rockwell paints a complete picture of him, portraying all sides of this very complicated man. Rickover was pragmatic; implacable in his pursuit of pure engineering perfection and one who expected total and absolute loyalty from his team. He never cared whether people liked him or not, just that they did their jobs and did them well. He could be hard on those around him and perhaps not so strangely, he became surrounded by a great number of people who could see the "fire in his belly" and deemed it an honor to work for such a man, somehow sensing the greatness of what he was about. Great men like Rickover can have that effect on people, despite the fact that some if not many, actually disliked the man. It seemed not to matter to him as long as they were deemed worthy to be a part of this farsighted work. However, I'm sure that did not altogether lessen "the stomach knots" in those people when personally engaged by him.

Stories abound about his famous or infamous interviews, depending on ones point of view, with prospective employees and Prospective Commanding Officers (PCO). The interviews were designed to test the prospect's ability to perform under pressure. He accomplished this in various ways, mostly by throwing the prospect "curve ball" questions that had little or nothing to do with the job at hand to see how they would respond; and God help the person who foundered about or lost his "cool." Those might be either summarily dismissed without so much as a "kiss my hand" or verbally dressed down, either one being a no-win situation.

Consequently, this behavior was difficult for some to deal with. All who faced him had to deal with his presence to the best of their ability, and it had better be good. He was not one to suffer fools or those who thought they could "talk around him" commonly known as B.S. He was much too informed on practically any subject one could think of, from the technicalities of nuclear science, engineering, and great literature and classical music. In his book, Rockwell also showed a softer side of Rickover, unknown to the public or subordinates, who had an abiding love for his wife, and in very close, personal company, showed a keen and sharp sense of humor. He also embodied very strong feelings concerning good education, starting with youngsters, with concentration on the sciences and engineering, which he advocated through his books and public appearances; a most admirable trait and one worthy of public support.

We in *Nautilus* certainly did not see that side of him. When he came on board, which he often did, sometimes on very short notice, he was all business. He did not have much use for ceremony and in all the three years, six months and five days I was aboard *Nautilus*, I only saw him in uniform once. That was during the New York City ticker tape parade in August of 1958 upon our return from the transpolar trip from the Pacific to the Atlantic. Otherwise, he always would appear in a somewhat rumpled, ill fitting, double-breasted grey suit that looked like it came right out of a 1920s movie.

I never personally saw him smile, but am told he loosened up a bit during the New York City parade and soon was seen waving to the tumultuous crowd, seemingly overcome by the adoration and response of the crowd towards "his" ship and crew. It certainly wasn't about him. It was a departure from his usual public persona. As mentioned before, he did not seem to care for public displays of any kind, most likely because it was a distraction from business at hand. However, there is a photo of him actually smiling. He was standing in *Nautilus'* Ward Room with Captain Anderson and Steward Walter Harvey, and was being presented with a chunk of pack ice that was collected from *Nautilus'* deck before heading to the North Pole. He was genuinely pleased, if not moved by that event, and showed it with a big smile.

Now, what of the KOG and me? Truth be told; very little. As the lowest of lowly in the boat, a Seaman, though a qualified Quartermaster watch stander and, best of all, qualified in submarines and privileged to wear the coveted dolphins, I was among the lowest rank in the crew. However, every time he was embarked, I lived with the fear that I might accidentally run into him in a passage way and be subjected to one of his famous inquiries, and consequently made myself "very small." That fear was largely unfounded because he spent all his time aboard either in the Wardroom or aft in the Engineering spaces, no doubt haranguing those 9955'ers (Navy Enlisted Code referring to those involved with nuclear engineering) to determine if they all were up to his standards and qualified in every case to operate "his" reactor. He took a personal interest in every single nuclear submarine, including going on sea trials; his motive, partially perhaps, to show that nuclear powered ships were perfectly safe. He never asked of others what he himself would not do. He also determined who would command every nuclear submarine until very late in his career.

My interaction with him was limited to those times when I had the Topside watch whenever he came aboard to review or confer with the

Skipper about the boats operation or upcoming deployment. During such times I never had to worry about his quizzing me on anything as the Quarterdeck was always a swarm with every officer in the boat all hoping, no doubt, that he would bypass them during his inspection, sparing them the uncomfortable gaze and questions.

He was, without a doubt, a man ahead of his time, much like Henry Ford; focused, determined, and resolute in his quest to bring nuclear power to the U.S. Navy. But to us *Nautilus* sailors at least, he'll always just be the KOG.

John "JC" Yuill, '57 – '60

1957 – Death Comes to *Nautilus*

It was a peculiar feeling I had several hours later on that fateful morning. *Nautilus* was entering Puget Sound en route to Seattle and I had just come off the mid watch, 0000 to 0400, as Quartermaster and had settled down in the Crews Mess for few minutes before hitting my rack. Sitting at the forward starboard table under the television set was Torpedoman's Mate 1st/class Theodore "Ted" Szarzynski. He was holding his head in both hands and complaining of a severe headache. I could see he wasn't in the mood for even casual conversation, but I did offer that he consider taking two or three APCs. We called them All Purpose Capsules (APC) but the initials really stood for the government's version of Aspirin. They were always readily available in the Crews Mess in a cabinet near the ever-perking coffee urn.

After a few minutes, I left to climb into my rack in the lower starboard bunk room, just through the watertight door separating the Forward Torpedo Room from the Crews Mess. It seemed I had hardly gotten to sleep when someone was shaking me and telling me to roll out, get dressed, take my "ditty bag" (toiletries) and leave the Torpedo Room. I was still pretty much in the fog of sleep, but did as told and joined a somber and quiet bunch of shipmates in the Crews Mess. It was then that I learned of the death of Ted Szarzynski from a massive cerebral hemorrhage and the need to clear the Torpedo Room of personnel to place his body until he could be transported ashore later in the day.

Ted was quite a bit older than I, in fact, he could have been barely old enough to be my father. He was riding the boat on temporary additional duty (TAD) orders and he came on board *Nautilus* either in

Tommy Robinson

San Diego or San Francisco, I don't remember which, bound for his next duty station.

He was a solidly built man who looked the part of a Torpedoman of the "olden days" when herding torpedoes around the cramped quarters of a Torpedo Room required a great deal of brawn and sweat. I also remember him as a quiet man, belying the fact that a Torpedoman rating sometimes produced men of, shall I say, a gregarious and boisterous nature. It seems incongruous, but his age alone probably allowed him a certain grace and calm that the younger men had not yet achieved.

I didn't know him well. In fact, I hardly knew him at all given that our duties kept us in different parts of the boat. We did bunk in the Torpedo Room, but there again, in different parts of the space.

He was on board for such a short time that I doubt many of the crew really got to know him well, though he seemed to fit in just fine, no doubt another credit to his vast experience in submarines. This wasn't his "first rodeo."

I wish I had known him better, perhaps enough to tease some sea stories out of him if he was so inclined. That goes for all the men I served with as they were, almost to a man, WW-II Vets. Being young sometimes has its drawbacks in that one doesn't always think of those kinds of things; things that can enrich one's life without even knowing it at the time.

Getting back to my first statement about feeling peculiar that day and every day afterwards that I remember him: I wonder if I was the last person alive to have spoken to him before he died?

John "JC" Yuill, '57 - '60

2 - CDR William R. "Bill" Anderson
and PANOPO'S

June 1957 – June 1959

1957 – Captain "A" – Part 1

The Skipper [Anderson] called me last night to thank me for sending him the article on *Lagarto*. He wasn't aware that the missing submarine had been found. Also, he said that the Bureau of Naval Personnel (BUPERS), by their reluctance to change orders, saved his life. Here is his story.

When Commander Lather received orders to leave *Narwhal* and go to new construction, he ask Anderson if he would like to go to new construction with him as third officer.

Anderson said, "Yes." When Lather passed through Washington DC on his way to *Lagerto* in new construction, he asked BUPERS for Anderson. However, BUPERS had already written orders for Anderson to report to *Trutta* and were reluctant to change them. Lather wrote Anderson and told him the bad news.

Sometime later Anderson learned that *Lagarto* hadn't returned from her war patrol and, as I said previously, he was unaware that she had been found in mid 2005.

Simply because of BUPERS reluctance to change his orders, Anderson's life was saved. We got him instead. Such is our gain! Much good for *Nautilus*, the submarine force, the Navy, the country and the world.

I mentioned to him what you [John Yuill] and I had talked about - that "Dutch," Jim and "Doggie" never talked about their past. I asked him if he has written his stories down and he said, "No." He started with another story, but said he would hold that for a later time.

Alfred "Al" Charette, '57 – '61

1957 – Captain "A" – Part 2

What a twist of fate. It can either play to ones advantage or against it. You are so right – in this case the world may blessed by this turn of events, none more so than we who served with Captain "A." I spent too many hours researching through my reference books looking for anything and everything I could find on the three boats you mentioned.

U.S. Submarine Operations WWII by Theodore Roscoe, has the most complete records that I have of all boats. Some tonnages and number of ships sunk have been charted and in some cases enhanced over the years.

USS *Tarpon* (SS-175), an older P-Class with only four tubes forward and two aft, only sank two ships, but racked up a record tonnage for those two ships – 27,910. Very impressive! USS *Narwall* (SS-167) (USS *Nautilus* (SS-168) sister ship) sunk seven ships for a total of 13,629 tons. However, this boat engaged in and survived some of the most harrowing missions of any submarine in the war. These stories read like fiction. USS *Trutta* (SS-421) was not credited with any kills in the book but was credited with one kill in another source, a much later book. As-is-all, any of the patrols that Captain "A" made in these fine boats must have been an experience. We got the "real deal" when we got him as skipper. That of course takes nothing away from Wilkinson and his history, of which I know practically nothing, but I believe Captain Anderson was the man of the time for *Nautilus*.

I'm glad you talked with him about "Doggie," "Dutch," and others and how their stories may be lost for eternity. I doubt that I would have the nerve to mention to him about his past but in light of your "opening the door," I will encourage him to put down his WW-II experiences. He is so humble it will take some real doing to get him to talk about himself.

Thanks for sharing the story about USS *Lagarto (SS-371)*. I hope someone can return to the site and film her for a documentary. Till next time, "Straight board."

John "JC" Yuill, '57 – '60

1957 – Transferred

I was mess cooking for Jack Baird, George Denny and Tommy Deane during the refueling at Electric Boat and I was told by the Executive Officer, Frank Adams, that I was being transferred off the boat. It seems they needed my bunk for some guys transferring to *Nautilus* from the prototype in Idaho. I was given a choice of a smoke boat [diesel submarine] or NUC School. I went to NUC School while you guys were making history. I feel left out!

George Boyle, '56 -'57

1957 – Ooooops! – I Think We Just Hit the Ice

I was bored to tears, nothing to do, just sitting there at the helm, with no head or stern way on the boat, while the Diving Officer struggled to achieve a hovering trim and neutral buoyancy. It was August 1957 and *Nautilus* was under the Arctic Ocean, returning from an aborted attempt to reach the North Pole. Dr. Waldo Lyon with Archie Walker, and their team of "Ice watchers" had spotted a polynya, an opening in the sea ice pack, on the up-ward pinging sonar. It was decided to attempt a vertical surface into the polynya. With a hovering trim finally achieved, the Auxiliaryman of the watch began pumping sea water from Safety Tank. Safety Tank is located at the center of the boat and kept full of water so that pumping it to sea produces a positive buoyancy making the boat lighter. The boat slowly began its vertical rise toward the polynya when there was a gentle shudder. Captain Anderson was seated at the periscope in the Attack Center above the Control Room monitoring the cloud–like vision of the approaching sea surface when he suddenly lost vision through the scope. He immediately ordered, *"Flood negative."* In that instant I was no longer bored but intensely aware that something extraordinary was happening. The Chief of the Watch reached past me and operated the lever to flood Negative Tank. Negative Tank has the exact opposite task of Safety Tank. Also located at the center of the boat, it is kept partially filled with sea water. In the event an emergency dive is required this tank is flooded and produces negative buoyancy making the boat heavier. After going deep, a subsequent surfacing attempt in another polynya indicated that #1 scope was also damaged. The submarine was optically blind.

The first thing needed was a complete assessment of the damage. We proceeded out from under the ice pack into clear water and surfaced. It was discovered that the damage to the upper portion of the sail was more extensive than first imagined. The top of the sail was crushed bending both periscopes back like broken straws.

A dilemma now presented itself. After fulfilling the Arctic Ocean expedition portion of our cruise, *Nautilus* was to proceed to the Atlantic and participate in a NATO exercise called, "Strikeback." Damage to both periscopes would preclude our participation in that exercise, resulting in an embarrassment to both *Nautilus* and to the U.S. Navy.

The #2 scope was beyond repair but Lieutenant Paul Early suggested to Captain Anderson that #1 scope might be straightened and made usable. Various crew members were assembled for this task, among them, John McGovern, Bob Scott, and John Krawczyk. After Herculean attempts with hydraulic jacks in bitter cold conditions the team managed to straighten out #1 scope, only to discover that in doing so, the scope barrel had cracked at the kink in the bend.

The inside of a periscope operates in a vacuum environment to ensure that no fogging occurs due to moisture. Another disappointment and challenge now faced the Captain and crew. Enter Jack Kurrus and Richard Bearden. *Nautilus* was blessed to have every manner of talent and skill available to the ship and so it was to have two qualified stainless steel welders on board. Welding stainless steel is difficult under the best of circumstances, but to do so in a howling wind and frigid cold presented a daunting task. For some twelve hours or so they labored to repair the crack, alternately welding, then applying a pressure test. After every failure they would grind down the weld and repeat the process – again and again until finally a pressure was maintained within the scope.

But a new problem now lay before the boat. How to reinstate a vacuum inside of the scope returning it to a usable condition? This time it was Jimmy Youngblood who came up with the solution. He suggested that a very high vacuum could be achieved within the scope barrel by rigging a hose from the scope, through the boat, to the engine room where that end of the hose would be attached to main steam condenser vacuum pumps. It was soon done and in a very short time the periscope was emptied of all air and moisture. A charge of nitrogen was then applied to the scope interior using the vacuum to draw it in. This, at last, insured that the scope was free of all moisture and would provide a clear view.

The whole project required some fifteen or so hours to complete and it's success enabled *Nautilus* to not only participate in the NATO exercise as scheduled, but to "kick some butt" while doing it.

I spent some amount of time on the Bridge as a Lookout during that incredible repair and how those men managed to work under those conditions remains a source of amazement to me to this day. It says something about the quality of those I was privileged to serve with in *Nautilus*. It is something I shall always remember, especially when the going seems to be difficult if not impossible.

John "JC" Yuill, '57 – '60

1957 – Hell Hath no Fury Like a Tempestuous Sea

Ah yes! If I close my eyes I can still vividly smell that first rush of salt air coming down the Bridge trunk upon surfacing. Some thought it stank but I liked it. Actually, I loved being on the surface as long as I had taken a dose of Dramamine beforehand. If not, I dreaded running on the surface for I became violently sea sick. On those rare occasions when I didn't have time for "my fix" I could usually be found retching into a #10 food can, wishing I were dead.

On this occasion *Nautilus* was on the surface between Scotland and Ireland, in the North Channel, returning with a damaged sail and periscopes from an aborted surfacing attempt under the Arctic ice. It was the autumn of 1957 and after the portion of our cruise north we were scheduled to participate in a NATO exercise. We were on the surface because the water in that area was not deep enough to run submerged.

My underway watch duties involved helm and planes watches. Being on the surface negated any duties on the bow or stern planes so three Seaman assigned to these duties would rotate between a one half hour turn on the helm and a one hour turn on the bridge as Lookouts.

As it happened, there was a huge gale blowing with seas running twenty to thirty feet with monster swells that would almost completely engulf the boat from astern in the following sea. The seas would sweep over us alternately placing us in a trough, leaving us to look up at the wave crests as one would stand in a valley gazing up at the mountains, then pushing us to the crest of one of these swells where it seemed one could see forever. So it was that I found myself on the Bridge as the Port Lookout. The Starboard Lookout and Conning Officer, Lieutenant Donald Fears, was also on the Bridge. The Bridge hatch was on the latch, shut but not dogged down, because of the heavy seas. It felt so good being up on the Bridge where I could keep my bearings, avoid seasickness, and gaze at these magnificent seas. So I volunteered to remain as Lookout for my entire four hour watch. That was a big hit with the other two Seaman because they didn't want any part of being topside in that storm. They were content to just alternate helm watches. To a young kid this was exciting stuff.

At times I thought the boat was diving out from under us as the swells would cover the entire hull leaving only the sail out of the water. On several occasions the swells came up the sail almost to the bridge deck, so high in fact that we Lookouts hoisted our feet off the platforms in anticipation of getting our feet wet.

After one of the swells rolled over us I looked aft and noticed a portion of the after deck was missing. I had to scream the observation to Lieutenant Fears in order to be heard over the roaring wind. With each passing swell the hole got bigger and bigger, even ripping away some ballast tank piping and miscellaneous gear. It's hard to imagine just what water can do to a metal ship. It was an awesome display of power by the sea when it gets angry.

We had to put in for temporary repairs alongside a submarine tender up the Firth of Clyde in the Scottish port of Rothesay. After repairs were made we proceeded to our assigned duties in the NATO exercise dubbed, "Strikeback." We were on schedule, with only one usable periscope and a huge steel patch on our after deck, but we proceeded to show the worlds Navies what *Nautilus* could do.

John "JC" Yulli, '59 – '60

1958 – Stick a Fork in Me – I'm Done

I hated to see it go, it was such a beautiful place, but the Panama Canal was now astern of *Nautilus* as she stood out into the great expanse of the Pacific. It was May 4, 1958 and we were beginning our second tour of the west coast.

Captain Anderson decided that since we were close to the equator and ahead of our speed of advance (SOA), (an average speed calculated to arrive at a designated destination) that we should cross that imaginary line in the ocean. It would give *Nautilus* an opportunity to initiate "Pollywogs" [sailors that have not crossed the equator] into that royal order of the deep known as "Shellbacks." Alas, it was not to be.

During the transit from Groton, watch standers in the Engine Room and Maneuvering Room had been complaining of watery and burning eyes but no cause could be found. It was Lieutenant Bill Lalor, the Main Propulsion Officer, who noticed a small wisp of smoke emanating from around the port main turbine. It was suspected that a small oil leak was responsible. As personnel began to investigate further the smoke became more prevalent and soon all those in the area began to have trouble seeing and breathing. News of the situation was passed to the Control Room and the announcement was made over the 1-MC (the boats main announcing system), *"Fire in the Engine Room."* Of all things that can happen on a submarine uncontrolled flooding and fire are the most dreaded.

Acrid smoke soon filled the Engine Room and Maneuvering Room but no flames were visible. The compartment was sealed off by shutting water tight doors at either end. Watch standers within the sealed compartment put on goggles and draped wet towels over their faces in an effort to breathe. Meanwhile, Frank Holland and Bill McNally donned portable breathing devices and entered the lower level section of the Engine Room in an attempt to locate the source of the smoke. Captain Anderson stopped the port turbine and brought the boat to periscope depth. He ordered the snorkel mast raised in an effort to ventilate the boat. It was to no avail – the engine spaces were becoming uninhabitable.

Realizing that the problem could not be fixed while submerged, Captain Anderson ordered *Nautilus* to the surface. The boat surfaced into a beautifully bright, calm, tropical sea and the Engine Room hatch to the after deck was opened to help evacuate smoke from the compartment. To assist in this effort, the "Dinky Diesel," a source of emergency propulsion and battery charging on the surface or while snorkeling was "lit off" (started up). The diesel engine took its air supply from the Engine Room and as such would draw the smoke from that compartment very quickly.

By now, it was recognized that *Nautilus* had a serious situation on her hands. The smoke was really pouring out of the lower level but by this time the source had finally been identified. Now began the process of removing the smoldering lagging (insulation) from around the port turbine then passing it topside where it would be thrown overboard. It was a very slow and tedious process and involved heroic and dedicated efforts on the parts of all those involved.

Meanwhile, the remaining members of the crew not involved in fighting the fire were allowed to go topside through the forward or Torpedo Room hatch. Since I fell into that category I went up on deck and, finding such a beautiful summer day, promptly stripped off my shirt to get "some rays" – a BIG mistake. I did not realized at those latitudes the rays of the sun came almost straight down and did not have the benefit of being filtered somewhat by slanting through more of the atmosphere such as was had at northerly climes. Soon, very soon, I began to feel the heat on my body and flipping up my sunglasses realized that I was already red. Get the fork ready, I was done. I looked like a lobster right out of the pot. I whipped on my shirt and went below but it was too late. I had the "Mother of all sunburns."

The next day my entire back was one big blister. Later, as the blister began to dry, my back turned into a crusty mass and each movement brought excruciating pain. I was completely embarrassed at being so stupid as to place myself in such a situation. The thought of my not being able to pull my weight, especially in light of what my shipmates had just gone though fighting the fire, was unthinkable. Also, disabling oneself to the point of not being able to stand ones watches was technically a court martial offense. I had to stand my watches and I did.

In retrospect, it was probably foolish and immature of me to take that action, but at the time it seemed like the thing to do. I was indeed fortunate that I did not suffer any infections or other complications that might have placed me on the "binnacle list" (sick list and off duty). That would have been a far more precarious position than if I had just gone to the Pharmacists Mate for treatment. It was a hard lesson learned, and since that day I've never gone out to get a suntan.

As for the fire, it was discovered that after a very long time, the lagging on the turbine had become saturated with oil, and when heated to higher temperatures because of the tropical seas, it had ignited and begun to smolder. The lagging burst into flames each time a piece of it was removed which exposed it to oxygen. Only the heroic efforts of those crew members who fought that smoky blaze saved *Nautilus* from a potentially disastrous situation.

Finally, *Nautilus* resumed her trip, not south to the equator as planned, but north to San Diego, California. Instead of becoming a "Shellback" I remained a lowly "Pollywog," albeit, a very well done "Pollywog."

John "JC"Yuill, '57 – '60

1958 – San Diego R and R

In 1958, on our way north (the North Pole), we pulled into San Diego for a little rest and relaxation (R and R). Since *Nautilus* "Was The First and Finest" every day was constant visitor tours. If you were on duty status you were automatically a tour guide for part of the day. During this time the shore patrol was informed the *Nautilus* crewmen were "hands off!" Needless to say many of the crew took advantage of that situation and would go from bar to bar without their hats or blouses on.

When we left San Diego and were rigging the boat for dive, it was found that the after escape trunk was filled with street construction barricades and flashing warning lanterns. I don't think they ever found out who did the dastardly deed but the crew sure heard about it and I don't think it was ever tried again.

John "JC" Yuill, '57 - '60

1958 – The Booze Flowed

We pulled into San Diego and arrangements were made to have a "Rate Grabbers" party for those recently advanced in rate plus those who had recently qualified. A tap room called "The Black Crow" was rented for the weekend. I say AGAIN – for the weekend! Booze was free and it got very drunk out, very quickly. At one point there was at least an inch of beer mixed with urine on the floor. The door never closed.

The local shore patrol had a very busy time. They took me back to the boat three times. The first time I was entrusted to the Topside Watch. Not a good play on their part. The next time they brought me back they tore up my liberty card. Sollenberger fixed that for me by issuing me a new card. The last time they brought me back I stayed on board because I simply couldn't negotiate my way back ashore.

There also was a time when the Officer of the Deck said I was too drunk to stand Lookout watch and I was ordered to go below. There were no spare bodies on the maneuvering watch to take my place so I just switched with Brigman. He went up on the sail as Lookout watch and I took over as Helmsman.

William "Bill" O'Neill, '56 – '59

1958 – The Golden Gate Bridge

Those on *Nautilus* in 1958 will well remember the Golden Gate Bridge as we passed under it 20 times according to my old letters home. We took on many VIPs during that visit to the west coast. It was terrible, seeing San Francisco so close, yet so far away. We all wanted liberty, including Captain Anderson, but the "Brass" overruled him. Back and forth we went, turning around just shy of Alcatraz to pick up another batch of visitors. Finally, the Skipper had had enough after two or three days of this and we headed for Hunter's Point. The landing there was one of our worst. The current was swift and kept sweeping us out to the bay, and as hard as the Skipper tried, we just couldn't seem to get into the pier, starboard side to. We must have taken in #1 line from the pier at least three or four times before we could get the timing right. I guess there was no tug assistance available. Of course, the pier was lined with every top Navy brass from the area. Kinda' embarrassing to say the least. After that we went up the bay to Mare Island Naval Shipyard to try to find a leak in the port condenser, but they never did.

Anyway, we had a great time for at least one night ashore. I spent it at the famous jazz club, Blackhawk, where I saw the fabulous "Modern Jazz Quartet" and Gerry Mulligan.

I also recall the trip to "Frisco" in 1957 and my first time at the Blackhawk where I saw Dave Brubeck. On that trip, while in Long Beach, Charlie Kates and I took a bus from Long beach to Los Angeles and knocked around that dismal town. We saw some good jazz there as well at the LA Jazz Concert Hall. I was mess cooking on that trip and didn't get to see all the topside stuff that I did in 1958.

John "JC" Yuill, '57 - '60

1958 – How I Almost Became Fish Food

Nautilus was in Mare Island Naval Shipyard in summer of 1958 during our tour of the west coast. It was here that I finally completed my submarine qualification (number 164 to qualify in *Nautilus*) and I was promptly tossed over the side into the murky river. I was a happy, happy kid.

It was a very busy time in the yard with much emphasis on finding and repairing the elusive leak in the port main condenser, which was never found, and a myriad of other repairs and upkeep items. This included some work inside the sail and a complete paint job of the boat topside. The day before we got underway, it fell to the Quartermaster gang to thoroughly inspect the inside of the sail for any loose gear adrift. That, in turn, meant me, the junior man in the Navigation Department. The submarine sail houses all the boats different masts; periscopes, radar, radio, ECM, snorkel, etc. The inside of a sail is a labyrinth of hundreds, it seemed like thousands, of angle braces going every which way imaginable, which support the sail structure, in and around all the masts. I spent better than an hour crawling and squeezing through this endless maze retrieving all the stuff I could find including shipyard fire extinguishers used during welding repairs. After the shipyard made their count, they were one short. Time was up and we finally got underway. Once outside the Golden Gate and into deep water we made a trim dive. Some banging and clunking was heard in the Attack Center but no one knew the cause.

I had the Quartermaster watch when we surfaced after the dive. It was normal to make radio transmissions while on the surface so the command came over the 21-MC to raise the starboard whip antenna. The comforting squeal of high pressure hydraulic oil coursing through the piping to the mast was suddenly broken by a loud bang followed by a roaring sound which lasted about a half a minute or so. Then silence. Next came a call over the 1-MC for the Chief Auxiliaryman to lay up to the Bridge. That would be Chief Frank "Big Daddy" Skewes, who went flying by me up the ladder to the Bridge, closely followed by other members of the Auxiliary gang. After a few minutes a call came over the 21-MC for Quartermaster striker Yuill to lay to the Bridge, on the double. I climbed up the 20 foot bridge ladder to come face to face with Chief Skewes who was as angry as I've ever seen a man to be. In his hand was the oily remains of our errant fire extinguisher. Lost and unseen in the jumble of angle braces it had become dislodged during our trim dive and then jammed near the starboard whip antenna mast. Upon raising the mast it severed the hydraulic line and broke off the extinguisher nozzle which promptly turned the entire area into some kind of oily winter wonderland. Not so wonderful for Chief Skewes and his crew who had to make repairs under those slippery and filthy conditions. Well, I'm sure that those present on the Bridge can attest to the fact that as Chief Skewes handed that dripping, slimy mess to me, with the order to lay down to the main deck and heave the beast overboard, every ounce of blood drained from my face. I clambered down the sail ladders with my slippery charge, opened the sail door, and was about to store the thing in the "green locker" when I heard Chief Skewes, livid with rage, holler down to me that if I knew what was good for me I would follow the damned thing over the side. NO ONE will EVER know just how close I came to doing just that. Even facing "Doggie" Rayl, my boss, afterwards was a relief.

John "JC" Yuill, '57 – '60

Tommy Robinson

1958 – The Condenser Leak

In trying to find the leak in the starboard main condenser, we snipes, except for the "can't get their hands dirty" members of the Reactor Control gang, were given the task to test for leaks on each individual tube. In four hour shifts and in pairs, I was teamed with James "Oink" Johnson, we began testing each individual tube. Main condensers are big and have several hundred tubes; repeat, several hundred tubes. The man hole covers forward and aft were removed (big heavy suckers). "Oink" was in the after section and I was in the forward section and we communicated via sound power phones. My job was to put a blank test plug in a tube and "Oink's" job was to place a testing plug in the same tube and apply air pressure to that tube. If the tube was good the air pressure would not drop. We both had blue prints and would indicate on the print which tubes were tested. The testing procedure was painfully slow and boring.

I know that this went on for a couple of days and the test results had found no leaking tube(s). Then a Chief Machinist Mate named Stu Nelson came up with the "Stop Leak" idea. It worked and the rest is history.

Later on, I believe, the name of the product was changed to Bar's Leaks. I always thought that was a bunch shit. I base this on the fact that right after the use of the product, Stu Nelson was nicknamed, by the crew, the "Stop Leak Kid." And, that name stuck with Stu for several years.

Imon Pilcher, '56 – '60

1958 – Bar's Leaks

Al [Charette] thanks for sending the invoice. It's coming back to me SLOWLY. I do remember having the Bar's Leaks on board. I think it was ordered in case we needed it under the ice. Something tells me that it was not delivered prior to sailing from Seattle, but we received it later, probably in Hawaii. I think it was stored in the bilges near the starboard main sea water pump along with Harry's rum. The bottles were not that big because it was heavy liquid and 30ozs was not a quart. By the way, those of us who spent countless hours plugging and testing the main condenser tubes never believed it was the Bar's Leaks that sealed the tubes. Our last tube plugs were never tested. But it a nice story anyway. God Bless "Nelly" we will always miss him.

Bruce "Zap' Aquizap, '57 – '62

1958 – Piercing the Pole

There I was, 20 years old, riding around under the Arctic Ocean in the most sophisticated and fantastic ship in the entire world, the nuclear powered submarine USS *Nautilus* (SSN-571). What could be better than that? How could that be happening to me?

The adventure of my life began with my graduation from submarine school in March 1957 and my subsequent assignment to *Nautilus*. After a shakedown cruise to Bermuda in April, the boat prepared for a trip to the north Atlantic and the Arctic Ocean where an unsuccessful attempt was made to gain the geographical North Pole. Several close calls were had while under the ice and much was learned from that experience.

Fast forward to the summer of 1958. This time *Nautilus* was on the west coast of the United States, departing Seattle, Washington, heading, or so the crew thought, back to Panama and on to our home port at Groton, Connecticut. Instead, orders from Captain Anderson, were to turn north upon leaving the Strait of Juan de Fuca. To our surprise we were on our way once again in an attempt to gain passage under the Arctic ice to the North Pole. Unlike the attempt in 1957, I was now "striking" for the rate of Quartermaster and I was a member of the Navigation Department. The ship was equipped with a much improved array of ice identifying sonar, an advanced gyro compass, the MK-19, and most importantly, an inertial navigation system once used in a guided missile. It was the first use ever on a ship. Unlike a gyro compass which uses the earth's poles as a reference, thereby becoming very unstable at high latitudes, the inertial system picks a spot in outer space as its reference and is not affected by this condition. It was a very complicated system requiring the almost constant attention of two North American Electronics engineers, Tom Curtis and George Bristow, assisted by two of our own ship's company, Robert Rockefeller and Barry Lerich. It was a "Jury-rigged" affair in the Attack Center with a maze of wiring and equipment which looked to me as if a telephone switch box had exploded. How those three guys made any sense of that mess was, and still is, beyond me. However, they did so and, to everyone's relief, it worked very well.

We submerged in the Pacific just off Swiftsure Lightship and began our journey north. For the first week or so, Quartermaster 2nd/class Rick Williamson, and I stood Port and Starboard watches, (alternating six hours on and six hours off watch). Meanwhile Chief "Doggie" Rayl and Quartermaster 1st/class Ron Kloch feverishly updated all the northern waters charts that had been clandestinely smuggled aboard earlier. This watch routine was a very tiring affair, the only upside being that neither of us had to perform any other duties while in this arrangement.

We soon passed through the Aleutian Islands chain and into the flat and shallow Bearing Sea. On June 13, we passed the Pribilof Islands and the following day, skirting the western side of St. Lawrence Island we encountered our first ice. This is when things started to get interesting. The ice became much thicker and more closely packed than originally anticipated. We squirmed around, going this way than that, trying to find a path under the enormous ice ridges that we were encountering. The ocean bottom in this area was about 180 feet deep. Ice thickness to 60 feet was recorded which left about 120 feet of navigable water. *Nautilus* was approximately 50 feet, keel to top of sail, so that left only 70 feet of water for maneuvering the boat – 35 feet above the sail and 35 feet below the keel. It was not a comfortable feeling.

We retraced our steps and passed around St. Lawrence Island to the south and began our next passage between that island and the Alaskan shore. This route posed its own set of problems, mainly, extremely shallow water. It meant that *Nautilus* would have to make the run just skimming above the ocean bottom. The water continued to shoal and Captain Anderson inched the boat ever upward until our keel depth was about 65 feet, placing the top of the sail just under the surface of the sea. We had only approximately 45 feet of water under the keel, not enough room to pass under any ice should the opportunity present itself.

We arrived at the Bearing Strait, passed though this watery slit between Russia and the Alaskan coast at periscope depth, entering the Chukchi Sea. This sea was just a flat and shallow as the Bearing Sea so the same degree of alertness was required to maintain safety. After much maneuvering to avoid ice floes we passed the Arctic Circle and I became a "Bluenose" for the second time.

It was now June 17th and once again I had the Quartermaster watch. There was a lot of ice overhead, so very close attention was being paid to the ice detection equipment and upward looking television monitor. It was around 2300 (11 PM) when there was unusual amount of activity around the ice detection sonar. Captain Anderson was immediately summoned from the Wardroom. We had just passed under ice 63 feet thick. Captain Anderson increased our depth to 140 feet leaving only 20 feet from our keel to the bottom and slowed the boat to just maintain headway. Meanwhile, sonar reported two massive ice ridges dead ahead over a mile wide. A hard turn was ordered and *Nautilus* began a slow swing away from the huge ice flow, which by this time was directly over us. The needle on the chart recording the ice thickness kept going down till, finally, it began to recede. We had cleared the ice by a mere 25 feet. Ahead of us still lay another piece of ice even bigger than the last one. Were it not for the humming of machinery all about us, I'm sure that if the proverbial pin were dropped, it would have been heard. We all stood stock still, transfixed, as the chart recording pen began another slide down the paper until it almost touched the reference line on the chart. That line represented the top of the sail. Finally the pen became stationary and then began to recede up the paper. We had escaped unscathed again but ahead of us lay even shallower water and much more ice. The handwriting was on the wall. We would have to turn back.

The news was disappointing to say the least. The prospects of returning though the ice to the miserable, shallow, featureless seas to our south, followed by a very long way home did not conjure up many happy thoughts, especially for the married guys, for whom the way north under the pole was the quickest way home.

After we had retraced our steps to clear water, Captain Anderson relayed a top secret message to the Pentagon reporting our situation. More ice was encountered and more maneuvering was required to evade these menacing obstacles. Finally, we received the anxiously awaited message from the Chief of Naval Operations (CNO) directing *Nautilus* to proceed to Pearl Harbor, Hawaii. Needless to say, this came as a quite a pleasant surprise to the crew, with the possible exception of some of those who were married. Be that as it may, we were headed for paradise.

The trip to Hawaii involved quite a bit of preparations. The true nature of our trip was top secret and any evidence of our excursion up north had to be completely erased. Beards had to be shaved and all letters home, foul weather clothing and survival gear, and any evidence which suggested a trip north had to be hidden away and locked up.

This included all ships logs, reports, records and charts showing northern waters, especially Arctic waters. New charts showing false ships tracks had to be drawn up to show *Nautilus* had been steaming about the mid Pacific doing general naval operations. All manner of cover stories had to be fabricated and rehearsed. The crew was sworn to secrecy and told to "forget" about what had just befallen us. I'm sure Captain Anderson, and perhaps others as well, crossed their fingers and prayed that time spent in Hawaii would not loosen anyone's tongues as to our real purpose. As it turned out, he need not have worried.

On the morning of June 28th *Nautilus* surfaced just off Diamond Head and several of the Seaman gang were sent topside to repaint the boats hull numbers in their appropriate locations. All identifying markings had been painted out before our initial dive upon leaving Seattle. The maneuvering watch was soon stationed and I took my usual place on the Bridge with the quartermaster's notebook. At 1000 (10 AM) I wrote in the log, "Moored port side to berth Sierra One, U.S. Submarine Base, Pearl Harbor."

It was quite a sight to behold; bands, naval and civilian dignitaries, and best of all, Hawaiian girls all in traditional attire, were there on the pier to welcome us. Fan-damn-tastic!

What can I say about Hawaii? I can tell you that it was a lot different then than it is now. It was not yet a state and it was still somewhat distant and expensive to reach. Though the tourist business was beginning to boom, there was still a real distant and exotic feel to the place. There were no interstate highways, only two-lane paved roads and dirt secondary roads which took one to any number of beautiful places. I teamed up with my "sports car" shipmate, Wally Durkin, and together we rented an MG-A roadster and drove practically everywhere one could drive a car. It was a wonderful and welcome change from Navy life at sea. We saw many fantastic sights, one in particular, a remote waterfall, "Angel Falls", was well back in the jungle at the foot of the ever pervasive and majestic mountains. There's probably a four-lane road to it now along with a "gedunk stand" [fast food and treats].

Since I was a fan of jazz, I spent time at the different lounges that presented that music. I remember in particular spending time with Bill Brown, a cool drink in my hand (The legal age for booze in Hawaii was 18), listening to the modern sounds of "The Four Freshman" a group very popular at the time. Another fantastic local musical group was The Martin Denny Band. It was a small aggregation and their music was unusual to say the least. It was composed of all percussion instruments featuring the Vibraphone. It featured music in a tropical vein complete with bird calls and all manner of jungle sounds interspersed with the music. It was very exotic and perfect in a setting such as Hawaii.

One of my regrets while in Hawaii was not taking time to see the other islands. I also wish I had visited the Royal Hawaiian Hotel, a place steeped in WW-II submarine history. I also regret not having taken the launch out to the remains of the Battleship Arizona to pay my respects. Ah, youth – wasted on the young.

All good things must come to an end and so it was with our stay in that beautiful place. The most important event of our stay in Hawaii was that not one single word of our trips true purpose was leaked by the crew. It was still a top secret.

On Tuesday night, July 22rd the maneuvering watch was stationed and once again *Nautilus* stood out to sea. Out of sight of land and under the cover of darkness, the Deck gang again painted out all identifying hull numbers and we resumed our interrupted covert mission to gain the North Pole.

The third trip north was without incident or fanfare with the exception of our grand submarine logging her 40,000th league (120,000 nautical miles). This achievement was twice the distance that Jules Verne's fabled *Nautilus* covered in "20,000 Thousand Leagues under the Sea." Dr. Waldo Lyon and his new assistant, Archie Walker, (Rex Rowray had left *Nautilus* for another assignment) crouched over the upward pinging ice detectors while Tom Curtis and George Bristow, with crew members "Rocky" Rockefeller and Barry Lerich again monitored the inertial navigational equipment.

We finally passed between Yunaska and Herbert Islands in the Aleutians and into the Bearing Sea but it was different this time – foggy and sullen.

This was the most tension filled time for me thus far. During my Quartermaster watches I had to spend a great deal of time on #1 periscope watching for anything out of the ordinary. It was not only stressful but incredibly boring. I would hang on the scope handles, peering through the eyepiece, and scan the water ahead to the horizon, if it were visible. I looked for anything that might endanger the boat such as floating logs or other debris. Also of very great importance was identifying any signs of human presence such as ships.

The seas were mostly smooth and glassy with nothing to see at all. It is sometimes far easier to be at ones best and sharpest when involved in a lot of activity. To stare endlessly into the eyepiece of a periscope searching for something, anything, was enough to make even the most wide awake insomniac fall into a deep trance after ten minutes. It required every once of energy to stay focused on that monotonous job. To make matters worse, when I took my eye away from the eyepiece for a quick rest and looked around the darkened Attack Center, the effect was dizzying. One eye was dilated and the other was not. The effect cannot be described but if one were to go outside on a bright sunny day, cover one eye while gazing about with the other, then take the hand away from the covered eye, one will get the idea. I felt as though I looked like the cartoon character Bill the Cat with one huge eye and one little tiny eye.

On July 29th *Nautilus* slipped between the Soviet Union and Alaska at the Bearing Strait and once again into the Chukchi Sea. Several attempts were made to penetrate the ice as far from shore as possible but because of the heavy concentrations it soon became apparent that *Nautilus* would have to find another route. The plan then was to skirt the northern shore of Alaska to about Point Barrow, where an existing sea valley was known to lead straight into the Arctic Basin. This entailed some risk of being detected but there was no other choice. Finally, on August 1st Captain Anderson ordered the Helmsman to make his heading north. Next stop? The North Pole – 1,094 miles dead ahead. I remember standing my watches with an ever increasing degree of anticipation, but without really knowing what to expect when the moment came.

As we got closer and closer to the pole, the tension throughout the boat increased. We were at 400 feet making over 20 knots. The Crews Mess was crowded with just about everyone off watch. As the final moment approached, Captain Anderson addressed the crew via the 1-MC concerning what was about to happen, followed by a few moments of silent dedication to all who had gone before us. Suddenly, he was counting down *"4 – 3 – 2 – 1 – MARK! August 3, 1958, Time 2315 (11:15 PM/EDST), For the United States and the United States Navy, the North Pole."* We had not only passed over the Pole, but in the words of Tom Curtis, *"We pierced the Pole!"*

At that moment the entire ship erupted with cheers and shouts of joy. A big party followed in the Crews Mess complete with a visit from Santa Claus, played by our perennial entertainer Bill McNally who dispensed a liberal dose of "tongue-in-cheek" admonitions for ejecting garbage, and other waste in his domain. A cake, along with a ceremony followed, including the first re-enlistment at the North Pole of James Sordelet. A contest to name this crossing of the pole was then announced. The winning designation was "PANOPO" (<u>P</u>acific to <u>A</u>tlantic via <u>NO</u>rth <u>PO</u>le). A great time was had by all and it was then that I realized just how fortunate I was. There are tens of thousands of "Shellbacks" throughout the world's history, but I would forever be one of only 116 people to be designated as "PANOPO." Some interesting statistics were noted in Captain Anderson's subsequent book, "Nautilus 90 North."

"We had assembled the largest number of men ever at one time at the North Pole, 116.

The water temperature at the pole was 32.4 degrees F.

The depth of water at the pole was 13,410 feet.

Our ice detection equipment noted the thickness at the pole was 25 feet".

Suddenly it was over, just like Christmas to a child – all that waiting and anticipation was gone, but unlike Christmas, this would never come again. A feeling of "post celebration blues" settled over me, but it didn't last long. There were watches to stand, equipment to monitor and maintain, and a long way to go before we were safe again in open water.

On August 5th we completed our transit from Pacific to Atlantic and surfaced in the Greenland Sea where Captain Anderson sent the now famous radio message, "Nautilus 90 North." The Skipper was air lifted off the boat by helicopter to nearby Reykjavik, Iceland and then flown by airplane to the United States for a meeting with President Dwight Eisenhower. We continued on to Portland, England, where to our great surprise, we were greeted by much pomp and circumstance. We had not yet realized the worldwide impact and the importance of our voyage. We were just happy to see land again and couldn't wait to set foot on it. We were certainly not prepared to be treated like "rock stars." People everywhere greeted us warmly and asked for autographs. One couldn't buy a drink. There were any number of official notices, proclamations, and ceremonies hailing us as heroes. Gaggles of giggling girls followed us everywhere we went. It was unbelievable.

A quick trip back across the Atlantic was made in record time and we arrived in New York City to the same adulation as received in England. We were honored with a ticker tape parade in New York City, luncheon at the Waldorf Astoria, free tickets to Yankee Stadium where the crew was acknowledged, and of course, free drinks and requests for autographs. It was almost too much to bear but somehow we managed.

One thing everyone wanted by this time was just to get home to Groton. As we slowly stood into the Thames River and passed New London Ledge Light we began to see the multitude of people on the pier at Electric Boat. When close enough, we read a huge banner which said, "Welcome Home PANOPOs." We knew we were home and we were happy. Life was good.

John "JC" Yuill, '57 – '60

1958 – Me and My Old #10 Can

I heard an ad for Dramamine the other day and it brought back some very unpleasant memories of my bouts with motion sickness. Now mind you, I did not hold the all time record for getting seasick while on *Nautilus*. That dubious distinction is reserved for, and is probably still held by Chief Ray Raczek, also known as "Chief Green." He would start turning green at the 1-MC announcement to, *"Station the Maneuvering Watch,"* prior to getting underway. I, on the other hand, would delay that coloration until #1 line was taken in.

That brings me back to the wondrous concoction known as Dramamine. It worked for me. In fact, it worked so well that an hour or so before getting underway, or if we were submerged and about to surface, my boss, "Doggie" Rayl, or one of the other two Quartermaster's, Ron Kloch or Rick Williamson, would notify me to take my Dramamine. I kept a stash close by me at all times in case the dreaded surfacing alarm was sounded in the next hour or so. I was a bona fide "Drama-junkie." One particularly sad tale went like this:

It was late August 1958. We had just gotten underway from New York City following our triumphant return from Portland, England and the North Pole. We had passed Ambrose Lightship abeam when the maneuvering watch was secured and the regular underway watch was set. It was just after 2000 (8 PM) and the seas were getting rough due to a large tropical storm just off the Atlantic coast. To my horror, the watch set was mine. It had to be a mistake – I hadn't taken my Dramamine. How could I have been so foolish to assume that I wouldn't be on watch until after we crossed the 100 fathom curve and submerged, which would be after midnight or 2400. Curses! I reluctantly retrieved my trusty old #10 can and relieved Ron Kloch as Quartermaster of the Watch. I fought it with all my might but mind over matter wasn't working. I managed to stay my normal color for about 45 minutes but soon I turned a pale white, then a lime green. I began filling up "my can" but very soon was as useless as the proverbial bull with mammary glands. "Doggie" Rayl was taking Loran readings down by the Radio

Shack and very soon either Kloch or Williamson (I couldn't tell nor did I care) had, for all intents and purposes, assumed my watch at the chart desk. The Navigation Center was located in the Attack Center, a step or two from the ladder that led up to the Bridge. It was customary for the Quartermaster of the Watch, if not busy, to accompany visiting dignitaries to the bridge if asked. I was, by this time, in a semi-conscious state, sprawled across the chart desk moaning away when I heard the familiar voice of Captain Anderson. I looked up at him and he down at me and then in a soft, almost apologetic voice he said, *"Oh, I was going to ask you to take 'Admiral Snodgrass' to the bridge but I'll get someone else."* At that moment Captain Anderson, next to my father, became my most favorite person. I remember saying, *"Thank you, sir"* but beyond that everything else was a blur. Of course, this tale was added to the many sea sick stories concerning me and to this day, every time Rick Williamson sees me he inquires after my #10 can. And, oh yes – the irony of ironies – just after my watch was relieved we submerged to the peace and quiet of the deep.

John "JC"Yuill, '57 – '60

1958 – Fan-damn-tastic!

That was an exclamation used in *Nautilus* to describe any number of things from a beautiful girl, to one of those great meals put down by Tommy Deane in the Crews Mess, or an occasional terrible submarine movie we would watch while underway, and telling the absolute worst "liberty" tale that anyone ever had while on the beach [Liberty]. I don't happen to know the origin of the term but I'm sure that it was coined by someone in *Nautilus*.

The beauty of the word was that, depending on the object of the exclamation, different emphasis could be placed on a different syllable in the word. For example, one might exclaim, "FAN-damn-tastic!" or "fan-DAMN-tastic!" or even "fan-damn-TASTIC!" If the event or object rated a special emphasis, one might stretch it out like a rubber band as in, "Faaaaaaaan-damn-tastic!" – using any one of the above combinations for extra effect.

It was used throughout the boat whenever deemed appropriate, and, when ashore, could even be used in mixed company, a great advantage when one considers the depth and range of a submariner's expletives.

However, the very best and most appropriate use of the term was uttered by *Nautilus'* esteemed Executive Officer (XO) Frank Adams on August 3, 1958, just after we passed under the North Pole. It was the ultimate use of the word and though I still use it on occasion but it has never had the same impact as it did on that day in August 1958 when the XO sail, *"Now THAT was 'FAN-DAMN-TASTIC'"!!!*

John "JC" Yuill, '57 – '60

1958 – Shipping Over

One of my favorite stories regards shipping over [re-enlisting] in the Navy. Apparently someone in the Wardroom came up an idea of having a crew member ship over at the North Pole. Jim Sordelet immediately volunteered with dollar signs in his eyes. He calculated the travel money he would receive, from Hawaii to New London via the North Pole, would be much more than what he would receive if he waited to ship over in New London. Travel from New London to New London = $0.00.

I don't remember the ceremony because I probably had to take his watch while he re-enlisted. In any event he did ship over at the North Pole. However, when we returned home to New London the Navy financial wizards said, *"Wait a minute. You guys left New London and returned to New London therefore he gets travel pay from his last enlistment address to New London."* I don't recall the location of his last address but it definitely was not Honolulu and Jim did not receive the big pay payday that he expected.

Joseph "Joe" Degnan, '56 – '58

1958 – The Ticker Tape Parade

A note of interest regarding the ticker tape parade held in New York City. After the parade a commemorative metal strip was installed in the side walk at 160 Broadway, New York City. It is very close to the former Westinghouse Building, manufacturer of Nautilus' reactor plant. The commemorative strip is engraved as follows:

"REAR ADM. HYMAN G. RICKOVER, COMDR. WILLIAM R. ANDERSON, AND CREW OF THE NAUTILUS, THE FIRST NUCLEAR SUBMARINE."

Alfred "Al" Charette, '57 – '61

1958 – The President and Admiral

I remember when President Dwight Eisenhower toured *Nautilus* in company of Admiral Hyman Rickover, the celebrated "Father of the nuclear Navy." Someone, whom was never identified, announced over the ship's 1-MC intercom system, *"Admiral Rickover, this is God. Request permission to let the sun come up?"* And the Admiral trumpeted back, *"Permission granted!"*

Charles "Chuck" Parshall, '57 – '58

1959 – How I Spent My 21st Birthday

It was Thursday, April 23, 1959, my 21st birthday, and I had just gotten off the Quartermaster mid watch. *Nautilus* was submerged about 600 feet somewhere in the Atlantic playing "cat-and-mouse" games with two "tin cans" (destroyers). I crawled into my rack in the lower starboard bunk room located in the Forward Torpedo Room, and immediately drifted off to sleep. It seemed I had just fallen asleep when I was jarred awake by the stern command, *"Surface, Surface, Surface"* over the 1-MC, the boat's public address system. This was followed by the usual three blasts of the klaxon alarm. On some submarines, at the Commanding Officer's discretion, the order "Surface" precedes the sounding of the klaxon alarm. That was not the case in *Nautilus*. Such a change in procedure rang an alarm bell in my head and I was awake and out of my rack in a heartbeat. The surfacing alarm was closely followed by the collision alarm and the words, *"Flooding in the Engine Room."* Now that really got my attention. I started up the three or four steps from the bunk room to the watertight door that separates the Forward Torpedo Room from the Crews Mess. Also at that location were the bulkhead flapper valves, ventilation valves that also separate one watertight compartment from another. They can be operated from either side of the bulkhead. Torpedoman's Mate William O'Neill had already secured both by the time I reached his side. We stood there, glancing at each other – wondering what had happened, as the deafening roar of 3000 lb air rushed into the main ballast tanks. The boat took an ever increasing up-angle until it was close to 45 degrees. Bill and I discussed whether we were going up or down while waiting for some tell-tale sense of motion. There was chatter in the background from the 21-MC, another communication circuit that connected the Forward Torpedo Room, Control Room, Attack Center and the Engineering spaces. It was clear while listening to the 21-MC that the engine room was taking on a lot of water. There was apprehension but no fear as we waited to see what would happen next.

During such times it is not unusual for the most bazaar and peculiar thoughts to occur. It certainly did with me. I remember jokingly telling Bill that if we failed to surface I would never get my first legal drink.

Finally, after what seemed an eternity, to our relief, we sensed an upward motion, much like one would feel in an elevator. Well, from the original 600 foot depth to whatever the maximum depth the boat attained during the flooding, (the depth could only be estimated based on the angle of the boat) the sudden positive buoyancy resulted in an ever increasing speed as she raced toward the surface. The destroyers that we were operating with, having been warned of our predicament via Gertrude, the under water telephone, promptly peeled off in some direction, turning away from where they thought we might surface. It must have been one hell of a sight to them as we broached from the depths like a whale and then slammed back onto the surface. It was determined that a 4 inch sea suction flex coupling in the Lower Level Engine Room had failed, filling the space with an almost atomized spray of water under intense pressure. Visibility must have been almost impossible under those conditions, but somehow the watch stander in that space managed to quickly locate and secure both the stop and sea valves to that coupling.

We were now on the surface, bobbing around while the Engineers tried to restart the reactor which had "scrammed" (shutdown) automatically upon rigging the boat for collision. Now another thought occurred to me. I was always prone to sea sickness and upon knowing beforehand that we were to surface I would take Dramamine. Well, it was too late now and the thoughts of barfing into a #10 can had already begun to make my stomach turn, no doubt the power of suggestion. Thankfully, our tired, old reactor was started up in about thirty minutes while repairs were made to the coupling and we bid adieu to the surface and dived into our proper element to continue our operations.

An interesting sidebar to this tale is about the power of the human body when it is fed vast amounts of adrenaline. While the Engineers were enabling all the systems to restart the reactor (go critical) it was discovered that some of the valves that had been shut by hand during the flooding casualty were secured so tightly that come-a-longs (a cable winching device) were needed to reopen them.

I'm sure that many of the crew, especially those who dealt first hand with the flooding, later reflected on the ramifications of the casualty that befell our fine submarine, but if they did it was done in private for I never heard anyone discuss the incident to any great extent. It was just something that happened. The casualty was dealt with and then it was back to business as usual.

Much later in my life, on April 10, 1963, to be exact, I listened with horror to the radio broadcast about the loss of USS *Thresher* (SSN-593) and thought, "There but for the grace of God went we." On board that doomed submarine were two of my former shipmates from *Nautilus*, Lieutenant John Harvey (Lieutenant Commander and Skipper of *Thresher*) and Electronics Technician 2nd/class John Smarz (Lieutenant in *Thresher*). A third former shipmate, Chief Ray McCoole (Lieutenant in *Thresher*) had escaped by remaining home on the day of the fateful cruise. But for the heroic efforts of all those who were on watch, *Nautilus* might have met the same fate as *Thresher*.

Since then I mark my calendar every year with the loss dates of all U.S. submarines and when those days arrive, I pause to reflect on those souls still on "eternal patrol" and how much different things could have been for us.

Epilog: Just this past month, the story of *Nautilus*' flooding surfaced again in a discussion with some old shipmates. I was able, at long last, to learn the names of most of those on watch in the Engineering spaces that day. I think they deserve to be recognized. They are: Richard Bearden who had the Upper Level Engine Room watch; Robert Albright was the Lower Level Engine Room watch and also was responsible for isolating the flooding; Frank Holland had the Reactor Compartment watch and Ed Dunn was the Reactor Watch Supervisor. It was those two that quickly restarted the tired, old reactor, keeping me from a three day appointment with seasickness. Last, but not least, Lieutenant Donald

Hall was the Engineering Officer of the Watch. The two destroyers were USS *Brownson* (DD-868) and USS *Willis* (DD-929).

John "JC" Yuill, '57 – '60

1959 – Emergency Scram Recovery

I know a Chief Petty Officer who saved *Nautilus* in 1959 from pre-joining *Thresher* and *Scorpion!*

He received a "Letter of Commendation" in his service file. Being aware of this, I nearly puked when I recently read about the Commanding Officers of a coupl'a "new boats" who were awarded THE SILVER STAR for hurling a few rockets into Iraq which was a planned and deliberate mission.

In 1959, just before I joined *Nautilus* she was at the end of the useful life of her reactor core and was heading into Portsmouth Naval Ship Yard for a year long overhaul and replacement of the reactor core. She was assigned to work with two destroyers to check out some sonar equipment just off the New England coast near Portsmouth, New Hampshire. After a day of operations she went deep for a trim check in preparation for operations in the AM. An Engine Room gauge line ruptured and caused a flooding in the largest compartment on the boat.

The watch shut a few valves which starved the reactor of cooling water and caused the reactor to SCRAM (shut down). *Nautilus* needed power to "drive to the surface." Without power she was sinking she and approached test depth and beyond.

With the reactor degraded the Engineering Officer of the Watch had to be extremely creative to save the boat with all hands. It should be known that at "Test Depth" it is virtually impossible to overcome sea pressure and BLOW water out of the tanks, thus the need for power to "DRIVE to the surface!"

It has to be remembered that Lola's [*Nautilus*] crews wrote the procedures and operating manuals! This procedure became known as EMERGENCY SCRAM RECOVERY - The CPO's name was Ed Dunn. God rest his soul.

Christopher "Chris" Pauli, '59 – '62

Steely Eyed Killers of the Deep

Here is a copy of the UNDERSTATED Commendation of the century! Ed Dunn without question saved *Nautilus* and all inside her! Here's the NOTE in his service jacket!

SS(N)571/pe

Ser 267

24 April 1959

From: Commanding Officer, USS NAUTILUS (SS(N)571)

To: DUNN, Edward Daniel, Jr., 227 41 40, ETCA(SS) (9955), USN.

Subj: Commendation

1. The Commanding Officer takes pleasure in commending you for your actions on 23 April 1959 during the casualty involving flooding of the lower level engine room, emergency plant shut down, and the following start up.

2. As supervisor of the watch your performance of duty during the flooding while at deep submergence left nothing to be desired. Following the plant shut down, a very limited time was available for start up due to the core age and xenon level. You proceeded to the reactor compartment and took charge of the reactor start up. Your vast experience and thorough knowledge of the plant enabled you to reach criticality and the power level in the face of extremely difficult circumstances, thus averting a long shut down period. Your technical competence, knowledge, and leadership were in keeping with the highest traditions of the naval service.

3. A copy of this commendation shall be made a part of your official record.

W. R. ANDERSON

Copy to: BUPERS

Christopher "Chris" Pauli, '59 – '62

Tommy Robinson

1959 – "Babalooie" the "Wizard" and Me

It was 1959 and *Nautilus* was in the Portsmouth Naval Shipyard in Kittery, Maine for a complete overhaul and nuclear core change after our 1958 trip under the North Pole. It was a magical time being ashore after being at sea for such a long time. There was plenty of spare time "on the beach" [ashore] to have fun and engage in one's hobbies. My outlet was my red, 1949 MG-TC sports car. When I wasn't driving it, I was working on it, and when I was driving it, it was usually in the company of several shipmates who also owned sports cars. The array included a red Triumph TR-3, a powder-blue 1955 Austin-Healey "four-banger," a couple of MG-As, and a magnificent red and black 1954, XK-E Jaguar, arguably the most magnificent and powerful of the lot. It was owned by Billy Kahl.

Though Billy was his name, everyone on the boat called him "Babalooie," why I haven't a clue. He was an A-ganger, although an Engineman by rate, his assignments were as an Auxiliaryman, maintaining much of the boat's mechanical equipment.

He also had a beautiful new BSA B-34, Gold Star single motorcycle which was a hotter cousin to my own BSA B-33 single, at home in Houston. He also owned a hot Ducati, an Italian bike which was quickly displacing the British bikes on the world's racecourses. As much as I loved my TC, I never passed up a ride in "Babalooie's" Jag. He let me drive it on several occasions. It possessed brutal acceleration, but handled like a tank at low speeds with very heavy steering (no power steering in those days) but it became much lighter and more manageable at higher speeds. By comparison, my nimble little MG-TC was easy to steer at any speed.

However, my greatest thrill was when Billy let me ride his BSA Gold Star. On one particular occasion in October of 1959, after working on his bike to solve a misfiring problem, I took off with no particular destination in mind and eventually ended up some 20 miles away in small village when the misfiring engine got so bad that it just stopped. Now what? Here I was on a borrowed machine and I didn't even know where I was. I pushed the bike to a near-by gas station and asked if they knew anywhere I could get it fixed. The gas station guy said, *"Oh yeah, take it over to the 'Wizard's' house"* He gave me directions saying I couldn't miss the place. Thank goodness it wasn't too far because the bike got heavier and heavier with every step. He certainly was right about not missing the place. As I approached the house, it looked more and more as if it were abandoned, with the front yard covered with weeds.

The house, a big one, must have had 10 or 12 rooms, and was probably a fine, gentile house in its day. However, it now was in an advanced state of disrepair, bordering on ram shackled. The lawn stood waist high in weeds except for two well-worn paths, one leading to the front porch and the other leading to a small barn in the back. In amongst the weeds and on the porch were all manner of junked items. I made my way on path #1 to the porch and there found at least 10 or 15 old, beat up, dilapidated, antiquated, ancient, medieval, broken, bent, twisted, and burned up motorcycles.

The "Wizard" greeted me at the front door and I explained my dilemma. He was as scruffy as the house wearing a raggedy old shirt, stained and greasy pants, and he had a head of hair that probably hadn't seen a barber in years. He waved me in and then he headed through the house as if in search of something. As we passed through this broken down museum of natural history, I observed an untold assortment of old television sets, picture tubes, cabinets and boxes full of vacuum tubes, tables, chairs, bed springs, castors, ash trays, hubcaps, and toys. There were also engine blocks, engine heads, valve covers, auto wheels, tires, and inner tubes scattered about with even more boxes filled with various auto engine parts, burned out exhaust valves, tools, bicycle wheels, spokes, radio transmitters and receiver parts, nuts, bolts, door hinges, locks, keys, and a lot of other unidentifiable stuff. Some of the rooms held a treasure of old refrigerators, stoves, kitchen and bathroom sinks, toilets, and bathtubs, all of which looked as if they came from before the silent movie era. In the back yard there were junked car bodies strewn about and even the remains of a wrecked airplane. The "Wizard" had prognosticated from my description of the breakdown that the magneto timing gear had probably slipped on its shaft and needed to be pulled and re-alined. Off we went into the barn where, amidst more mountains of boxes and stuff he quickly found just the right gear-puller. He tore the machine down, pulled the gear, re-positioned it to achieve the correct ignition timing and in an hour and a half and a few dollars lighter, I was off and bound for Kittery.

It was among my most memorable motoring experiences. Even now I can't fathom how lucky I was to be led to the "Wizard's" door that afternoon. If I hadn't chanced to cross his path I would never have gotten that bike running again.

On September 16, 1960, I departed *Nautilus*, my only Navy home for three years, six months and five days, for the last time. I saw Billy at our shared garage in Groton, Connecticut. As I pulled my TC out from alongside his Jag I said so long but not goodbye.

I saw him twice after that day. Once he rode his BSA to the home of my intended wife for a visit. Then several years later, during a white-out snow storm, he called from the Providence, Rhode Island bus terminal. I immediately jumped in my 1963 red VW bug and slushed my way through the deep snow to pick him up. We enjoyed a nice dinner and visit, whereupon I repeated my course to the bus station and dropped him off. I never saw or heard from him again.

Over these many years at the *Nautilus* reunions, all who knew him always asked about him, wondering where he was and what he was doing. Where in the world was "Babalooie?"

On January 1, 2012, we all learned that he had departed on "eternal patrol" December 30, 2011. According to his obituary, he led a varied Navy and civilian life, prospering in both and continued to enjoy his motorcycles and fishing in several of his boats. He also left a fine, loving family in his wake. I and my shipmates who knew him only regret that we never got to share in his life after *Nautilus*. So many stories to tell; so much time passed. He will be missed but not forgotten. Same for the "Wizard."

John "JC" Yuill, '57 – '60

1959 – The Aft Air Expulsion Head

What is the most dangerous thing and/or operation on a submarine? Charging the battery? Messing with a MK 16 torpedo? Refueling or diving after Charlie Green rigged a compartment for dive? I say the air expulsion head [toilet] in the After Torpedo Room. A chamber is located in the lower part of the crapper. You do your potty business – so far, so good. Then you open the water flush valves, open the valve that deposits the material into the chamber and shut the valve. From now on we are talking about something as serious as defusing the most hideous booby trap the Viet Cong ever imagined.

Pressurize the thing, insuring that you closed everything that was supposed to be closed. There are no interlocks for the unqualified. Discharge the contents into the deep blue sea. Now comes the hard part. In order to return the system to normal, you must go through a critical venting procedure. No slack is cut. You must return the shitter to a

Steely Eyed Killers of the Deep

usable condition, and venting in sequence is critical. Depending on the depth of the expulsion operation, the lurking monster in the "chamber" can reach a destructive potential of biblical proportions. The velocity of the remains in the chamber (the whole thing if you didn't do the first part right) can reach the velocity of some of those little thingees that whiz around in the accelerator in Switzerland (CERN). The situation is worse when you can't get the door open and have to withstand the full wrath of the air monster. One advantage is that you only have the volume of a small chamber to come to local ambient pressure.

Up forward it's a different story. Any malfunctions will result in the full fury of the whole sanitary tank. I never understood why we called it a "sanitary" tank? Its everything BUT sanitary!

I remember when we were in dry dock with *Thresher* and the Mess Cooks blew sanitary tank. The yard birds were changing the screw on *Thresher* and the sanitary tank discharge line blew off, spraying crap all over the yard birds. I was topside and I never saw yard workers move so fast. I wish I was back to those days when life was so simple – keep the water out of the people tank, stay out of Hymies way, and keep "Doggie" happy when he was the Duty Chief - and check after Charlie Green.

George Clancy, '58 – '63

3 – CDR Lando Zech, Jr. *and* Lando's Commandos

June 1959 – April 1962

1959 – Cumshaw

The motorcycle season [in Alaska] is short, even for us hard core riders. I remember when "Babalooie" had a stainless steel exhaust system made in the shipyard for his sports car. Now this starts me to thinking about all the stuff you could get made in the yard for pound of coffee, or better yet, TORPEDO FUEL! (180 proof grain alcohol). We went into the yards with lots of "Gilley" [Torpedo Fuel], about 200 gallons I think. "Red" Sommes ran the torpedo shop at Portsmouth. He was a retired Torpedoman and hard hat diver. He must have been on the boats during WW-I. He dove on every boat sinking except *Squalus*. He also ran the decompression chamber that was in the torpedo shop. He had a distilling unit built into the piping system of the decompression chamber. You bring him all your denatured alcohol torpedo fuel, he cleaned it up for a cut and you got it back for trading material. I think he drank up all his cut. That must have been the most highly classified system in the submarine force - Top Secret, No Officer Pukes (TSNOP). You could look at the decompression chamber and never tell it's real function. The barter system was only managed by the old timers that had been in and out of Portsmouth on other overhauls. Our agent was "Dutch" Dichard. I got to carry all the contraband, no doubt as the senior Torpedo Room bilge attendant. The preferred barter material was alcohol, followed by coffee. If you had plenty of time and filled out requests, perhaps, someone would show up for your request. Of course, with "Gilley," shipyard response was instant. Smaller jobs, such as painting the Torpedo Room, "Dutch" took care of with doughnuts to a favorite painter. Every morning I took doughnuts down to the dry dock and fed our "Wildlife." We never touched a paint brush the entire overhaul. The enlisted supply system works!

George Clancy, '58—'63

1959 – Lobster Restaurant and Sea Gulls

I remember the lobster restaurant across the channel from Portsmouth Naval Shipyard. All the seagulls that had any senior status would sit on the roof and when the restaurant workers dumped the shit out through the window into the drink all the gulls swarmed down for a snack. We got some "Gilley" and soaked bread in it. The gulls liked that. In about an hour, every piling in Portsmouth had a drunk seagull sitting on it. I think we did the same thing to the pelicans in Key West. I hate

Tommy Robinson

@#$%^&* seagulls. I also remember standing Topside watch at State Pier in New London. When the tide was out the gulls got shellfish and then dropped them on the boat to break the shells. Then they did a "fly bye" just to shit on you. Some of the gulls were pretty accurate even compensating for cross winds.

George Clancy, '58 - '63

1959 -- Lobster Feeds

I also remember the duty section lobster feeds during the first yard trip. "Dinger" and I went over the side with the diving gear and got lobsters from under the barge. We dumped them in a big metal milk container, the kind farmers use, then stuck a steam line to the container bottom and when the top lobster was red it was PIGOUT! One of the yard birds was a part time "fish cop." That's what we call Game Wardens here in Alaska. They are State Troopers with brown uniforms instead of blue and can be big trouble. Anyway, he knew we had a preference for under sized lobsters, but he couldn't do a thing about it.

George Clancy '58 – '63

1960 – Gunners vs. Seagulls

As memory serves it was on a duty weekend at the yard and "Babalooie," "Chimp" Sandborn, and myself were lounging on the work barge looking for something to do to amuse ourselves. This already was a bad sign – Three A-gangers looking for something to relieve the monotony.

It all started very innocently. Lets feed the Sea Gulls by throwing bread out on the water for them. This lasted for awhile, about five minutes or so, then we took it up a notch by soaking the bread with hot sauce. No immediate effect was seen. Apparently hot sauce doesn't bother sea gulls.

Then we became cannoneers (Clancy would have been proud). We determined that if we could find a way to shoot at the gulls without using conventional weapons, whose noise would bring Marines and civilians guards, that it would liven up the event. While looking around the barge for a launching device we found a couple of 20lb CO_2 fire extinguishers that might do the job. The cone was removed for a starter. Now we needed a projectile. Aha, welding rods! By grinding the tips to a point, a primitive arrow was produced. Next we had to figure out how to reduce the end of the extinguisher hose down to snugly insert the arrow. A rather exotic reducing connection was made.

Next came a few test firings to see how well our device worked. A few rounds were fired into the wall. Low and behold the arrows actually stuck into the wall. Success!

Once again we began throwing pieces of bread out into the water to attract our prey. Taking careful aim we fired the first round. No hits. In fact it didn't even phase the gulls. So, the "You may fire when ready Gridley" order was given and the big event began.

The final score was Big N gunners zero - Sea Gulls six loaves of bread. It was not good shooting for having used over 20 CO_2 fire extinguishers. When the shipyard Fire Department came around the next day to pick up spent CO_2 bottles and saw all the empties we just told them that we had a lot of "Fire Watches" on the boat over the weekend.

Barry "Dan" Danforth, '60—'61

1959 – The Huge Hand

"Chimp" Sanborn, some others, and I took rubber gloves, packed them with dry ice, tied the wrists shut and threw them out in the river. They would get to be a huge - HUGE hand just floating downriver before they'd finally pop.

Gary Brown, '59—'62

1960 -- "Chimp"

I remember Ginger, "Chimp's" first wife, and his mother-in-law. "Chimp's" mother-in-law came from southern Italy. She lived with them and used to nag him in Italian and he shared that with us. When we were in La Spezia, Italy, "Chimp" and I decided to go to Rome. Down to the train station we went, having a few drinks on the way. Some of this is a bit foggy considering the language barrier. Well "Chimp" was a piss poor tour guide. We wound up in Genoa going in the wrong direction. How we ever got back to La Spezia has always been a mystery. I think I must have a jam proof navigation system that served me well after I went into Special Forces. I don't believe we ever bought train tickets. I suspect the conductors just didn't think it was worth all the paper work. At least it was a change from hauling Brady around in Spain. If our crew, at that time, could be transported into the current submarine force we would all be the subject of congressional investigations. The officers who led us would be labeled "Not Retainable." In fact, *Nautilus* would probably be forbidden to carry explosives or small arms.

George Clancy, '58 – '63

1960 -- Reactor Operations 101

Hell, by today's naval standards the whole *Nautilus* crew from the Commanding Officer down to Seaman Dave Ross would have been "Sent Home." We would have been classified as, "Unreliable, Nonconforming, Failure to Comply with non-harassment directives." And for the O-gangers "Lack of Confidence" in their lack of ability to conform to today's "Do not offend anyone" policies. It would be real interesting to have one of today's Operational Readiness Safeguards Examination (ORSE) team members question Bob Stroud, Stu Nelson, Bill Wolf, Admiral Carr, Commander Zech, Bruce Aquizap, John Chelstad, Don Brady, Mick MacGovern, even Malcom Snellgrove and rest of the NUCs about reactor safety operations. I can hear the reply, *"Look Sonny, who the Hell do you think 'Wrote the Book on Reactor Operations 101' - We were conducting 'Fast Scram Recovery' before you were born."*

Barry "Dan" Danforth, '60 – '61

1960 – Snow Removal

A tragic event occurred circa 1960 at the Portsmouth Naval Shipyard. A bunch of us were relaxing on the barge, where we held quarters every morning, watching a snow removal operation take place. I don't know where the snow removal was originating from, but the workers would scoop up snow and place it in dump trucks. The dump trucks would take their load to the end of the pier, back up the truck and dump the snow in the river. As we watched one particular truck back up, it continued over the edge of the pier and down into the river. We ran down to the site of the accident and could clearly see the tracks of the truck where it went into the water. A big ass crane must have also seen the truck go over the edge and it was making it's way to the scene of the accident at about one mile per hour. The box on the truck extended over the cab and made a perfect place to allow the hook on the crane to grab it. Eventually, the crane arrived and lowered the hook down into the water and snared the box on the first try as I remember. Up came the truck with the driver inside the cab. The crane placed the truck on the pier and the medical personnel had already arrived. When they opened the door of the cab and extracted the driver, we could tell it was too late for the poor driver. He was really blue and had a leather jacket on. That was a bummer of a day for everyone.

Wayne Hock, '59 – '62

1960 – Sideboy for Admiral Rickover

When I first came on board I was a sideboy during a visit by Rickover. The officers found a Ship's Bos'n and had the Admiral properly piped on board. When the pipe stopped I brought my right hand down from the salute. Unknown to me, Rickover had stopped and turned to my side. My hand hit his hat and his scrambled eggs [cap insignia] and all went in the drink. I was standing by for the worst but not a word was said by anyone and they all went to the Wardroom.

Fredrick "Reds" Knouse, '60—'62

1960 – Admiral Rickover Photo Op

Speaking of Admiral Rickover, I also had the Topside Watch one time when he came aboard. Of course, Commander Lando Zech and several other brass were there to greet him.

John Krawczyk was ready with his Hasselblad [camera]. As the Admiral crossed the brow, John kept backing up to frame his shots. He backed into, and almost fell over, the sonar dome on the starboard side. Rickover laughed at him just as John shot the photo.

Rickover immediately said, *"Krawczyk, I want that film right now!"* John obediently removed it, exposing it to light, and handed it to the Admiral.

Apparently it had been the only photograph ever taken of Rickover smiling.

Gary Brown, '59—'62

1960 – O2 Generator Technical Representative

Electrician's Mates 1st/class John Lewis and Dick Cox, both NUCs were the two electrical O2 generator guru's along with Sanborn, "Babalooie", and myself. Many thought that the O2 generator was a device created by a mad scientist. It contained all red, green, flashing yellow lights and hissing sounds when it was running, which wasn't very often. While we were still in the yards the machine developed and electrical problem. Dick Cox told the wardroom that he could fix it but he was told that the Command and SupShips were in the process of getting a technical representative from the Treadwell Corporation to come and take care of the problem.

At this time Cox was a short timer and he got out of the Navy a week later. The next part is classified as a "White Hats Dream." Treadwell hired Cox and who shows up to fix *Nautilus'* O2 generator, none other than Mr. Cox, the new civilian Treadwell Technical Representative.

Cox went into the Wardroom sat down and had the Steward pour him a cup of coffee. A couple of the O-gangers came in and looked at him with a "What the Hell are you, an enlisted sailor, doing sitting at our Wardroom table look?" They ask, *"What can we do for you Cox?"* Dick very casually and politely stated, *"The name is Mr. Cox and I'm your Treadwell Technical Representative. I'm here to fix the problem with your O2 generator. Oh yeah, and by the way, you could have had me do this for free while I was still on active duty now it's going to cost you over $500.00 dollars a day and a minimum of three days for me to fix it!"*

A few years later I spent some time, four days to be exact, with John Lewis during new construction on *James K. Polk*. He came on board as Treadwell's Factory Representative to commission our two O2 generators. John informed the Engineer that I would be working with him getting the generators commissioned for a least a week. It took us about one or two days to get them up and running and the rest of the time, operator training was conducted at the ElBo Club outside the main gate reminiscing about the good old days on the *Big N*.

Barry "Dan" Danforth, '60—'61

1960 – Swim Call in Key West

There was a narrow channel and it took a long time waiting in line to get out to sea. We'd often slip out early and hold swim call while the Destroyers and other surface ships got into formation. We had a gunner on the Bridge watching for sharks. Once they appeared he shot a few before the wardroom decided that wasn't a good idea for us to be in the water. Somebody got some scrap meat, and threw it into the water. Talk about a feeding FRENZY!

Gary Brown, '59—'62

1960 – The Base Player

Another Key West caper comes to mind. I recall Wayne Hock used to play the bass electric guitar, a Fender Stratocaster, I believe. We were out on Duval Street making the rounds of the local establishments trying to find all 110 bars supposedly in Key West. We were in Tomato Patch and found out their band's bass player was ill. The group's leader made the apologies. We told him that we had a guitar player with us who left a promising career as a professional bass player to "Serve his Country." They let Wayne come up onto the stage to see if he really was that good. It took just a few minutes for Wayne to warm up and when he got into his groove he brought the house down.

Barry "Dan" Danforth, '60—'61

1960 – Miss *Nautilus*

The Class of 1960 at Seabreeze High School dedicated their annual yearbook to USS *Nautilus* (SSN-571) and ask the crew to select one of several students to represent the boat as MISS *NAUTILUS*. Captain Zech's letter in response:

Tommy Robinson

Dear Mr. Yates,

You are to be congratulated on the large number of lovely young ladies who attend Seabreeze High School. All hands agree that it has been a pleasure and an honor to pick the winner in your "MISS NAUTILUS" contest.

Briefly, the contest was run as follows: Our ship's photographer made a Polaroid copy of each photo and mounted it on the enclosed board. A list of the crew was posted beneath the board, and each man voted beside his name.

In spirited balloting, Miss Marie Fajardo was elected "MISS NAUTILUS, 1960." The election was extremely close, as the choice was difficult.

I am enclosing the montage used for the voting, as well as a photographic copy for each participant and one for your annual. The winning photograph of Miss Fajardo is enclosed. If another copy could be returned, along with any others of "MISS NAUTILUS", I am sure that the crew would be deeply appreciative.

Our hearty congratulations to the new "MISS NAUTILUS", and the other lovely participants.

Very sincerely,

L. W. Zech, Jr., LCDR, U.S. Navy, Commanding Officer

As an ironic sidelight, the previous Commanding Officer, Commander Anderson went on to become a U.S. Representative from Tennessee for eight years from 1965 through 1972. During the latter part of his tenure, Commander Anderson's correspondence was handled by none other than our own MISS *NAUTILUS*, Marie Fajardo Ragghianti.

Contributed by Phil Stockhausen, Class of 1960

1960 – Bermuda Scooters

One of our guys rode a scooter right off the dock into the drink. If *Nautilus* ever returned, I bet they weren't ever able to rent scooters again! When we came back from Bermuda, we were filling out customs declarations to verify all the liquor we had bought was tax free. One of the forward Electronic Technicians, either Mandeville or Testerman, asked Frank Skewes, the Chief of the Boat (COB), if he had to declare something he had stowed. The COB said, *"What booze is that?"* The guy replied, *"The stuff in my locker."* The COB gave him this really gruff look and said, *"I damn sure better not find out about it!"*

Gary Brown, '59—'62

Christopher "Chris" Pauli, '59—'62

1960 - Hurricane

The very word can make the hair on one's neck stand on end, especially if one is destined to be in the cross-hairs of one, either at sea or ashore.

I've been pretty lucky in that I've only experienced four in all of my 73 years; all ashore. The fourth and last one in 2011, "Irene," technically a tropical storm when it made landfall around Long Island near New York City, was pretty nasty in that it took down so many trees and resulted in Cumberland, Rhode Island being without power for 79 hours. That was enough outage to spoil all the refrigerated and frozen food in our house.

The third was "Bob," a category 2, in 1991, a bit of a blow hard "wanna-be." Still, watching it take down a big Oak a hundred yards from our front door was a little unnerving. We escaped "Bob" unscathed.

The second one that I recall was "Gloria" in September, 1985 and it was even worse than "Irene" in tree damage and power outages. We were again without power for three days and reaped a lot of winter fire wood because of her.

This brings me back to my first experience with a hurricane during my waning days in the Navy. It was September 10, 1960, when "Donna" came roaring up the Thames River in Groton, Connecticut.

USS *Nautilus* (SSN-571) was fresh out of overhaul with a new reactor core and had just completed a short shakedown cruise. We had returned to her home port and tied up alongside the submarine tender, USS *Fulton* (AS-11) at State Pier in New London. Word soon came that a hurricane, "Donna" by name, once a category 4 storm and soon to make landfall as a category 2, was heading for our area. That meant that *Fulton*, affectionately known as "Building 11" because she hardly ever got underway and was suspected of being aground on old coffee grounds, would have to get to sea for her safety. That in turn meant that we would have to move up and across the river to the U.S. Submarine Base.

A submarine being much different than a "surface skimmer," need not worry about being tied up at a pier during a storm surge. Whereas a surface ship would have to continually lengthen her mooring lines to the pier as she rose higher and higher in the water until she rose higher than the pier resulting in terrible damage to the structure and herself. Never mind that it would be impossible to handle lines on a flooded pier. For a submarine it was a "no brainer" because we could flood down as the water rose around us.

September 10th dawned with an ominous sky and an uneasy stillness in the air. Soon the wind began to freshen. The maneuvering watch was set, meaning that the boat was ready in all respects to get underway. All underway stations were manned; the Helmsman was in his seat in the Control Room with all the attending personnel. The Lookouts were on the Bridge along with the Conning Officer and the Maneuvering Room was ready to answer all "bells" - power to turn the screws in order to move the boat. All were ready except the line handlers on deck and the pier. They were not needed because as the storm serge came in and raised the water level, the boat simply "flooded down" accordingly to maintain our same position at the pier.

My maneuvering watch station, being the junior Quartermaster, was usually on the Bridge with the Quartermaster's notebook, the official ships log, to record all maneuvers the boat took while moving seaward upon departure or visa-verse. However, in this case the log was being kept in the Attack Center at the navigation desk where it was nice and dry. Consequently, I was expendable, and was sent into the elements on the Bridge with ships anemometer to record wind velocities and consequently, to see firsthand what it was like to be in a hurricane.

Soon the wind really began to howl, whipping the river into a frothy spindrift. Then the storm serge began to roll up river, past New London, to where we were, and then on up river to Norwich. As it did so, the Control Room would occasionally flood the main ballast tanks so as to keep us even with the pier at the direction of the Conning Officer on the Bridge.

It was an amazing sight, almost surreal, watching the water rise as if it were a cake in the oven. I almost felt as if I were watching stop-action photography. The water engulfed the pier quickly, bringing along with it tons of flotsam of all kinds. Soon the pier and the adjoining land were covered in roiling water. Our submarine became an island with only the sail poking out of the water. All the nearby buildings had been sand bagged to prevent water from entering them so they were as protected as they could be.

The wind by then was screeching in our ears, tearing the words from our mouths and hurtling them away, making us appear to be mute. The rain drops felt like sleet against our faces so we tried not to look into the wind, but it was like watching a train wreck; one just couldn't look away. My trusty old anemometer was spinning away for all it was worth, but I can't recall the maximum velocity I recorded. All I know that it was windy as hell.

After a time, as the eye passed to northwest of us, the wind began to lessen and the storm serge began to reverse itself. Now all kinds of flotsam began its rush down river to the sea. Whole trees along with all manner of stuff came flowing past our stern headed for God knows where. The water receded from the pier almost as quickly as it came, leaving behind tons of junk, littering the ground and piers.

As the water receded, the ballast tanks were subsequently slowly blown empty, returning them to their original state.

Later that day the sun appeared in the west and things began to return to normal with a flurry of activity on the lower base to assess damage and clean up the mess. The maneuvering watch was secured, the duty section watch was set, and we all returned to our normal activities. I went to the Crews Mess for a hot cup of coffee and dry clothes. The following day it was almost impossible to believe that a hurricane had passed through the day before.

Still, to this day when I hear the word, "hurricane," I always think back to my first experience with "Donna" and her visit to the submarine base and *Nautilus*, and I think, "been there, done that," and I didn't even need to take my Dramamine.

John "JC" Yuill, '57 – '60

1960 – Stroud's Liberty

I remember a story about Stroud. One morning either at quarters or just after, Stroud appeared. He was banged up; cuts, bruises, and a black eye. Apparently, he had gotten "wiped out" at Ernie's and a few other drinking holes along Bank Street then "borrowed" a taxi to get back to the boat. He thought it was a good idea at the time. Stroud, of course, crashed the taxi and then gave the local police a good ration of crap when they came to the scene. They hauled him to the "pokey" and "allegedly" beat the crap out of him. I don't know what happened to him with regards to the wrecked taxi, but I'm sure someone, unofficially, made good to the cab company, probably taken out of his pay, so the whole thing went away. There is a sorry foot note to this story. I heard much later that he had been killed in a car wreck. Not so ironic.

Joseph "Joe" Degnan, '56—'58

1961 – The Stroud Saga

I wonder how Captain Zech's diary dealt with many of his and our adventures? We were at Electric Boat preparing to get underway. Stroud the "Sheep Herder" was holed up at a bar at the head of the pier. Tugs had arrived, lines singled up, and no Stroud! The Chief of the Boat and Commanding Officer walked up to the head of the pier and encouraged him to join us. Otherwise Brady and one other Reactor Operator would have to stand Port and Starboard watches.

Christopher "Chris" Pauli, '59—'62

I was with Stroud in that bar outside Electric Boat. We had been given advanced paychecks for the three months we were to be at sea and we had just received checks for the trip we had recently returned from. Way too much money in our pockets for such a short period of time. After the officers brought us back to the boat we were all given a mast (not in our records) and we were confined to quarters [the boat] for the duration of the passage to England. I think we made port in Portsmouth where we went ashore.

Fredrick "Reds" Knouse, '60—'62

Continuing with the Stroud saga. Another event occurred during our Mediterranean run when we were anchored in Valletta, Malta and John was missing once again from quarters. One of the Limey shore patrols asked if we were missing one of our mates. He had seen an American sailor sometime around 0600 (6 AM) at the local Trotters race track trying to hitch a ride back to the boat and he was really "bitchin." The

Shore Patrol said the Yank was really pissed and told him, *"Those Damn horse drawn cabby's would not stop to pick him up."*

Barry "Dan" Danforth, '60—'61

1960 – Burning Bread and Qualification

Bridges ALWAYS let the bread burn. He would come watch a movie or start bullshitting with somebody in the Crew's Mess and when we smelled smoke he would go running to pull the bread out of the oven. He blamed all the combustion in the food on, "Those Dammed AC ovens."

Bridges made the Mediterranean run. Too bad we didn't take up a collection while we were in Italy and have a contract put out on him. "Gunner" Callahan wanted to hone his skills with the Thompson and use Bridges for target practice. "Big Daddy" Skewes tried to get "Doc" Cobbs to declare Bridges' food "Unfit for human consumption." They used to say if you could cut his bread you could use it for hockey pucks.

On the other hand, Clyde Miller, the Chief Cook, was, without a doubt, the Navy's best cook. Nobody ever provided better meals - but he flat out said he was not going to qualify, and I don't believe the wardroom made him qualify. He was the only man I ever heard of who never qualified but was allowed to stay on board. I think eventually he was even allowed to pin on a set of dolphins, which was just wrong.

Gary Brown, '59 - '62

George Clancy, '58 - '63

Barry "Dan" Danforth, '60 - '61

Michael "Mike" Harmony, '59 – '61

1960 – Barbara Cartocci

Speaking of Italy – just before we pulled into La Spezia, I got called to the Captain's Quarters. Captain Zech asked me who Barbara Cartocci was. I was very surprised that he knew the name of the Italian girl who had been a foreign exchange student in my high school. She and

I had dated a little. I explained to him who she was, and he produced a typewritten Naval Message:

"08 Nov 60, TOR/TOD HOCK RM3(SS) from NAVCOMSTA WASHDC to USS NAUTILUS. UNCLAS GARY J BROWN ET3SS BARBARA CARTOCCI ... [gave her address in Arezzo, Italy] ... MAY BE AT SCHOOL IN FLORENCE. WE ARE FINE. MOM AND DAD."

Captain Zech informed me that my parents had sent an unclassified telegram that revealed our ship's movements. He admitted it was okay to tell our families where we were going but they shouldn't send a telegram containing that information. I still have that message, framed and hanging on my wall.

I missed all the crew's antics in Italy because I took a train to Florence, met Barbara, and we then went to her parents' home in Arezzo. Her dad got me very drunk on home made wine.

Gary Brown, '59 - '62

1960 – Did you Drink your Dolphins?

Yes, I did drink my dolphins, TWICE! I qualified on the Mediterranean cruise. We stopped at Malta and I and several other newly qualified went to THE GUT. We stopped at a seedy bar where there were several other older shipmates. The bartender took a large water glass and filled it up with a little of everything. Think Zombie. The four of us dropped our dolphins into the glass, drank it and held the dolphins in our mouths. I foolishly kept my drinks down. The other three went to the head and stuck a finger into their throats, barfed, and then left.

About 30 minutes later Lieutenant Commander Cummings, the Executive Officer, came into the bar. He saw me with the older shipmates and asked, *"Ross, did you drink your Dolphins?"* I said, *"Yes, sir!"* He replied, *"Well I didn't see you do it."* And with that another glass was filled, thanks to my older shipmates, and I drank my dolphins again. Sick is nowhere near descriptive of my condition afterward.

David Ross, '59 – '61

1960 – Don Brady

Don Brady was another Big N legend in his own time. I don't remember who arranged the event but it was another one for the "memoirs." During our infamous Mediterranean run we docked in Genoa and a couple of the sailors paid some little Italian sweetie to drive down to the boat while the crew was mustered topside for quarters. She got out of the cab holding a young kid, pointed to Brady and told the kid, loud enough for everyone to hear, *"That's your Papa!"*

Without a doubt the crew back then was a very resourceful and creative bunch.

Barry "Dan" Danforth, '60 - '61

1960 – Random Bouts

Who did Clyde Miller get into the fight with in Italy? It seems his name started with an "S." Miller wore a black eye for a few days and he did not want to talk about it. I remember them "duking" it out on the pier. It was quite a scene.

I also remember Butler decked John Lewis in the barracks at Portsmouth Naval Shipyard. Lewis was standing next to one of those metal racks and grabbed the edge of a thin metal piece after Butler nailed him and opened up his hand.

He had to go to infirmary and get patched up. I was sitting on the crapper at the end of the sleeping quarters when Butler came in and told me all about it. Butler also decked Stroud one time and afterwards they became good buddies.

Wayne Hock, '59—'62

1960 – Italy

I had the bow watch with Clancy at the brow. All day long my grandfather's people were celebrating some holiday that turned out to be Feast Day of the patron saint of the Italian Navy.

Italian enlisted sailors were in rowboats attacking their flagship *Garibaldi*. They hurled bottles of paint at her side while the crew on *Garibaldi* tried to sink the row boats with water from fire hoses. Enlisted men ask officers for smokes officers saluted the enlisted sailors. It was just a topsy-turvy kind of celebration.

That day could have been noted on the U.S. Navy's calendar as the day that "Clancy Lowered the Boom!" I don't think Italians are protected, sort a like the Catholic church is fair game. So, I say, a mass of Wops ran down the pier heading for *Nautilus*. George with his Tommy gun in hand was not about to trifle with the fools. I quickly proposed that we haul in the brow then call the Duty Officer. George stood down. Thanks be to God! Amen.

Christopher "Chris" Pauli, '59 – '62

1960 – Italy Continued

Lieutenant Wolff was the Duty Officer when *"Repel Boarders"* was passed over the 1-MC. I came topside with a Tommy Gun. We were tied alongside the Italian flagship *Garibaldi*. It's the only Italian ship the British didn't catch and sink during WW-II. One of their sailors came crawling up one of the mooring lines. Mr. Wolff said, *"Don't let those Wops on board."* I went to the mooring line in question, waited until the sailor got within two feet of the muzzle, and then cocked it. A Thompson makes a loud click. The sailor looked up and at this point and was staring right down the barrel. He sobered up in less than a microsecond, let go of the mooring line, and fell into the harbor. I seriously doubt the harbor in La Spezia is on the approved bathing list.

When we tied up along side *Garibaldi* it was a lash up. The Italians didn't have piers like we do, just a long stone wall. Their ships back in, drop both anchors, run two lines over to the stone wall, tighten everything up and put the gangway over from the stern. With our rudder set-up we couldn't do that, and we only had one anchor. So we came in bow first and put lines over to the cruiser, the stone wall, a float located between us and the cruiser, and anything else that looked strong enough to take a mooring line. We had to bring up all the spare mooring lines. We normally used four lines but we had at least six over. We didn't have enough rat guards for that many lines. Gunners Mate 2nd/class August Fuller, was in charge of Topside and I was helping him install the rat guards. We decided to locate the rat guards between us and the cruiser thinking that had the best potential for keeping the rats off of *Nautilus*. There were no rat guards on the lines running to the stone wall.

So, with mooring lines running all over the place and rat guards between us and the Italian flagship, let's think about rat guards. They look like a big split funnel that can be slipped over a mooring line or anchor chain and lashed down, however they are directional. If a rat climbed up the small end, it could jump down on the line and continue it's mission of "tour de ship." The rat guards can also be put on backwards. Our choice was to keep the Italian cruiser rats away from *Nautilus*. I later learned the Italians were rather disturbed about our choice of location, i.e., insulted.

In this day and age, Fuller and myself probably would have been shot; a formal apology issued by Obama and Hillary; *Nautilus* forced to fly the flag upside down; loss of submarine pay and the Captain relieved.

"Reds" Knouse and myself went over on *Garibaldi* soon after docking and left holding our noses. It smelled like the Paris public urinals in August. There was no flushing water. If two submariners are overcome with stench you know it's bad.

George Clancy, '58—'63

1960 – My 21st Birthday in Paris

Okay, here goes another salvo. I don't have any more Czech beer in the fridge, but a little cheap white wine should help me remember. The key players in this story are Chief Quartermaster and Assistant Navigator, Lyle "Doggie" Rayl and Chief Fire Control Technician John Krawczyk, both WW-II submariners entitled to ware the War Patrol Pin. John was also a world class photographer.

It's Spring of 1961 and I had just turned 21. I shipped over, had received my re-enlistment pay, and won the anchor pool. *Nautilus* was tied up in England and we were going to Paris. *Nautilus* was on it's way up North to the "tourist free, non recreational, submarine use area." I don't recall how it started, but someone decided that a trip to Paris would be nice. Having already been up to the "tourist free area" on a diesel boat, I decided that this might the last chance to see Paris, or any place for that matter.

Krawczyk had been to Paris before so he was our tour guide. The tour members as I remember were Gregoire, Krawczyk, "Doggie," Marchal, Raso, and a few others. We flew from London to Paris and then things started to unhinge. "Doggie" was a world class drinker and he was about half gone before boarding the plane and had a few drinks on the plane which increased the threat level considerably.

When we landed in Paris "Doggie" put his suitcase on one bus and got on another. As luck would have it, both buses went to the same place, so we were able to retrieved his stuff. But it gets worse. Krawczyk lost all his cameras. Krawczyk had his hands full with "Doggie" and when we all got to the hotel, Krawczyk had left his cameras in the cab. The cab left for other points and fares. A short time later, the French Police came to the hotel with all of John's cameras. I guess the cabbie was so shocked he turned everything over to the cops.

We checked into the hotel and "Doggie" was about 7/8's gone at that point. Marchal and I took one room, "Doggie" and Krawczyk had another, and so on. Have you ever see a bidet? It's an item common in Europe, but uncommon in the USA. It's a bathroom item usually located next to the toilet. It looks similar but there the similarity ends. A toilet has a big drain and a bidet has a small drain. "Doggie" had to take a dump and used the bidet as opposed to the toilet. Krawczyk was quite upset at this point and to make matters worse, the maid showed up with more towels. She really lost it when a turd was discovered in the bidet. She was saying some really bad things about the U.S. Navy. I think she was about to call INTERPOL or maybe something even worse. It's possible that shitting in a French bidet is an automatic trip to the guillotine. I told Krawczyk to give her some Francs. Earlier in the evening we were trying to figure the difference between "New Francs" and Francs. Krawczyk gave her a fistful of Francs and she immediately shut up. She whisked up the offending turd in a towel and vanished. "Doggie" never did realize what had happened.

A few days later, we went to the Lido Club. Now this is really big caliber stuff. We were all seated at a large table with some guy and his wife. She spoke some English and we learned they owned a sports car factory in Italy. They bought us dinner and drinks. It was great, you know, show the flag and the might of the U.S. Navy. A big floor show was going on, dancing girls with minimal or no clothing, clowns, the whole works. Every set of tables was higher than the ones in front, like a movie theater, but with tables instead of seats. Now this couple must have been good customers because at least three waiters were hovering around, ready to attend to our every want. The champagne flowed like water and it was taking it's toll on "Doggie." At least three bottles were on the table in ice buckets with the tops on, ready to be opened and pressed into service, like ready service ammunition during a Kamikaze attack. One round was expended, ready for the next to be opened by the waiter. The waiter reached for a bottle, but "Doggie" got to it first. A few seconds expired while the waiter and "Doggie" went back and forth over the bottle. Finally the waiter got it away from "Doggie" opened it and started to put it back in the ice bucket. Doggie grabbed it again and now it's OPEN. It foamed over, and champagne went over the balcony down onto the people below. It went dead center down some gals low cut dress, right between her boobs. After hitting those warm boobs it really foamed.

At this point I'm not sure if we were kicked out or if we just decided to go elsewhere. Outside the club, Marchal and I were trying to flag a taxi, while Krawczyk had his hands full with "Doggie." Limos were pulling up and all the rich and famous were getting out wearing fur coats, etc., just like in the movies. At this point "Doggie" needed to urinate so he pissed on the side of the building. A stream of urine slowly worked its way across the sidewalk in the direction of the ladies with the fur coats.

The next day, we went up to Mormarte, a big church on a hill, surrounded by the artists section. People were running over to Krawczyk calling *"John, John."* He knew them all. But I must say there were some strange looking people in that group. Anyway, John spent the day taking pictures of them. We toured the Eiffel Tower, the Louvre, Notre Dame, Napoleons Tomb, and other sights. If anyone ever wants to celebrate their 21st birthday with re-enlistment pay, I recommend Paris in the spring.

George Clancy, '58—'63

1961 – Water Skiing

I picked up a boat which I had just paid for that morning and headed out for Long Island Sound with Butler and Stroud to do some water skiing. Today, I would never ever consider doing that with those two.

We were out in the Sound with a couple cases of beer. Butler and I had urinate so we pissed over the side. Stroud rocked the boat and we both went overboard head long into our own piss. I thought we were back in Italy. Later that day we went up the Connecticut River to water ski. I was on the skis and Butler was driving the boat. Stroud was laying down on shore. Boat traffic on the river was heavy, so Butler was going to ease into traffic but he was too close to shore. He piled into a pier and flew onto the bow of the boat. He and the boat was held up against the pier because the engine was wide open. Butler and the boat were held in this position at a steep incline against the pier for quite a few seconds. Butler was finally able to scramble back to the throttle. When he backed the throttle down the bow hung way down in the water. We limped it back to shore and put it on the trailer. Buy it in the AM - Wreck it in the PM.

Wayne Hock, '59—'62

1961 – Green Ice Cream

St. Patrick's Day always reminds me of this story. I was standing Auxiliary Watch in the Control Room and we were underway with celebrities on board. The Diving Officer ordered a 30 degree up bubble. The night Cook had made green ice cream for the soft ice cream machine. He was standing next to the machine and filling it as the boat began to rise sharply. He held his apron to the side to catch the mixture as it spilled out. He obviously failed and came screaming into the Control Room covered in green from his chest to his toes. I do not remember who the Diving Officer was but he did apologize. The Cook then went back into the Crews Mess to clean up.

Fredrick "Reds" Knouse, 60—'62

1961 – Painting Out the Numbers

We were heading out on a Special Operation from the Submarine Base and were steaming down the Thames River. The Commanding Officer (CO), Commander Zech, had told Jamie [A Junior Officer] to "paint out" the hull numbers on the sail after we passed Edge Light. Meaning for Jamie to instruct a member of the Seaman gang to do the job. We had just passed the railroad bridge and were approaching *Fulton* when the CO asked, "Does anyone smell vinyl paint?" One of the Lookouts, I think Leo Amero, looked over the side of the sail and informed the CO that the smell was coming from Mr. Duel who was painting out the hull numbers. Mr. Duel was summoned to the Bridge and what transpired between the CO and Jamie would have, in today's Navy, been just cause for being "Relieved of Command for lack of Confidence." The severe chewing out of a junior officer's ass in front of the troops.

Barry Danforth, '60 - '61

1961 – Lieutenant Green

I served most of my tour on *Nautilus* under Lando Zech and one of my shipmates was Lieutenant Charles Green. "Lando's Commandos" as we were affectionately known made up a song, *"There once was a guy named Green who had a marvelous pumping machine... "* The song continued to describe Mr. Green's routine habit of ordering the Auxiliaryman of the Watch to start and stop moving water from fore to aft and/or aft to forward, constantly giving trim commands and stopping them before the Auxiliaryman could move more than a few gallons of water.

Lieutenant Green also had the Conn on one occasion when *Nautilus* departed, or attempted to depart, from alongside the submarine tender *Fulton* at State Pier. The port screw went into the *Fulton's* hull. The *Fulton* Officer of the Deck yelled down to us from *Fulton*, *"Can you please stop your port screw? It's in our storeroom!"*

Sigfrid "Sig" Hauck, '60 - '62

1961 – Spaghetti, Brass, and Fishing

Let's not forget Jamie's, or maybe it was Charlie's, spaghetti puke on the side of the sail. We were returning home from the Mediterranean, coming alongside State Pier, and all the Brass was awaiting us. The people on the pier was staring at something on the side of the sail that we on deck could not see. The last Officer of the Deck while coming into Long Island Sound had eaten spaghetti for a meal and lost it overboard. It was dried out and all over the port side of the sail.

Barry "Dan" Danforth, '60 - '61

All the "Brass," as I recall, was the Under Secretary of the Navy and some NFL Football team. We were going to take them to Quonset Point, Rhode Island then return them to New London, Connecticut.

Tommy Robinson

Some of us made a quick run to *Fulton's* ship store and purchased every cigar in stock. While underway, we managed to turn the Under Secretary and his groupies into a most ill group of fellows with cigar smoke. I'm sure I heard them praying for relief to the Greek God ROOOOOOOK! They ate every cracker we owned! At Quonset Point they all decided to take a bus for their return trip and we proceeded to RACE back to New London for a long overdue reunion with family members!

Lando also dove in a fishing net area. He ordered, *"Battle Stations"* and *Nautilus* became the catch of the CENTURY for a fisherman out of New Bedford. We surfaced and Lando hailed him. The fisherman said, *"I was maintaining position at 'full throttle' when suddenly my deck became awash and I was lucky to have an axe handy to cut my nets or we would have been dragged under!"*

There was an article in the *Boston Herald* that mentioned me and Chris Cunha as local sailors assigned to *Nautilus*. The Navy bought him new nets. Between the nets and the crushed Normal Fuel Oil tank I don't believe Lando would ever have gotten his TWENTY in this NEW CANOE CLUB - let alone made Admiral!

Christopher "Chris" Pauli, '59 - '62

Biggest Fish, It's A-Powered

Reprinted from the Boston Globe

The crew of the New Bedford dragger *Stanley Fisher* netted the biggest fish they ever saw, last Thursday, it was disclosed last night. It was worth $55 million.

Then they had to give it back to the U.S. Government. It was atomic-powered.

George H. Fisher of Oak Bluffs, the skipper, reported that his vessel's steel-mesh net snared the atomic submarine *Nautilus* 80 miles south of Block Island, R.I.

Mate Herbert Snowden of Vineyard Haven said the net cables "screeched."

Steely Eyed Killers of the Deep

Cook Emmanuel Thomas of Edgartown said the 101-ton, 72 foot dragger almost capsized as the giant steel-fish fought the net.

The cable broke; the net was lost; the dragger righted itself and the *Nautilus* was freed.

When the submarine surfaced, Comdr. Lando W. Zech, Jr. hailed the fisherman to make sure it was in no danger.

Assured by Capt. Fisher that all was well except that the fishing was over, the *Nautilus* submerged and resumed it its routine cruise.

The dragger returned to Fairhaven for repairs to its nets.

The *Stanley Fisher* netted the submarine at a depth of 1020 feet as it trolled for lobsters. There was no threat of a collision.

The Navy remained mum on why the submarines radar [sic] equipment did not detect the nets ahead and warn the submarine from its course.

But the Navy Department said it would pick up the tab for repairs to the dragger.

A Navy spokesman described it as a "really mild incident" and likened it to a "guy's car going through a clothesline." He did not say what the car would be doing in a back yard.

An air of secrecy was maintained about the accident yesterday at the request of the Navy Department. The fishermen were asked not to discuss it with newsmen.

In May 1959, the *Nautilus* ran afoul of a net from a New York trawler and dragged the vessel backward until the cable snapped.

The submarine suffered only scratches to its hull in both cases.

The Navy noted that two Bay State men are currently serving aboard the first nuclear-powered submarine *Nautilus* now operating in the Atlantic. They are

Christopher J. Pauli of Dorchester and Christopher V. Cunha of Medford.

Christopher Chris Pauli, '59 – '62

1961 – *"Blow Negative"*

While transiting the North Atlantic on patrol I was aroused out of my pad in the Chief's Quarters to go on watch in the wee hours of the morning. It was my turn as Diving Officer. I noticed that we had a couple degrees of down bubble. When I was ready to relieve the watch I walked uphill to the Control Center. All appeared quiet and calm. I ask, *"What's going on?"* The drain pump was undergoing repairs and because the boat leaked like a sieve the previous watch had pumped the boat light. We was transiting at moderate speed with a small down bubble to hold us on an even keel at approximately 200 feet while the Auxiliary gang continued to work on the drain pump. I received other watch information. We were scheduled to slow, make our depth 100 feet, clear baffles, and come to periscope depth. The raise the football antenna [VLF Loop] and copy CW [Morse Code] radio broadcast messages on the next hour. I relieved the Diving Officer.

Right above the Helmsman's head was a brass voice tube that we used to communicate with the Conning Officer. We would get his attention by cupping a hand over the tube opening then give it a couple of thumps. The Conning Officer would typically respond immediately.

The forward diving planes were set slightly down to compensate for the missing weight and that's what gave us the down bubble. So all is quiet while watching the clock and waiting for Conn to order Maneuvering to *"slow to 1/3"* speed and order Control to *"make your depth 100 feet."*

Nothing heard. I waited for a couple more minutes, still nothing heard. I gave the voice tube a couple hard hits "Thump, Thump" and all of a sudden the Conn hollered the anticipated commands.

It appeared that we might be late for the broadcast. Instead of waiting for the ship to slow and the Diving Office's instructions to change depth, both Bow and Stern Planesmen immediately put on rise and the ship started up very quickly.

We put dive back on the planes but *Nautilus* continued to rise. We flooded sea water to increase our weight but it was no help. Over the

Steely Eyed Killers of the Deep

1-MC, *"Put all water tight doors on the latch."* It looks as if we might broach. I requested Conn to get our speed back but that takes a lot of time. I looked behind me and the Skipper was sitting on the stairs leading to the Attack Center watching the events unfold. He gave me the okay to continue as Diving Officer. The shallower we got the faster we rose. I quickly flooded negative tank for additional weight - no help yet!

Word was passed over the 1-MC that we were going to broach just before we bobbed out of the water. While flooding negative tank it was also being vented into the Control Center and we were immersed in a thick fog and very loud venting noise. When we broached I ordered the Auxiliaryman to open all the ballast tank vents to vent off trapped air. What we heard then was so much air venting that is was like we had purposely put 3000 lb air on to blow the tanks. We are now sinking with too much weight and not enough speed with loud noise and poor visibility in the fog.

The next step was to blow negative tank, which probably had not been done in years, to get rid of that weight. Then start pumping out sea water that we had flooded in to hold us down, and wait for the turns to build up. I couldn't pump out because the drain pump was out of commission. Now that we blew negative it had to be vented and, of course, it again vented right back into the Control Center generating more noise and lots more fog. All of the people in the Control Center were now focused on the depth gauge and the ships speed. We went down a lot further than we wanted to go but finally the power plant got us out of trouble with more screw turns.

So what happened? It appears that high pressure air had been leaking the into the ballast tanks and as we were rising this air expanded. As we rose we were literally blowing the tanks. That's why we heard all of the air movement when we opened the vents. In hind sight – I never considered Safety Tank as an option to help us out and maybe that was good.

I went off watch with my left eye lid jumping up and down and I had a tough time calming down. It was a close call.

Vernon "Vern" Mitchell, '61 - '62

4 - CDR Jeffrey "Jeff" C. Metzel, Jr. *and* Crew

April 1962 – October 1963

1962 – Sleeping and Stuff

It took seniority and some time on board before I got to sleep UNDER the flash cover with my bedding. I slept EVERYWHERE over my three plus years on board and started out in the upper starboard bunk room. I was sleeping on my back in a top bunk during my first dive. I was exhausted and sleeping sound and nearly woke up with a "SPLIT PERSONALITY." As the down angle increased, I slid head first toward the torpedo tubes, on top of the flash cover and only stopped when the bunk chain halted my forward progress! Talk about an OWEEEEEE! I never did that again! After that "hello" and "welcome aboard" I always slept with my toes between the flash cover and rack-case.

Then we had a First Class Machinist Mate non-qualified puke (NQP) who bitched to the Chief of the Boat about me, a qualified Third Class Petty Officer assigned a bunk, while his NQP ass was roaming from sleep area to sleep area. Shortly afterward he was seen exiting to the Wardroom via Crews Mess hatch, never to be seen again.

When I slept in the Stern Room I had a locker with a 150 watt light bulb installed to help abate condensation. I put my clothes in extra heavy weight plastic bags and drilled holes in the locker bottom to let water run into bilge.

Thank God I missed out on this new Navy! I'm normally a beer drinker, but one of the best hard liquor drinks I ever had was on our way home from Bermuda. Someone mixed Canadian Club into the ice cream. I remember an unnamed Lieutenant who said our Ice cream in the Crews Mess was MUCH better than theirs in the Wardroom.

One of my most moving religious experiences was during a Sunday Lay service when it dawned upon me; fantastic engineering is this atomic power BUT who provided MAN the ability to do these calculations? Build me a human or a butterfly. Now that's ENGINEERING!

Could one of today's Captains lead a Lay Service? Play tapes of Arch Bishop Fulton Sheen? I think not. What a DAMN shame!

Christopher "Chris" Pauli, '59 – '62

1963 – The Bat Cave

Here is a short history of the Bat Cave. Do you remember the Batman fad of the early 1960's? My son had a batman book with stickers of the bat signal, a black bat on a yellow background. So, prior to a scheduled Northern run we put the stickers on our red phones, a hot line between the Radio Room and Conning station. In Radio we would answer the red phone, *"Bat Cave, Robin."* So that's the background. One day I answered the red phone in the usual manner, *"Bat Cave, Robin."* The reply from Conn was, *"THIS IS BAT MAN."* Now, who said Captain Metzel didn't have a sense of humor?

Leonard "Len" Scherer, '63 - '65

1962 or 1963 – Reactor Scram?

Nautilus had many unique problems. I remember when all the rods dropped but there was no alarm until they hit the bottom. I had the Conn and I remember the Reactor Operator who was on his first watch saying in a puzzling manner, *"Reactor Scram?"* We were running at 102 percent reactor power when this occurred and we entered that in the incident report. Rickover never said a word, but the system was changed so that the alarm went off when the rods started to drop instead of waiting until they had dropped all the way to the bottom.

In this incident when the rods fell before giving an alarm. I was Senior Watch Officer and Frank [Slattery] had the Engineering Officer of the Watch, something which I had never done before, putting Frank and myself on watch at the same time. It was the middle of the night and the Skipper both heard and felt the ship slowing. He rolled out of his state room and said, *"I relieve you,"* and pushed me towards the Reactor Compartment. The reactor water was dropping fast and as I entered the Reactor Compartment from forward the Engineering Chief of the Watch, who had worked for me in Idaho, came running into the Reactor Compartment from the Maneuvering area. He pointed to the right and both of us headed to the two valves needed to get water into the reactor, and opened them just as the water level was disappearing. There was never a dull day on the "Queen Mother."

Harold Glovier, '61 – '63

1963 – Loss of Thresher

On April 10, 1963 we lost a submarine, USS *Thresher* (SSN-593), and many fellow submariners. Three who perished at sea that day were former USS *Nautilus* (SSN-571) crew members. They are:

>SSN-593 LCDR John W. Harvey, Commanding Officer
>SSN-571 '55-'58, LT, PANOPO

>*SSN-593 LT John Smartz*
>*SSN-571* '58-'58, ET1(SS)

>SSN-593 HMC(SS) Andrew J. Gallant, Jr.
>SSN-571 '59-'60, HM1(SS)

Our departed shipmates are missed but not forgotten. Sailors rest your oar!

>Tommy "Robby" Robinson, '63 – '67

1963 – A Little Known Fact

Chief Raymond McCoole was my Leading Chief in the Interior Communications gang on *Nautilus*. He later became the Reactor Control Officer on *Thresher*.

Ray was commissioned in Pearl Harbor just before we left for the 90N mission. Captain Anderson wanted Ray to make the trip because the gyro compass was acting up. Ray wanted to get on with his new career and was transferred.

Ray was the Lieutenant that stayed home the day *Thresher* was lost because his wife had been involved in a home accident. The sad part of his side of the *Thresher* story was that Ray blamed the loss on himself. He believed that had he been on watch when the reactor scrammed he would have restarted the reactor, not by the book but, by pulling all the rods up at once, thus regaining propulsion power.

Perhaps, SSN-571 would have met a similar fate during the flooding incident in 1959, had not Chief Ed Dunn thrown away the book in order to restart the reactor on that fateful day. Ed received a Letter of Commendation for his actions and Rickover never complained about the lack of procedure. I received a copy of that letter from one of Ed's kids a few years ago. He had found the letter in Ed's stuff after he went on eternal patrol and did not know why his dad had received it.

Imon Pilcher, '56 – '60

1963 – SCRAM

I was working with a metallurgist who was called out of retirement to get a welding program up and running on a job here in Alaska. Now comes the interesting part. He was called into the investigation after *Thresher* went down - cast fittings - produced in Arizona, New Mexico, or Nevada? They were PORUS. Legal? And filled with something to fill the pores. Still legal? It was found that the silver brazers had brazed one half of a joint on one day shift and brazed the other half of the same joint on the next day shift. This results in un-brazing the other half that was previously brazed. The "filling" in the porous castings did not help the situation. Just a little squirt of water in the wrong place; a reactor SCRAM, a Main Ballast Tank (MBT) blow system that didn't work; a ship that was thirty feet too short, and we all know what happened next.

I remember on *Nautilus*, the feeling of sinking backwards with no propulsion, a SCRAM, and a few other minor problems - but the MBT blow worked. For anyone to think that *Thresher's* crew got it quick, has not consider watching the depth gauge come up and up with bigger and bigger numbers when all they could get out of the MBT blow was "Pssst" and then silence. There was no familiar sound of the high pressure air moving tons of sea water out of the ballast tanks.

Do those of you that were not around in the early days of nuclear power know what SCRAM means? When I got to the Comanche Peak Plant, it was called "Reactor Trip." I must admit, as a Torpedoman coming off a diesel boat, the first time I heard "Reactor SCRAM" I was a bit concerned. When Enrico Fermi was doing his thing under the stadium at the University of Chicago with the graphite moderated pile, (Manhattan Project) one rod was held out by a piece of rope (Safety rod). If the things got out of hand, the operator of the axe (Safety Control Rod Axe Man), cut the rope with the axe, the rod dropped and "scrammed" the operation. Now you know the "Rest of the Story."

George Clancy, '58 – '63

5 - CDR Francis "Frank" Fogarty, USN *and* Crew

October 1963 – April 1967

1963 – ERG's

It was 1963, and *Nautilus* was moored outboard of *Fulton* at State Pier in New London. Richie Burke and I had been working on the URC-32 [radio transmitter] and needed a part. We figured we could "liberate" the part from the electronics shop on the tender. So off we go. Richie walks up the brow and steps onto the tender. I'm right behind him and I get an immediate dressing down for wearing "Dirty, Dirty" shoes. I don't know what possessed me, but I told the Watch it was because of the "ERG's." Richie looked at me, swallowed hard, and turned his head so the Watch could not see his grin. I proceeded to explain that we had been in the Reactor Compartment and as usual I had stayed and talked to the Reactor Operator. The length of time I spent there was enough to collect many ERG's, which accumulated in the leather of my shoe's. I further explained that "ERG's" always seek the lowest part of the body. He bought it and let me pass. By this time Richie was around the bulkhead bent over with his hand covering his mouth to keep from laughing out loud. Oh, by the way, we "found" what we needed in the Electronics shop.

Leonard "Len" Scherer, '63 – '66

1963 – Hamilton, Bermuda

I was Duty Section Leader and Lieutenant Cox was the Duty Officer on our first night in Hamilton, Bermuda. Just about everyone in the Wardroom and crew were on liberty. Only the duty section and a few others was on board. A British ship was tied up directly across the pier. Of course, they had their grog rations and a lively group of Limeys were partying on the pier. They were jumping off the pier into the water and swimming around the pilings. As *Nautilus* sailors begin returning from liberty that evening they joined in the fun.

The Topside Watch rang me up to come topside. He pointed down the pier and strolling toward the boat was Lieutenant Smith with a couple of cases of beer on his shoulder and a jug of rum swinging in one hand. I met him as he approached the brow and I ask that he please stay on the pier with his beer and booze. I think that was his intend because he readily agreed. The pier party was at its peak. He did say, "Robby, send ice and juice to the pier." A Mess Cook provided pitchers of the needed ice and mixers and we were able to keep the party confined to the pier. As the revelers began to fade they were brought aboard and dried off. "Doc" Bonner cleaned the coral cuts and the happy sailors turned into their bunks to live another day, albeit with a headache and a bit of soreness.

The next day was my turn. Richie Burke and I went on the beach. We visited a British pub or two, shot darts, and was introduced to a yard of ale, my penalty for loosing at darts. Our liberty was cut short in the afternoon by a television announcement that all American sailors were to immediately return to their ships. President Kennedy had been shot. *Nautilus* got underway shortly afterward.

Tommy "Robby" Robinson, '63 – '67

1964 – Tank Re-certification

"Doc" Bonner drove a bunch of us, in a Navy bus, from Portsmouth Naval Shipyard at Kittery, Maine down to Submarine Base New London in order for us to re-certify in the submarine escape tower [Blow and Go] Of course we had to have fuel so we stopped and bought a few cases of beer, well maybe lots of beer. We were pissed up when we arrived at the tower but the divers took us in anyway. After re-certification, we left New London and immediately began looking for a bathroom but couldn't find one. By the time we got on the expressway from Boston to Portsmouth I was begging Bonner to pull over. "Doc" was half pissed himself, so he says, *"Hang it out the window Foreskin."* I was dying, so I opened a window and pissed a yellow stream. All the cars behind us turned on their windshield wipers even though it was a bright sunny day. We all laughed so hard I had to piss again. Yep, out the window!

Gerald "Gerry" Forseth, '65 – '69

And now for the rest of the story. The Massachusetts Department of Highways has been repaving a section of northbound Route 95 every year because of some unknown acid spilled in the late 60's. They have been trying to find the cause so that they can recover the cost. Just recently a citizen found a picture of a U.S. Navy bus travelling north past *USS Constitution* in Boston with sailors hanging their weapons out the windows. The State Police and FBI are investigating in an attempt to ID the sailors. So far it is reported that their faces are not recognizable due to grins, smiles, and laughter. They are asking others to look for pictures.

Edward "Ed" Montague, '69 - '72

1964 – The Big Heist

We know how resourceful *Nautilus* crew members can be and how we submarine sailors adapt. These are actual events that happened to members of the Radio Shack in 1964 during the overhaul at Portsmouth Naval Shipyard. The culprits are Rich Burke, Tommy Robinson, Len Scherer, and Ken Shelton.

We had to remove 90% of the radio equipment from the Bat Cave [Radio Room]. Well the shipyard assigned us a large space above the Bank as a work area. Each of us were given a key which lead to that space and the Bank, which had a separate locked door. The Bank was located just inside the main gate about 150 yards. Pay days were weekly for the shipyard workers, ours was every other week, so there was a huge amount of money in that Bank when both the shipyard and Navy were paid. I mention this as background for this event.

Our working area was huge with a phone at one end. We moved all of our equipment into this space aside from a few items left on the work barge. We stowed some of the sensitive equipment in locked cages and began the arduous tasks that are inherent during overhaul. Well it soon became apparent that our facility although spacious was working against us. The phone would ring constantly. We, of course, had everything at the other end of the space so it was a race to the phone. Well, being "The Best of the Best" we decided to rectify this situation by appropriating an additional phone, which we did. The new phone was "paralleled" to the existing phone line and we no longer had to endure our 100 yard dash, just a simple reach and we were on line, or so we thought.

One afternoon Base Security happened by (they had not bothered to visit before) and just shot the breeze but they did ask us one rather off hand question, *"Did we have or were we having trouble with our phone?"* With our most innocent faces we answered in the negative. I remember one of the officers asking if he could use the phone. We of course made sure that it was the "legal one," the other was in one of the near by work cages. He lifted the receiver, dialed a number listened for a few seconds, put the phone back in it's cradle. He said, *"Thank you"* and left with his buddy.

That was enough, it was obvious to us something was wrong. I picked up the phone and it was dead, I dialed anyway and it was still dead. No rocket scientist was needed to figure this one out. With the acquisition and covert installation of our new phone we somehow fouled up the phone system (later we found out it was just at the bank). We checked our new phone connection and found that bare wires were shorted against the cage. We taped the connection and dialed the phone again. It worked. So much for that, we were clean, and we all went back to work. The next day, one of us went to the Bank for a transaction and found that on the previous day the Bank's alarm system had failed and prompted base security to check the building, but just as mysterious as the failure, the system had returned to normal. The Bank's alarm system was on the phone circuit and we had disabled it! Our acquired phone disappeared immediately, everything was put back the way it was and we all breathed a sigh of relief – SAFE!

But there is a bit more to the story. Acquisition is the way of life in the yards, theft is not! Only a court of inquiry can determine the fine line between the two. At first we treated the whole thing as a joke and could not believe that it was so easy to disable the Bank alarm. A routine test of the alarm was done daily at the bank by employees of the bank and they were the ones who alerted base security. You have to be a submariner to understand how our minds worked at this point. With this knowledge we now conceived how it would be possible to simply relieve the Bank of it's money. The main vault was in the middle of the Bank from floor to ceiling (our floor). We knew exactly the spot. Although we did not investigate any safety measures that surrounded the vault we did develop this scenario for our potential heist:

1. Do it early on Friday about 0100 (1 AM), on the odd week when both civilian and military are paid. The armored car came on Thursday afternoon with money for pay day.
2. Short out the phone which would disable the alarm the Bank alarm.
3. Cut through the floor/ceiling into the Vault. Of course, we were confident we could do this – just didn't know how as yet.
4. Get the money – simple, right?
5. Immediately leave the base.
6. *FORGET ABOUT THE WHOLE THING!*

Of course we knew we could do it, or so we thought! What was scary to us is here we are, the elite of the Navy, submariners, each one of us with a Top Secret security clearance, protectors of some of the most sensitive information our government had. Crew members of the best damned boat in the Navy; able to run rings around "skimmers;" protectors of our Country; and stemming the "Red Tide."

It was just one of those fantasies that our overactive minds dreamed up from a situation that occurred during our yard period. It was an exercise that helped relieve the stress and/or boredom of a simple yard period that kept getting extended. We had a good laugh and nothing more.

Leonard "Len" Scherer, '63 - '66

1964 – Fire Watch LLRC

During the 1964/1965 Portsmouth Naval Shipyard overhaul non-NUC crew members who primarily resided forward of frame 45 where pressed into service to aide their NUC shipmates by standing fire watches in the Lower Level Reactor Compartment (LLRC). This policy was designed to minimize the radiation exposure of nuclear trained personnel and save them for more important work in the Reactor Compartment.

Being a non-qual Radioman I simply followed my NUC shipmates instructions. *"Suit up dummy, put these booties on, here's your dosimeter, don't let the welder catch on fire."* The process, of course, was much more complicated because NUC engineers had procedures for everything; even procedures for writing procedures.

But in I went! I figured I was going be in there for awhile so I plopped my butt down on an outboard heat exchanger and settled in while the welder went about his business. About fifteen minutes or so into the mission I looked at my dosimeter. It was pegged so figured it was time to crawl out of the LLRC.

Apparently the outboard heat exchanger was "hot" and not considered an approved seat. That ended this Radioman's brief career in the Reactor Compartment spaces aft of frame 45.

Tommy "Robby" Robinson, '63 - '67

Tommy Robinson

1964 – The Cigarette Lighter

Off hours boredom on the living barge was stifled by diversionary projects. One of these projects was the "cigarette Lighter." I don't recall whose brain child it was, but this idea started out as a collaboration between the forward Electronic Technicians and Radioman and soon the Sonarman were helping.

The intent was to create a unique way to light a cigarette. I think this all started because someone had to bum a light and there was none available. There was a wealth of spare electronic parts mostly available from cannibalized electronic equipment. We started out with a simple 102v ceramic light socket and a screw in heater element which glowed red hot with applied voltage, a simple on/off switch gave us the lighter.

Well anyone could build that simple device. So we decided that the hundreds of thousands of taxpayers dollars which went into our education and training should be put to better use. We needed to improve that simple device. I supplied a variable time delay, a couple of relays, one being an air operated relay from the URC-32 transmitter, a thermal switch and an old blower motor. The other rates supplied their share of goodies and we went to work.

Because this was a cumshaw project all serious work took a secondary role. It did not take long to build upon our project. Submariners are very efficient. Although It's been over thirty-five years, this is how I remember the operational sequence to get a "light."

First have cigarette in hand, then push the red power on button, a flashing LED signified that lighting sequence has started. There was a time delay, approximately 5 seconds, then a panel of LED's lit in sequence, followed by another delay, and another LED sequence. There was some relay noise as I believe eight relay's sequenced. A small light lit and the heater element glowed. At this point you had to be quick with the cigarette because as soon as the element got hot enough to light the cigarette a blower motor came on and shut the whole process down.

The lighter disappeared in a week. I still wonder who has it?

Leonard "Len" Scherer, '63 - '66

1964 – The Cannon

The living barge had a machine shop area and just outside of this space was a large lathe. Being a Radioman I didn't have a clue how to operate it so it was of no consequence to me. One day, in the tin benders shop, I was negotiating a deal for some stainless steel trim work for the Radio Room. I offered a can of coffee and promised of one of those crummy, all you can eat meals, that Wes Behning was so famous for on Fridays. You remember, steak and lobster, baked potatoes, corn on the cob and some other junk you had to force down. For some odd reason one of the tin benders in Shop 17 took my offer. Yard birds are a strange lot, aren't they? He promised to use only "scrap" stainless for the job. Well the bribe worked. He did a lot of work and so did some of his buddies. You can still see the results if you look through the door into the Bat Cave (Radio Room) on the Big "N."

But I regress, I found a brass bar in that shop about two inches in diameter and a foot long. I didn't know what to do with it, but it was shiny so I brought it back to the barge. About a week later someone was using the lathe for a home project. I watch the process and it seemed simple enough to me. You just put your material in the chuck and cutting tool in the holder at a certain angle, push the start button and start creating. Well to make a very long story short, and not to disclose my ineptness at machining, I proceeded to make a brass cannon. I actually got pretty good at it in time. Of course, I did not have a plan. I just cut metal and formed a general shape of an old fashion muzzle loading cannon. Well I had this cannon blank, why not make a cannon that actually shot?

After looking around I found a whole bunch of 9/16 inch ball bearings. Now I had my shot. I drilled a 5/8 inch bore; drilled and attached a brass bolt into the bore; and drilled that to the bore to fit a fuse from a fire cracker. I cleaned the whole thing up with a crocus cloth. It looked pretty good but would it fire?

I took my creation to the shop area where there was a large vise attached to a work bench. I believe my ordnance testing was on a duty weekend, probably Sunday, because the work barge was generally deserted. The ball bearings slid into the bore and I elected not to use a patch to make sure there where no unplanned explosions. How much powder and where do I get it? That was my the next problem. Answer, buy a box of .22 shells and some firecrackers for fuses. Now all that remained was figuring out how much powder to use. Being brilliant, I decided trial by error was the best method. It's a wonder I didn't kill myself.

We had some bunk bottoms and mattresses stowed in the overhead of the work barge. I got a bunk bottom and two mattresses and set up the bunk bottom and one mattress by the loading doors on the starboard side of the barge. I broke open one .22 shell and pored it's powder into the bore. Then I lubricated a ball bearing with DC4 and holding the cannon with the muzzle upwards inserted the ball. I secured the cannon in the bench vise and aimed in the general direction of the bunk bottom and mattress and tightened the vise down. Then I placed a fuse into my touch hole, stepped behind the other mattress and lit the fuse. It went off with a loud bang and scared the life out of me. I looked at the target and there was no indication of a hit. I felt that by hearing the report of the firing it was safe to inspect the cannon. The ball was missing. I found it on the deck in front of the target. Was my charge too light? Did I need more powder? I experimented whenever I could, finally firing my last shot. If the barge was inspected today you could find a neat 5/8 inch hole through one of the oak loading doors.

I still have that cannon and it has some pretty serious vise marks on it's barrel.

Leonard "Len" Scherer, '63 - '66

1964 – The Pink Lady

Shortly after arriving at Portsmouth Naval Shipyard in 1964 Stewards Mate 2nd/Class Donald Wilson affectionately known as "Willie" purchased the Pink Lady, a pink Chrysler convertible, reportedly for $25.00. Although "Willie" could drive he would not due to a very bad auto accident in years past. So after his purchase, "Willie" canvassed the brown baggers [married men] who had left their wives in Groton in order to put together a crew who would take turns driving him and the other brown baggers between Kittery and Groton on non-duty weekends. "Willie" was very proud of his cadre of white chauffeurs. That ride became known as the "brown bagger's special" - going home to get some loving. Len Scherer, Chimp Sanborn, Joe Thompson, me and a few others were selected by "Willie" to drive.

Each Friday after Benny's big Steak and Lobster feed, we, with a case or two of beer and a jug of wine, would pile into the Pink Lady for the trip south. The consumption of beverages was in direct proportion to the number of pit stops. I believe every state trooper between Maine and Connecticut knew the Pink Lady and her crew and they pretty much gave us a free pass. We would arrive in Groton in various states of inebriation; usually dumped Chimp at his house and tossed all the empties on his lawn; Occasionally Len's dog Lassie would chase "Willie" around the yard and back into the Pink Lady; and there were new adventures with each trip. The Pink Lady ran like a top and never failed us.

Tommy "Robby" Robinson, '63 – '67

1965 – The Crypto Room

In the early 1960s someone at Commander Naval Telecommunication Command (COMNAVTELECOM) decided that submarines should have their own Crypto Rooms. We Radiomen questioned that logic. The foremost reason being that our Radio Room, or Bat Cave, was already designated a secure space with cipher locks and Officers and Radiomen had been conducting Crypto operations for years in the sanctity of our small space with no problems. Radiomen perform the majority of Crypto Operations but occasionally an "Officer Eyes Only" message requires an Officers attention, normally either the Communications or Operations Officer responds. But the orders came down from high, work commenced during the 1964/65 overhaul, and eventually we Radiomen became dubious owners of a Crypto Room within the Radio Room.

Physical space, as you know, is severally limited in a submarine and the Radio Room is no exception. Our Radio Room, located on the starboard side of the Control Room, was basically a narrow passageway with transmitters aligned against the pressure hull. There were two Morse Code (CW) operating stations and radio receivers located inboard. A few feet of space inside the Radio Room just forward of the door from the Control Room, was designated Crypto and partitioned athwart with a heavy metal vault door. The result was a metal closet roughly the size of a very small WalMart toilet stall. Our Crypto Room contained a small safe, a chair and KLB-47 Crypto device for encrypting and decrypting messages. A skinny person could just manage to squeeze into the chair with his knees knocking against the KLB-47. The vault door had to be shut and locked from inside the Radio Room essentially trapping the operator in his stall.

Sea trials followed completion of the overhaul at PNSY and we were very happy to finally be at sea. It was shortly after sea trials and during normal operations that we Radiomen discovered an anomaly with the Crypto Room. As *Nautilus* descended beyond 200 feet in depth, the pressure hull compressed, the Crypto Room vault door jammed shut, not to be opened until the boat ascended shallower than 200 feet. Occasionally we "trapped" an unsuspecting officer in the vault for the duration of a deep dive. It wasn't long before this flaw became general knowledge in the Wardroom and our fun at the O-gangs expense was over. The flaw, however, remained a Radio Room qualification question for years.

Tommy "Robby" Robinson, '63 – '67

1965 – Anti-Semitic Executive Officer

The entire Jewish population on board *Nautilus* in 1965 consisted of Donald Worobe and Alfred "Abie" Shuman. Don received orders to transfer off the boat that year and as he departed he made the following 1-MC announcement.

"Now hear this – Sadly, I report to the crew that the Executive Officer is anti-Semitic. He signed my orders, transferring me from Nautilus, and with that simple stroke of his pen, he coldly eliminated 50% of the Jewish population on board this fine submarine – Carry on!"

Then Don reported to the Pentagon where he frequently got lost in the miles and miles of corridors.

Tommy "Robby" Robinson, '63 - '67

1965 – Man Overboard

One day, as we were leaving the work barge, three shipyard workers were just walking up the gangway from *Nautilus* to the pier. One of them let out a yell and fell into the water between *Nautilus* and the pier. The pier was about twenty feet higher than the water, and *Nautilus* was about ten feet higher than the water. This was in the dead of winter, the water was very cold and the sixty year old worker was wearing heavy foul weather gear that would soon pull him under water.

His two buddies raised the alarm right away, and *Nautilus'* Topside Watch passed the word *"Man Overboard"* throughout the submarine.

A shipyard crane immediately moved to where the worker fell into the water and lowered it's hook toward the now sinking individual. He was able to grab and hold onto the hook but that's all he could manage. He was too cold to hang on tight enough to be pulled out of the water.

Another crane (cherry picker) rolled up in about one minute and lowered a basket with two other shipyard workers in it down to the individual in the water. They, as best they could, held the fallen individual against the basket. They could not get him out of the water and into the basket. The wet foul weather gear coupled with his weight was more than they could lift. They held on to him while the cherry picker and crane simultaneously lifted him out of the water and onto the pier. The individual left in an ambulance and he was back to work the next day. We, in the submarine crew, were amazed at how fast and efficiently the shipyard workers responded to the emergency. If anyone had waited 30 seconds more to respond, this guy probably would not have made it, as he was sinking very fast.

As it turned out the gangway hand rail had broken. The shipyard worker fell into the water after he leaned on the broken hand rail.

George Hofferber, '65 - '67

1965 – Systems Testing

As *Nautilus* neared the end of her shipyard refit period, more and more preparations were being made for the first trip out to the diving area for sea trials. As the last of the systems were turned over to us, we tested them and operated all of the gear to make sure that it would work as designed. This was a busy time for us and we often worked from 0700 (7 AM) in the morning until very late at night to get the systems tested, repaired and operational. After a system was turned over to us, it was up to us to fix anything that was wrong with it, unless it required major work or repair. In that case we would turn it back over to the shipyard to fix or repair but this time we were responsible to make sure that the work was performed correctly. The shipyard workers did not care for us looking over their shoulders while they worked. But we did just that. Several systems and components were turned back over to the shipyard for final repair.

George Hofferber, '65 – '67

Tommy Robinson

1965 – Fast Cruise

During hot trials [fast cruise] we performed as if we were at sea but actually we were tied up to the pier the entire fast cruise. We closed up the submarine for three full days. No one went in or out as we simulated being at sea and submerged. The game was not broken by anyone. No one went in or out during these three days. We turned the shafts as if we were steaming along and did everything except actually dive. All systems were rigged as if we were at sea and we disconnected from electrical shore power. The only connection to the shore was the mooring lines that held us next to the pier. We held every imaginable drill. Drills ran 12 hours during the day and several more times during the night and the crew responded to all drill scenarios.

It was a long three days and we spent a lot of time working on equipment to get little things repaired and/or getting things to operate as they should. Unfortunately, on the last day of the "fake" sea trials, the reactor water system sprung a leak. We had to shut down the reactor plant, cool it to room temperature, and de-pressurize it. The shipyard workers came back on board and spent another week fixing the leak. Because the leak happened before the end of the "fake" sea trials we were required to drill again for three more days. The second three day trial alongside the pier went smooth with very few problems.

George Hofferber, '65 – '67

1965 – Flooding in the Park

Work required to correct various equipment malfunctions was extensive during the week it took the shipyard workers to fix the leak. We were working all day and sleeping on the work barge or on *Nautilus* at night. I was just too tired to go to my trailer which I had rented off base. But at the end of the second three day fast cruise, I happily went to the trailer as soon as we were released from the submarine.

However, when I arrived I found all the carpeting removed from the trailer and both doors open. I went in and was followed very closely with one of the workers from the trailer park. They had been installing a trailer in the space next to the one I was renting when they looked over and saw water running out of the front and back doors of my trailer. The heat had gone off and the water lines had frozen and broke. They were in the process of drying everything out and had tried to get all of my possessions up off the floor. I was amazed that nothing was missing and they had done a good job of protecting my stuff. I was so tired that I slept in the soggy humid trailer. It was still better than the living barge.

George Hofferber, '65 – '67

1965 – The Sound Pier

After fast cruise *Nautilus* moved to the sound piers. This is where the submarine is isolated from underwater sounds in the bay by placing large partitions all around the submarine after it is tied to the sound pier. Then every motor in the submarine is shut off. The hundreds of motors on the submarine are not intended to be all shut off at any one time. The people on the sound pier would say, *"I still hear several motors running"* and we would continue to look for them. Small fans in gyros, small cooling fans in all kinds of sonar, radar, radio equipment, etc. You get the idea – NO motor in the entire submarine could be running. After we finally found and shut off all motors, the sound pier would ask for a specific motor to be turned on, and it was up to the electricians to figure out how to turn on each motor in the sequence requested.

In some cases systems had to be lined up to operate (hydraulic oil system pumps) and part of the line up often specified that other motors needed to be operating. We had to figure out how to operate only the one motor that the sound pier requested. We also had to walk in stocking feet and talk in a whisper so as not to interfere with the sound readings being recorded by the sound pier personnel. When we finished, two days later, after working 24 hours a day, the sound personnel could identify exactly what motors were running on the submarine and what the operating configuration was at any particular time. No matter what we did, they could tell us what we were doing, and/or which motors were running.

George Hofferber, '65 – '67

1965 – Sea Trials and Dreams

As sea trials for *Nautilus* drew nearer, someone figured out that *Nautilus* was the only submarine that had been in the Portsmouth Naval Shipyard

[PSNY] in a refit that actually took longer than *Thresher's* and, of course, *Thresher* sank while on sea trials after her lengthy refit period. *Nautilus* had actually been in the shipyard two full months longer than *Thresher*.

Then the stories started flowing about how *Nautilus* was in the same dry dock as *Thresher* and there were many other unsubstantiated stories that paired the two submarines. By the time we actually pulled away from the pier some of us were nervous wrecks.

Several nights before we went out on sea trials I dreamed that we were sinking and the Officer of the Deck (OOD) started reciting the Lord's Prayer over the 1-MC system as we were going down. I woke up yelling out the Lord's Prayer as loud as I could, and several shipmates spent time trying to fully wake me and calm me down. The thought of sea trials was weighing heavy on my mind and I was not the only one that was concerned.

A final footnote regarding my dream came several years later when I was instructing at Nuclear Power School in Idaho. I overheard another instructor tell his students that things got so bad on *Nautilus* once during sea trials that the OOD started saying the Lord's Prayer over the 1-MC system. I just smiled because I knew exactly where this sea story originated.

George Hofferber, '65 – '67

1965 – Sea Trials Shallow Dive

We left the shipyard and went on actual sea trials to the shallow dive area which was less than 500 feet deep and performed our first shallow trim dive to periscope depth. No Problem. We did all kinds of drills and performed several more dives and surfaces in the shallow dive area over two full days. We replayed the three days of drills that we had just concluded during the fast cruise. Actually these two days were quite easy and the drills were no problem even though we did not get a lot of sleep. When we did go to bed, we were tired enough to sleep, no matter what was going on around the bunk areas in *Nautilus*.

Then after two days of diving and surfacing in the shallow water area we transited as fast as *Nautilus* could travel underwater to the deep dive area. *Nautilus*, in spite of her age, was still able to dive much deeper than the old World War II diesel submarine *Rock*, but we could not go as deep as *Sam Houston*, my previous boat. *Nautilus* was originally a brand new diesel submarine that, while being constructed, was cut in half and a reactor plant was added to the hull. It still had most of the manual valves and hull configuration that the old diesel submarines had, only the reactor plant and propulsion plant was different.

George Hofferber, '65 – '67

1965 – Sea Trials Deep Dive

We started the deep test dive at periscope depth and went down in 50 foot intervals stopping at each interval to completely check all areas of the submarine for potential problems. We manned battle stations in order to efficiently use all available manpower for this episode. Every crew member would be on the station they were most familiar with during the entire evolution. It was estimated that it would take a couple of hours to complete the deep test dive.

After reaching a predetermined depth, the entire submarine was rigged for deep submergence. Everything that has sea pressure applied to it and is not necessary for the evolution being carried out is shut so that sea pressure is not needlessly affecting equipments and gauges. After rigging for deep submergence we continued down at fifty foot increments.

My battle station watch was the bell recorder for the propulsion panel. I recorded the speed ordered by the Control Room, the time the speed was ordered, and the time the propulsion panel operators (two personnel - one for each shaft) were able to establish the ordered speed. I was wedged into a space just wide enough for me to sit on a low ledge behind the propulsion panel operators. In that location I could see all that happened in the power plant control panel area. I also wore a headset connected to the ships sound powered phone system and I relayed to Maneuvering Room personnel various communications being said on the phones.

All went well until we reached the last 50 foot plateau. Just as the Control Room was passing the word over the ships 1-MC system, *"We are at Test depth, check all spaces for leaks and/or damage,"* we in Maneuvering heard an ominous very loud sound from the Stern Room, the compartment directly aft of Maneuvering. I heard an extremely loud bang then the deafening sound of streaming water. It was a terrible ominous loud roaring sound.

A watch stander in the Stern Room was screaming into the phones at the top of their lungs just to be heard. The deafening roar of water in the background almost drown out the talkers voice, but it was clear that he was screaming, *"Flooding, Flooding in the Stern Room,"* over and over again. I repeated the alarm several times very loudly to the watch standers in Maneuvering. Then came a loud metallic bang from the water tight hatch that separated the Stern Room from Maneuvering. It was slammed shut and dogged down tight by someone in the Stern Room.

The propulsion panel operators heard my first report and started speeding up the shafts from the 1/3 speed they had been ordered to maintain. The electrical panel operator turned and looked directly at me and I repeated, in a louder voice than necessary, *"Flooding in the Stern Room."* He actually heard the first report, but didn't believe it until he saw me say it. He then tapped the Reactor Operator on the arm and said, *"Pay attention to George,"* at which time the Reactor Operator realized what had been said and what was going on without asking again.

Now the shafts were speeding up, dragging more steam from the reactor plant. It was up to the Reactor Operator to keep up with the power level changes so the shafts can turn as fast as needed in order to drive us to the surface, if possible. The Reactor Operator John Livingston (John later transferred to *Scorpion* and was lost at sea) placed one hand on the battle short switch, ready to hold it into the battle position which would override any automatic shut down of the reactor. This would allow the reactor to be used at all costs to provide power to the shafts. This was an excellent move for him to take.

The Engineering Officer of the Watch ordered the shafts sped up slowly until we receive a bell order from the Control Room. He then informed the Control Room of flooding in the Stern Room over the ships 1-MC intercom system and recommend an all ahead emergency on the shafts. Almost immediately the order came back via the engine order telegraph to go to all ahead emergency. The propulsion panel operators responded to the bell as fast as the Reactor Operator would let them. During the ten seconds or so that this sequence is happening, the stern room phone talker is still screaming at the top of his lungs, *"Flooding in the stern room,"* over and over. He cannot hear the ships 1-MC intercom system because of the deafening noise of water flooding into the Stern Room and he does not know if the flooding alarm has gotten out yet. It's an understatement to say that I could hear the concern and alarm in his voice.

Steely Eyed Killers of the Deep

After the shafts were moving at all ahead emergency, and the steam plant was no longer in transient power levels, there was nothing for us in Maneuvering to do but turn and look at the depth pressure gauge. It was located right behind the propulsion panel operators and immediately over my head. It was indicating about 250 pounds per square inch sea pressure and it was not moving.

Nautilus had a steep up angle and the twin screws were turning very fast directly under us causing major vibration. The Stern Room phone talker was quite. He had shut off his phone and headset and we could no longer hear what was happening aft. The sea pressure indicator should decrease as the submarine moved closer to the surface indicating that we were not, in fact, sinking. It seemed like an hour that we sat staring at that pressure gage, noting that it was not moving at all, which meant that we apparently were not getting any closer to the surface. Time to worry! Actually we sat like this for about 20 or 30 seconds, but it seemed like hours.

Suddenly the up angle on the submarine came off, the bow dropped, and the Control Room ordered a 2/3 speed bell. We could feel the submarine gently rocking back and forth which meant that we were on or near the surface. Only then did we realized that the pressure gauge we had been staring had been shut when we rigged for deep submergence. It was displaying the sea water pressure at the time we rigged for deep submergence and not the greater pressure at test depth when the flooding occurred.

The Stern Room phone talker came back on the phone and there was no background noise as before. In a very shaky voice he reported, *"Flooding in the stern room is secured."* Then the water tight hatch between the Stern Room and Maneuvering flew open and some very shaken sailors stepped into the Maneuvering Room. They just needed aplace to go away from the scene. They were jumpy and could not stand still for several hours.

The Stern Room had actually flooded for about 15 to 20 seconds we ended up with four to six feet of water in the bilge. We proceeded to pump out the water as we listened to the submariners from the Stern Room recount what had happened. Here is their story.

All went well going down to test depth. There are very few hull penetrations in the Stern Room so the impact of going to test depth is not great. The Auxiliary gang, used to combat flooding in the after half of the submarine is stationed in the Stern Room during battle stations, thus the crew of trained personnel was in the right place at the right time. When *Nautilus* reached test depth the Stern Room personnel heard the 1-MC announcement, *"We are now at test depth,"* over the speaker and flooding occurred immediately after the announcement.

Two operators were in the lower level of the Stern Room where the carbon dioxide scrubbing equipment and carbon monoxide cleaning equipment is located. There were about six personnel and the phone talker in the upper level where the crew bunks. The chemistry lab and the oxygen generator are located there. When the flooding started it was in the lower level shooting upward from below the deck on the starboard side of the submarine all the way at the back end of the lower level compartment. Water was shooting up from the floor all the way to the ceiling and hitting the ceiling extremely hard. The ceiling of the lower level is the metal floor of the upper level, thus all the noise. The metal floor plates were rattling with the high pressure sea water hitting them. The only way to the area where the water appeared to be coming from was to go down the ladder on the port side rear end of the compartment which was the opposite corner of where the water was coming up. After going down the ladder, you had to turn around and go forward about fifteen feet, then cross over to the starboard side between the scrubbing equipment then turn and come towards the back of the submarine about ten feet.

Three people immediately went down the ladder and traversed the course to the starboard side and dove into the high pressure water in an attempt to find where the water was coming from. The space is very small and confining, thus the picture of this pile of sailors in a mass of frantic searching is not comforting. The fourth person down the ladder by accident looked to the right of the ladder as he was descending to the lower level. He spotted what appeared to be a pipe extending all the way down the side of the hull and did not remember a pipe being there before. On *Nautilus* the sailors qualified as if they were on the old diesel submarines and knew many details in many compartments in addition to their own watch stations. Of course this sailor was on the damage control team at battle stations and it was his job to recognize problems and he did.

The pipe running down the side of the submarine was not a pipe at all. There was indeed a short pipe extending downward about two feet from the overhead and sea water was flooding into the Stern Room through that pipe. From the end of the pipe, sea water under great pressure at test depth, appeared to be a long pipe when actually it was hard running water. The water went down the curved hull of the submarine, and as luck would have it, the water went right through a cutout area at the keel line of the submarine, hit a floor brace about five feet past the keel line, and sprayed straight up to the overhead on the other side of the Stern Room. The Auxiliaryman that spotted the problem took two steps back up the ladder and shut the stern tube flushing valve, thus securing the flooding in the stern room.

The stern tube flushing valve and pipe is used to flush dirt out of the stern tubes where the shaft goes through the hull. This valve should have been shut before the submarine was placed back in the water from the dry dock. Even though the valve was checked shut each time we rigged for dive, twice during fast cruises and once on sea trials, it apparently was not completely shut or somehow defective. In any event it was now shut and the flooding was secured.

An Engineman found a rag in the bilge as sea water was being pumped out so he retrieved it. A theory soon developed. The rag had red lead hull paint on it. Apparently it had been stuffed into the stern tube flushing pipe hole to prevent paint from being sprayed into the stern tube area while the hull was being painted while in dry dock. Evidently, the rag was not removed from the hole by the ship yard painters. When *Nautilus* left the dry dock and returned to the water, the rag apparently moved up the pipe to the valve. During one of the times the valve was exercised to verify that it worked the rag must have moved into the valve itself. Thus when the valve was checked shut, it was actually seated on the rag, andthe valve was not completely shut. The great pressure of deep submergence was enough to force the rag out of the valve and cause a lot of us on the submarine to have to change our skivvies at the first opportunity.

After a short period of discussion, the powers to be accepted the deep dive as complete, and ordered us to do the thing that we all hated the most - angles and dangles.

George Hofferber, '65 – '67

1965 – Angles and Dangles

Angles and Dangles is the art of going at high speed, with a large down angle, travelling to test depth, then returning to periscope depth while making an all ahead full bell. During angles and dangles we looked at the engine order log, which I was tasked to maintaining at battle stations. The log tells the whole story. The order for the 1/3 bell, which was given at the start of the deep submergence dive and used continuously while we went down incrementally to test depth was written into the log clearly, plainly, and neatly as required by procedure. The all ahead emergency bell, which occurred about 10 or 15 seconds into the emergency, was also written into the log clearly, plainly, and neatly as required by procedure, as was the time and rotation speed of the shafts upon reaching the all ahead emergency bell. At this point I was following procedure and had no time to think about what was going on. At the completion of the high speed run up to periscope depth the order given was a 2/3 bell and the log reflected exactly how I was feeling at that time. The entry was almost illegible.

The other Maneuvering Room operators laughed when they looked at my log sheet and started to give me a hard time about the illegible entry. But then we compared logs and when compared to the reactor operator, electrical operator and steam plant operator logs, we all had made entries at the start of the event, and well into the event keeping up the log with our actions was no problem. After we watched the non-moving pressure gauge and thought about what was going on, all log entries were almost unreadable.

After sea trials we took *Nautilus* back into the Kittery, Maine shipyard for a couple of weeks to finish up on some superficial work that needed to be done and some repair work that were identified while on sea trials. Nothing spectacular happened during this time. We then moved down to New London, Connecticut, the Home Port of *Nautilus*, where we resumed normal operations with the fleet.

George Hofferber, '65 – '67

1966 – Flooding in AMR 2

I reported to *Nautilus* while she was in the Portsmouth Naval shipyard in Kittery, Maine. After my first couple of days aboard I was not very impressed so I'll move on.

Nautilus was the next boat to dive to test depth after *Thresher* went down. The rider list changed a lot on *Nautilus*. In addition to shipyard supervisors the men who did the work were also on board. Rickover rode us to 200 feet then we surfaced, he got off, and then we went to test depth. At about three quarter of the way down, with things getting pretty tense for the riders, some residue that covered one of topside emergency vents blew off in After Machinery Room (AMR 2). The water went down behind a scrubber or burner and when it hit the bulkhead it made AMR 2 a hard place to see anything. In the Control Room, where I was on watch, a lot of people were on their knees asking for help. One of our fine highly qualified Auxiliaryman quickly found and shut the open valve. We only took on a few hundred gallons of water if I remember correctly. Once the flooding was resolved and everyone stood up we quietly slipped to our test depth. I didn't have control of the dive but I did know where the Chicken Switches were located for the Emergency Main Ballast Tank blow. That's my story. Remember the *Thresher, Scorpion,* and all the other boats we have lost over the years past. Were we lucky, or good, or both?

Joseph "Joe" Thompson, '65 – '66

1966 – Loadout

Shortly after our overhaul period at Portsmouth Naval Shipyard, we began making preparations for a long, planned 60 day patrol which actually lasted 67 days. We took on a full load of torpedoes after off loading our practice torpedoes. We also took on a full load of food and supplies. Food was packed everywhere in the submarine. Tins of non perishable goods such as coffee and canned goods were stored in every nook and cranny that was not taken up with equipment and other supplies. The walk-in refrigerator was packed solid with items that needed to be cool and the freezer was packed solid with the frozen items. The cooks packed the food in the reverse order that it would be needed for meals. Think about that for just a minute. Enough food was loaded for 120 crew members for three meals a day, a snack each evening, again at midnight, and a soup snack at 0400 (4 AM), each day for 60 days. The Cooks had to store food in the chill box, freezer and other storage areas around the submarine in the reverse order that it would be needed so they can get the food out quickly as it is needed.

That's not a small task, by anyone's standards, and it was all done by four Cooks and one Mess Cook (dish washer and potato peeler). At least "Benny," the lead Cook, brought milk along for the patrol. I remember on *Sam Houston* for the very first meal, out of Holy Loch, we only had cool aid to drink. *Nautilus* brought enough whole milk for us to drink for each and every meal that was served and then switched to cool aid (bug Juice) - YUCK! I learned to hate bug Juice. But, for the most part, the meals were excellent. The Navy provided good provisions and the Cook's did a great job preparing meals for us submarine sailors.

George Hofferber, '65 - '67

1966 – "Borrowing" Contraband

On the last night before we went out on patrol (we left the pier at 0500 (5 AM)) a couple of Electricians went to a house in Groton, Connecticut and broke an eighteen inch cement Owl off of a brick post that stood in front of the house. They brought this 20 plus pound cement Owl on board for the patrol. However, that was not the worst item or the most daring item that went on patrol with us.

The most daring theft was pulled off by the Auxiliary gang. They went on Main Street in New London, Connecticut, and stole - oops, pardon me, "borrowed" the eight ball from a sign in front of a billiard hall. This eight ball was actually a heavy rubber inflated eight ball that weighed several pounds and was about sixteen inches across. Since they selected the sign on Main Street, in the middle of the night, they had a much greater chance of getting caught and arrested for theft.

Another "borrowing" incident, that probably would have had the worst consequences if the owners had figured out who borrowed their possession, was pulled off by the NUCs. They went next door to *Nautilus*, at the same pier, in the middle of the night, and took down the four foot long mermaid sign on the Navy Seal Team Barge. If those Navy Seal Team members had caught them, they would have really been a hurting, not just a little, I mean really hurting. Those Navy Seal Team guys were a mean bunch of sailors that took no guff whatsoever. This incident would not have been funny if they had been caught.

George Hofferber, '65 – '67

1966 – The Owl

Paraphrased from "History of The Owl" [www.ussnautilus.us]

Steely Eyed Killers of the Deep

The Owl first surfaced years ago aboard *Nautilus*. Being a crew member at that time, myself, "Jiggs" Kronenwetter, Jerry "Foreskin" Forseth, and Phil Zahl had been to the Newport Jazz Festival in Rhode Island the night before we were to leave on patrol. Phil had the idea that we take this statue of an Owl along with us then return it when we got back. This is a common practice for submariners. They always take everything not nailed down with them on patrols. So we took the Owl. Other crew members took the Navy Diver's mermaid, a huge mistake, but, that's another story.

The Owl was displayed in the Crew's Mess on board *Nautilus* as we were steaming in from patrol. Me, "Jiggs" Kronenwetter, Ted Trafka, Frank Webb and Bob Holst surrounded the Owl. We all were sporting beards including the Owl. The Owl spent most of the patrol in the Maneuvering Room after a short abduction by the Enginemen. The Owl was there for all of the Maneuvering Room watches.

After patrol the Owl went ashore to his perch in New London. He missed the next trip to Bermuda but he would soon return to the Big "N".

It was during the 1966 Bermuda trip that we got involved in a life changing event for most of us. During a war game, *Nautilus* was run over by the aircraft carrier *Essex*. It was not fun! As a result the Owl cartoon was born. His first appearance as a cartoon character was taking booze intravenously after the collision. After we limped back to New London, we re-acquired the Owl and returned him to his perch in Maneuvering. He was a veteran of a patrol and a shipmate. Needless to say, the Owl was the mascot of the electricians.

After that incident, the Owl cartoons literally showed up everywhere on the boat, even inside of machinery that was disassembled for repair. The only way to see the cartoon was to disassemble the machine.

When I departed the Big "N" at the end of May, 1969, the Owl was resting comfortably in his watch standing space on board *Nautilus*. I was even given a citation upon my departure from the Navy for creating the cartoon character of the Owl. I don't know what happened to the physical Owl afterward nor do any of my shipmates. I am sure he is somewhere contributing to the morale of those around him. I went off to college and got a bachelor's degree in Art, and a master's degree in Educational Media. My friends and I have had a lot of fun, over the years, with the Owl. Due to my cartooning and interest in graphic art, I have managed to feed myself many years doing visual communication.

At this stage of my life, I am focusing on cartooning, hoping to do nothing but draw cartoons soon.

James "Jimbo" Neaves, '66 – '69

1966 – Berets, Beards and Earrings

"There is a touch of the pirate about every man who wears the dolphins badge." Commander Jeff Tall, Royal Navy

Just before we departed Groton on our Northern run in 1966 "Doc" Bonner suggested we do something unique to commemorate the trip. He took up a collection, just a few bucks, from those of us who wanted to participate in this adventure and he purchased a rather large quantity of black berets and gold earrings. After being underway for a few days "Doc" determined the time was right and he set up an all night ear piercing operation in his office. "Doc" was very professional. As I recall he held an ice cube behind my earlobe and ran a syringe needle through the lobe, pulled it out, and inserted the earring. "Doc" was also thrifty. He didn't waste many things so that was probably the same syringe that he used to inject gilley into oranges just before the movie in the Crews Mess. When the watch was relieved sailors would stop by "Doc's" office for their piercing, earring, and beret. The Skipper had already authorized beards but this was long before earrings became fashionable for men and Admiral Zumwalt's days as Chief of Naval Operations (CNO). The next morning a motley looking crew of bearded pirates was waiting for first call in the Crews Mess sporting new earrings and black berets. Not a word from the O-gangers, just smiles.

Tommy "Robby" Robinson, '63 - '67

1966 – Games we Played

During the entire patrol, we played games with the "prizes" that were brought on board the evening before leaving port. I think they started writing rules for the games on the first day out of port, and the rules got rather complicated as the patrol went on. Every gang on board the submarine; Electrician gang had twelve crew members, Chemistry gang had six, Engineman gang was fourteen, Auxiliary gang was eight, Torpedoman was six, and Cooks consisted of four full time personnel

Steely Eyed Killers of the Deep

and whoever was assigned as Mess Cook. I think every gang joined in the fun, with exception of the officers, who just sat back, watched and laughed, or shook their heads in disbelief, as we played the games.

The idea was to steal each item that was brought on board from the gang that had control of it. That had to be done without any one catching you stealing it. Then you had to hide the item and attempt to have your gang keep control of as many items as was possible. One additional rule was that the item had to be in plain sight at all times. You could not hide it such that it could not be seen. For example, the Owl was kept by the Electricians in their work area. It was in plain sight in that if you went up to the stainless steel mesh door that was used to lock up the space, you could see the Owl through the mesh on the stainless steel door. The Electricians thought that no one would be able to get into their work area to steal the Owl, but how wrong they were. When it came up missing, the first thing the Electricians did was go through all the Electricians to see if they could determine if anyone let someone else into the work area unsupervised. No one had and finally it was determined that it was possible to climb over some pipes and get into the work area without unlocking the door. Again the Owl had to be in plain sight but no one could find it.

After several days of looking the Owl was spotted locked inside the chemistry control cabinet. The Chemists almost broke the rule as the Owl was only visible through a one inch crack in the stainless steel door hinge area. But it was visible, if you looked into the area with a flashlight, so it counted. Now it was up to everyone else to figure out how to get the Owl out of that cabinet without getting caught.

I don't know how the Electricians got the Owl back, but one night I was sleeping, and a Electrician came running past my bunk and handed the Owl to me to hide. No one saw the exchange and the Owl stayed in plain sight on my bunk for several days. I had to sleep with this stupid cement Owl, and keep it hidden without covering it up, but it was worth it. I caught hell from the other Electricians the day I went to my bunk and the Owl was missing. We never found it again until the end of the patrol. The Auxiliaryman had hidden it in a place that was harder to see than the chemistry locker. Their hiding place was deemed inappropriate. But the patrol was over so it didn't anymore. Actually, the Auxiliaryman had all of the items hidden by the end of the patrol, and the appropriateness of the hiding places was questionable. We all got our items back the day we came into port at the end of the patrol. The eight ball was returned to the billiard hall, unfortunately it was deflated.

The Owl was returned to the stanchion at the house in Groton. It, of course, had a blue nose and beard glued on it before it was returned. I took a picture of it several weeks after it had been returned and it still had a blue nose and beard. The mermaid also went back to the diver's barge with a blue nose and beard. Never did hear a word from the divers. Oh, the things sailors did to amuse themselves.

George Hofferber, '65 - '67

1966 – Bluenose

Nautilus crossed the Arctic Circle while on this patrol, an event that is worthy of a party. All sailors who cross the Arctic Circle are initiated into a club called "Bluenoses." Sailors who had crossed the circle in the past initiated the rest of us into the wonderful world of Bluenoses. Thus, another evening of fun was had by all. Admittedly, the initiation was at the expense and pride of us new Bluenoses, but good fun anyway. Actually, it was not too bad, because there were only a handful of crew members that were already bluenoses, and, as luck would have it they were not ones that would make things too hard on us new Bluenoses.

George Hofferber, '65 - '67

1966 – A Lesson in Leadership

During my first 1966 cruise aboard *Nautilus*, while transiting the frigid Atlantic, north of the Arctic Circle, en route to perform a classified mission, this young 19 year old sailor witnessed leadership and attention to detail first hand.

A small radio antenna had broken and needed repair, a task capable of completion only on the ocean's surface. Since nuclear submarines spend most of their time hiding submerged for months at a time, unplanned surfacing exposes these boats to enemy eyes. Since the antenna was essential to our mission, however, the order was given to "semi" surface and do the repairs. So we pop up on the surface, with only four-to- five feet of the submarines sail sticking above the water.

Because of the extreme cold and with Arctic waves splashing over the sail, soaking Lookouts and technicians, everyone Topside had to be strapped in place and were allowed only 20 minutes exposure to the harsh elements before being rotated below decks for recovery and clothing changes. The repair required almost two hours to complete. I worked three rotations as a lookout.

What stood out in my mind most in that frigid Arctic air with freezing water spraying all over us was the Captain, Commander Frank Fogarty, standing there the entire time constantly vigilant for our Cold War enemies and for ice obstacles while also personally ensuring the repair went well. Here we are Topside for 20 minutes, then we rush back down inside for a cup of coffee and he just stood there through out the entire process. That was dedication to the ship and it's crew. I really respected that. It taught me early on what senior officer leadership entailed.

Lonnie Barham, '66 – '68

1966 – Thanksgiving in the North Atlantic

I remember celebrating Thanksgiving Day on *Nautilus* in the North Atlantic in heavy seas off the coast of Iceland. Sea state 8, I believe. We were conducting operations with a tin can (destroyer) and a P-3 Orion (aircraft), providing anti-submarine warfare (ASW) services. Chief Slebodnick, with his #10 can (barf bucket), was the Diving Officer. Each time we came to periscope depth to communicate with the aircraft or destroyer the boat sustained heavy rolls. Many of the crew members were green around the gills and we all wanted to go deep.

At periscope depth, we established Gertrude (underwater telephone) communications with the tin can and UHF (radio) communications with the aircraft and after a brief discussion all parties decided to call it a day. The Skipper, Commander Fogarty, ordered a depth of 500 feet. We descended into the peaceful quite of our normal operating realm. The rolling and pitching stopped and Chief Slebodnick re-stowed his #10 can. The crew was most "Thankful." Benny, the Cook had his Mess Cooks take the turkeys out of the oven. What a wonderful calm Thanksgiving dinner we enjoyed in the deep. Those poor tin can sailors were lucky if they had cold sandwiches. Just another of the many reasons I volunteered for submarine duty.

Tommy "Robby" Robinson, '63 – '67

Tommy Robinson

1966 – Rosy's Stash

Denny "Rosy" Halstead, and occasionally known as "Buckskin," said at a reunion, in front of all present, that while underway from Bermuda to New London he offered Joe Thompson and I (off watch) a sip or two from his 1/5 bottle of Chavis Regal just before he assumed the Electronic Countermeasures Watch with the understanding that we would save some for him. When "Rosy" got off watch he found his bottle empty. I recall Joe and I taking a couple of sips but after the ninth or tenth, I certainly don't remember an empty bottle.

I suppose, after all these years that have passed, in order to make an old shipmate happy, that instead of donating to my favorite charity this year, I will have to purchase a bottle of scotch to appease him. Of course it will have to be one of those little tiny bottles, similar to what they served on airlines. Inflation since 1966 has been staggering. One would think with all those AKA's that Denny used he would be doing hard time in some upper state New York prison instead of legally dealing drugs out of a pharmaceutical store in Michigan.

Tommy "Robby" Robinson, '63 – '67

Robby cannot seem to remember the occasion. It was on our return from our northern run, not the Bermuda trip, that my classic, expensive, and very special blend of Ballentine Scotch was consumed by two old salts. Those two top sailors showed neither regard or remorse in reference to my humble special request to please leave one small sip for me. This was a huge learning experience for me but well worth the loss of one tiny, yes tiny, sip of a world class Scotch whiskey.

Enough said, it would once again be my honor to provide any adult liquid refreshment to two great gentlemen and their beautiful ladies.

Dennis "Rosy" Halstead, '65 - '67

1966 – Final Quals

A suggestion, if you are a non-qualified puke NEVER report for duty to a submarine just before it enters a shipyard for overhaul. In my case, I reported to *Nautilus* October 15, 1963 immediately after submarine school and was handed my first qualification card. I immediately qualified Topside watch just in time to freeze my ass off in the winter months while moored at State Pier on the Thames River.

Nautilus entered Portsmouth Naval Shipyard at Kittery, Maine January 17, 1964. Topside watches ceased and living barge watches began. The winter weather did not improve. Qualification card #1 was collected and I was handed qualification card #2 with instructions to continue to qualify during the shipyard overhaul with the understanding that I would NOT be "qualified in submarines" while the boat was in the shipyard. I admit the overhaul presented a great opportunity to trace systems and qualify in compartments not normally accessible while underway such as the Lower Level Reactor Compartment (LLRC). Yep, I stood fire watches in the LLRC but that's another story. I got to know the boat pretty well BUT 17 months later still no dolphins.

Nautilus departed shipyard on May 2, 1966 and I was given qualification card #3. Now that we were at sea it was time to operate and/or demonstrate operation of systems. My two plus year qualification saga finely ended on August 16, 1966 when the Engineer walked me through the boat and Captain Fogarty signed on the bottom line. I drank my dolphins at "Ernie's on the Thames" a custom no longer permitted in the submarine force. I chose a 8 ounce Zombie instead of a pitcher of beer – less volume, drank it down, clenched my dolphins in my teeth, grinned, immediately went to the head and puked. What a grand day!

Tommy "Robby" Robinson, '63 -'67

1966 - Wake Up Calls

While underway in 1966 Richie Burke was making wake up calls for the oncoming watch. The Executive Officer (XO) had left a note to be awakened at 0545 (5:45 AM). Richie allegedly made this wake up with the unwritten approval of the Officer of the Deck (OOD) who apparently didn't believe he could pull it off. Richie, who was always the joker, opened the XO's stateroom door and loudly shouted, ***"XO, wake up you son-of-bitch."*** He could be heard below in the Control Room. The XO, a very heavy sleeper, sat bolt upright, still groggy from sleep, and mumbled, *"What, what did you say?"* Without missing a beat Richie replied, ***"XO, wake up Sir, it's a quarter of six"***.

Another of Richie's famous wake up calls was made in the ten man bunk room. I don't recall who his victim was, but, as the story goes, he also slept soundly, laying flat on his back with his feet forming a perfect "V." Richie removed the red lens from his flashlight and placed it between his feet, shinning a bright light in his face. Then, in his best rendition of a moving locomotive, Richie began whispering in his ear, "Choo-choo, Choo-choo, Choo-choo," growing ever louder and ending with a shrill train whistle, "Whooo-Whooo." His victim opened his eyes, saw the light bearing down on him, set bolt upright and smacked his forehead on the bunk bottom directly above. Richie always looked for innovative ways to wake up the oncoming watch.

Tommy "Robby" Robinson, '63 - '67

1966 – Perils of Pauline

During our northern run in 1966 the Radioman and Sonarman, and maybe a forward Electronic Technician or two, put our heads together and decided to record a soap opera using the RD-219 reel to reel tape deck, located in the "Bat Cave." We intended to entertain the crew during the noon meal. Script writers were assigned, sound effects people and actors were named.

The plot consisted of three main characters; a very sexy and amorous Pauline, her husband, a Gloucester fisherman, and her lover boy who was a long haul trucker from Texas. Pauline lived in a second floor apartment above a fish factory She preferred the quaint smell of diesel fuel on her grimy trucker lover more than the fishy aroma of her salty sea going husband.

In a typical episode Pauline would be in bed with her trucker whispering sweet nothings in his ear while teaching him various forms of horizontal folk dancing. All of a sudden the squeaky hinged fish factory door would slowly begin to open, "Creeeeek." Pauline blurted out in a very high falsetto voice, *"Oh no! It's my husband, he's home from the sea, and he's looking for me. Quick, out the window my dear trucker lover, jump down into the alley, you must run!"* In a deep southern drawl the trucker replied, *"Gee Ma'am, I ain't got no clothes on."* She again urged, *"Hurry, jump!"* Then the sound of cans rattling and, *"Aaarrgh, there's nothing but garbage and fish guts down here."* Pauline's husband, in excellent down eastern accent, hollered out as he ascended the stairs, *"Pauline, muh dearie, where you be sweetie? Ah can't wait to come along side and tie my dingy up next to your thingy – Oooh, Pauline where are you?"*

The crew had some fun trying to figure out who played the various parts and the sound effects were great. We aired a few episodes on the old reel to reel entertainment system in the Crews Mess before the

O-gang censors found us out and cancelled further production of the "Perils of Pauline."

Tommy "Robby" Robinson, '63 – '67

1966 – *Nautilus/Essex* Incident

I was on watch in the Radio Room, starboard side of the Control Room, just below the Attack Center in *Nautilus* on November 10, 1966. *Nautilus* was operating as part of an anti-submarine warfare (ASW) exercise with *Essex*. The carrier was being protected by a screen of destroyers.

Essex was being refueled by *Salamonie*, an oiler. *Nautilus* was submerged on a parallel course at a depth of about 200 feet. *Nautilus* had already made three or four successful penetrations of the destroyer screen that morning. We had maneuvered into firing position and launched flares indicating to those on the surface that we had "killed" *Essex*. Apparently Essex turned to port upon completion of refueling which put her on a collision course with *Nautilus*.

Nautilus penetrated the destroyer screen again made her approach for the next run. The Officer of the Deck (OOD) was ordered to bring the boat to periscope depth for a "quick look."

As *Nautilus* ascended to periscope depth I heard the ever increasing noise of *Essex's* screws beating very loudly through the starboard side hull in Radio. I counted a spread of four individual screw beats as the noise amplitude continued to increase alarmingly. I knew *Nautilus* had to be very close to *Essex* for the screw noise to be that deafing.

I had a sinking feeling in the pit of my stomach as I jumped to the Radio Room door to see what was happening in the Control Room. I immediately heard the Captain exclaim, *"Oh my God! Flood negative! Take her deep!"* I can only imagine that he was looking a rivet on the bow of *Essex*.

Simultaneously the Diving Officer opened negative tank vent and ordered *"Full Dive."* At that instant the bow of *Essex* crashed into the forward starboard side of the sail. *Nautilus* was filled with a deafening shriek of grinding metal and metal scraping against metal as the force of impact rolled *Nautilus* about 45 degrees to port and downward. Coffee pots, charts, and other loose gear was flying around the Control Room.

I was thrown across the Control Room and into the Diving Officer. We both were bent over the TPTR (hull opening indicator) panel. A single red light indicated that the upper bridge access hatch had been carried away. All other indicators were green. The lower bridge access hatch held and kept water out of the "people tank."

I made my way back to Radio and manned the sound powered phones. Collision bill procedures were carried out automatically. Sound powered phones were manned throughout the boat, bulkhead flappers were shut, and watertight doors were shut. Although I don't remember hearing the collision alarm it may have been sounded. *Nautilus* came under control at a depth of about 150 feet. Damage control reports were coming into the Attack Center from each compartment. No major internal damage was reported. Lew Petty, a Mess Cook, sustained a injured arm, thought to be broken, when a watertight door slammed shut on his arm. Several other crew members received scrapes, bumps, and bruises.

The Stern Room was ordered to load and fire a red flare to warn surface ships away from our surfacing area. Ballast tanks were blown and we slowly surfaced. Of course, the normal routine would have been for the Quartermaster of the Watch to open the lower then upper bridge access hatches so the OOD and Lookouts could take their stations on the Bridge, but there was no Bridge. The Captain and a few selected crew members went Topside through the Forward Torpedo Room hatch to access the damage.

The seas were calm and the men on deck took quick stock of the damage. The entire upper forward part of the sail had been sliced off and mangled metal hung dangerously from the sail's port side. Chief Machinist Mate Art Gogan lead a team into the damaged sail to cut away the dangling chunks of metal.

The Control Room was ordered to test all masts. A few began to rise but jammed and couldn't be lowered. The communication masts were inoperable. I sent Radioman 2nd/class Richie Burke into the damaged sail area to clamp an emergency whip antenna onto an upper metal ridge. The lower bridge access hatch was sprung and had to be forced open. Sea water that flooded the trunk drained into the bilges. A coaxial cable was drawn from the emergency antenna through the wreckage and threaded through the lower bridge access hatch into the Control Room and Radio Room. With radio communications re-established we informed Commander Submarine Group Two of the collision and also communicated with *Essex*.

The *Essex* Commanding Officer sent a message to her division that it had struck a submerged object but had sustained no damage. Later *Essex* was found to have an approximate 30 by 60 foot hole in her bow below the waterline.

Nautilus made the five hundred mile trip from the Atlantic off North Carolina to New London under her own power making about ten knots on the surface. We were accompanied the destroyer *Furse*. *Essex* put into Boston for repairs.

A board of inquiry into the event was convened. As I recall the board found *Nautilus* to be at fault in some degree as does the Navy in nearly all situations where a submerged submarine is struck by a surface ship.

Tommy "Robby" Robinson, '63 - '67

1966 – *Essex* Collides with *Nautilus*

It happened 10 Nov 1966 while refueling from *USS Salamonie (AO26)*. During the refueling, instead of steering a straight course while alongside the Salamonie, the Admiral got a wild hair and had the ships change course to port one half degree at a time. This put *Essex* and *Salamonie* a considerable distance from where *Nautilus* thought we would be, and when *Nautilus* came up to periscope depth, she was directly in *Essex's* path. Although *Essex* shuddered from the collision, it was not much worse than some of the waves we hit at times. Of course emergency breakaway was instituted from *Salomie* because no one was certain what had occurred and it was not until quite some minutes later that we learned what had happened. This is the best of my recollection of the incident and what I entered in the Quartermaster's Log at the time – although after 43 years memories can fade (I wish I had a copy of the Log from that watch).

Quartermaster 3rd/class Franklin B. Williams – USS Essex (CVS-9)

1966 – *Essex* vs. *Nautilus*

I was in the Sonar Room when the incident occurred and was later questioned by the board of Inquiry. This is what I remember.

Tommy Robinson

We were operating with *Essex* and a couple of destroyers after we left Bermuda. We had come across the stern (Starboard to Port) of the carrier while she was refueling a couple of destroyers. We continued on course opening up the range and then turned on a parallel course. We increased speed and were going faster than the carrier which eventually put her in our starboard baffles.

About that time both destroyers broke off from refueling and kicked it in the ass speed wise. They made an amazing amount of noise at fairly close range. We could not get decent bearings to either destroyer. A little time passed with the destroyers opening their range, and unknown to us, the carrier had turned to port and was headed straight for us, giving us a zero angle on the bow (AOB). When that happens, her hull develops an acoustic shadow zone where her acoustic energy is shadowed by the pointy end of the ship. In addition, she was still in our baffles. As I recall, the Executive Officer (XO) and Navigator, Lieutenant Commander Bachman, called Sonar on the 27-MC and said we were coming right and up to periscope depth for a quick look.

I immediately requested that we clear baffles first. My request was on the tape in Sonar which I had with me during the inquiry. The XO said negative, we are just coming up for a quick peek. About that time the Commanding Officer (CO), Commander Fogarty, raised the scope and the rest is history.

When I walked into the board of inquiry, I had never seen so much brass in one place at one time. By the look they gave me I thought I was going to be fed to the wolves. I was one scared puppy during the questioning. They asked me if I was able to tell the difference between the heavy's (carrier) and the light's (destroyers) and many other very pointed questions. Apparently they felt sorry for me and nothing was ever done to me.

From what I recall, the board of inquiry awarded the XO a letter of reprimand. I don't think Captain Fogarty got anything. [He was toward the end of his tour as CO and was relieved during a scheduled change of command.]

In typical submarine "rag hat" humor this event became known as the "Bachman Zero Ranging Technique."

John Shook, '64 – '67

1966 – The Phone Call

I was home on leave when *Nautilus* was hit by *Essex*. Mother was at work and dad was taking a shower. The phone rang and I answered it with a hearty, *"Hello."* The caller asked, *"Is this Mr. Alex Hofferberger,"* and I replied, *"No this is his son."* The caller identified himself as an officer with Commander Submarine Flotilla Two (COMSUBFLOT TWO). Mom and dad would not have a clue what that stood for. He again stated that he really needed to talk to Mr. Hofferberger. I realized that something must be wrong and I said, *"Alex Hofferber is busy but I am George Hofferberger can I help you?"* This dufas replied, *"Oh, are you a brother or something?"* I realized this officer must be calling with bad news about *Nautilus* and I became quite shaken myself.

I said that I was stationed on *Nautilus* and I was home on authorized leave. The officer said, *"Oh, I have the shipping manifest and you are listed as being on board. Sorry to have called you."*

I asked, *"What is wrong and why are you calling families of Nautilus crew members?"* He replied, *"There will be a national news release regarding Nautilus at noon today and we wanted to contact all families before the news release. Nautilus has been involved in a collision at sea but they are all right. They are on the surface, performing repairs to the superstructure, and will be returning to New London."* I asked the big question, *"Was anyone hurt?"* The Officer, admittedly a Junior Officer, tasked with phoning families who probably had no training in these kinds of emergency messages replied, *"Yes, one crew member was hurt but we do not know who or how badly."*

Taking a chance that this officer may take offense, I said, *"Are you telling me that if I was on Nautilus this very minute that you would be telling my parents that Nautilus was in a collision, one sailor is injured and you don't know who or how badly? Is that what you are doing"?* He said, *"You are correct. Before we make any more phone calls we need to get that information."* I said, *"Thank you,"* and hung up.

An hour later the news release was on National television and, as expected, mom and dad both were upset. I was happy to have intercepted the phone message before they received the news and, of course, because I was home they did not have to worry about me.

George Hofferber. '65 – 67

Tommy Robinson

1966 – Injured Sailor

I was the night baker at the time of the *Nautilus/Essex* collision and I was in my rack, lower left berthing, when we were hit. The boat pitched sharply and I was tossed out of my bunk. When I looked toward the Mess Deck, I saw water hitting the bulk head and I thought we were flooding. Later I found out it was the Mess Cook's dish water. I went up the stairs and tried to close the hatch between the Mess Deck and the Forward Torpedo Room. As the boat came back to center, I released the latch holding the hatch and lost control of the door and it slammed on my arm. When I got my arm out of the way I did get the hatch shut and secured. I was air lifted by helicopter over to *Essex* for an arm x-ray to see if it was broke. It wasn't broke so they brought me back to *Nautilus* by helicopter and dropped me on the aft deck.

Lewis "Lew" Petty, '66 – '67

6 - CDR Norman "Earl" E. Griggs, USN *and* Crew

April 1967 – January 1970

1968 – Filling the Pot

What is this? Well, after the new core was put into place by a heavy crane at Portsmouth Navy Shipyard, and the Top Hat (reactor) with all the control rods is lowered and bolted down and all the electrical is made to the rods, and after the primary was sealed up and a valve line completed, we could get town to filling the primary system with primary grade fresh pure water. Well it's a bit more involved than that.

There had to be a crew member and a yard bird at every valve and pump and watch station, an officer from ship's force in Forward Machinery where the charging pumps were, plus the Engineering Officer of the Watch (EOOW) in Maneuvering and an officer over on the barge where the fresh water was located with it's own pump, etc. The catch was, only ship's force could operate ship's machinery valves and only yard birds could operate their stuff, plus Westinghouse and Code 08 (Naval Reactors) wanted to watch all of us.

We finally got started and I was stationed to control the charging pump locally from Forward Machinery when directed via sound powered phones from Maneuvering. The flow rate on the pump, since it was designed for high pressure charging was small, about 10 GPM. So we were looking at three hours or more to fill the reactor and the piping to the primary loop TH and TC stop valves. The idea was that the stand pipe, which shows water level in the reactor core, would visually tell us how much water was present and the two pump flow meters would tell us the rate, and the level indicator on the barge would tell us how much we had pumped.

After three hours, no water level and our readings indicated that we had pumped over 1000 gallons from the barge to the reactor vessel. The word is past, *"Secure pumping. Hold on stations."* This of course means stop and wait. And wait we did, while Westinghouse called Bettis at Pittsburgh trying to figure out what was wrong and what to do next. And we waited. Finally the word came to pump in another 50 gallons by meter in Forward Machinery where I was. So the yard bird opens the valve, notes the time, and everyone agrees. I open the discharge valve and turn on the pump and put in 50 gallons by meter. Still no indication by the site glass, all hands secured from pumping, but stayed on station.

Another three hour call to Bettis and another 50 gallons and still nothing. It's appropriate to explain that we were also monitoring the bilge levels in the Lower Level Reactor Compartment. There was no leakage. The Engineers were stumped. The core configuration was new but we still had the same control rod configuration. So we should have seen water by now. After more waiting, the order came to continue filling until water was visible at the top of the stand pipe. After another 45 minutes we got the required level and called the pot full.

We were never told why or what happened, but some civilian must have really screwed up on that one because ship's force didn't.

Bruce Kinne, '68 – '71

1968 – Olly, Olly, Home Free

Nautilus was at sea playing a Russian submarine for a group of destroyers and *Haddo* in order to practice anti-submarine tactics. The exercise began and *Nautilus* maneuvered to avoid the hunters. I was in Sonar and Lieutenant Melvin Lyman (Retired as a Captain) was the Conning Officer. While trying to lose the hunters, Lieutenant Lyman called Sonar and asked, *"Is there any open waters out there?"* I didn't see any so I told him via the 27-MC, *"Not really"* and that the northwest was now clear of contacts. He said, *"I guess I'll let you drive awhile"* and changed course to the northwest. We figure that when we made the course change we past under a destroyer and emerged in her baffles and the hunters lost all contact with *Nautilus*. Later in the exercise we lost all contact with the destroyers. We had ended up about 20 miles away from the hunters. It was time to end the exercise so we came to periscope depth and Lieutenant Lyman announced our presence on the radio with a transmission that all of us who have ever played hide and seek know and understand, *"Olly, Olly, Home Free."*

Jon Sutton, '66 – '68

1968 – Scorpion Lost

On May 22, 1968 we lost a submarine, USS *Scorpion* (SSN-589), and 99 fellow submariners. The Navy declared *Scorpion* "presumed lost" on June 5th. Four submariners who perished at sea that day were former *Nautilus* crew members. They are:

Steely Eyed Killers of the Deep

CDR Francis "Frank" Slattery, USN, Commanding Officer
SSN-571, '61 -'66, LCDR

MMCS(SS) Richard "Dick" Kerntke, Sr., USN
SSN-571, '63 -'65, MMC(SS)

MMC(SS) James "Jimmy" Wells, USN
SSN-571, '61 -'64, MM1(SS)

ET1(SS) John Livingston, USN
SSN-571, '64 -'66, ETN2(SS)

Our departed shipmates are missed but not forgotten. Sailors rest your oars!

Tommy "Robby" Robinson, '63 – '67

1968 - Lost Shipmates

I knew them well. Jimmy Wells slept in lower port in the Torpedo Room. John Livingston was a great guy and Commander Slattery was top shelf. While in the yards in Portsmouth Naval Shipyard, I lost my ID card. Someone found my card and turned it in. Lieutenant Slattery, at that time, was filling in for the Executive Officer (XO). He called me into his office and asked me about my ID card. I told him I lost it. He said, *"Your card is government property and you are responsible for it."* Then he opened the desk drawer to return it but he couldn't find it. I said, *"XO that ID card is government property and I think you just lost it."* He smiled, told me to see the Yeoman and get a new ID card and to get the hell out of his office. He was one of the best officers I had the pleasure of serving with in my 30 year career.

John Wahl, '63 – '66

Tommy Robinson

1968 – My Nautilus Sea Story

My first day on *Nautilus* was May 20, 1968, when she was in Dry dock #2 at Portsmouth Naval Shipyard. A new reactor had been installed, and the engineering task of the day was starboard loop fill, as events were moving toward the initial start-up and power range testing.

Earl Griggs, a fine Virginia gentleman, was the Commanding Officer, and the Wardroom included (this is from memory, so apologies for any inaccuracies) Executive Officer Bob Bachman, Nolan Burke, Ed Von Fischer, Payson Whitney, Mel Lyman, Bob Boyd, Pete Pandolfi, Jim Allen, Dave Musolf, Andy Prince, and Fred Broberg. It was mostly a loose and happy group, and "Rye on the Rocks" was a much-discussed favorite haunt for some of the team.

The backbone of the Navy is the Chief Petty Officers, and on that score our crew was blessed. Senior Chief Radioman W. W. Robinson would become my mentor when I became Communications Officer a few months later, and he had a great way of teaching a green young officer how to do things. The Engineering Department had two real bulwarks in Senior Chief Electrician Howard and Senior Chief Machinist Mate Edmonson, and Master Chief Electronics Technician Parker knew as much about reactor controls as anybody needs to know. His retirement ceremony in New London was a memorable event, but I'll let others fill in the details. Chief Torpedoman Lincecum knew all the ropes in the Weapons Department, and was a great mentor, as well, when I became Weapons Officer.

There was uneasiness in the air at the time, as people learned that *Scorpion* was overdue on its return from the Mediterranean. Just about everyone on board seemed to know and admire Frank Slattery, *Scorpion's* skipper, who had served on *Nautilus* for thirteen years, which took him back to the famous era of the trip beneath the North Pole. When it was finally announced officially on June 8 that the ship had been lost, gloom pervaded, as many had lost not just fellow submariners, but personal friends. My own Naval Academy classmate, Lieutenant (JG) Michael Odening, went down with *Scorpion*. Everyone who was not on duty attended a very solemn memorial service at the Portsmouth Chapel, which was made all the more poignant by so many people's close relationships with Commander Slattery and others.

While we mourned the loss of fellow submariners from the loss of *Scorpion*, we had to get on with our job of finishing the refueling outage and getting *Nautilus* back to sea. This included the normal examinations by a team from Naval Reactors (NR) before we could start the new reactor, and some of the real old-timers from NR seemed to want to see *Nautilus* again, so several of them were part of the team. As the newest and youngest officer on board, I was not qualified to stand watch yet, and was able to sit in on the exams without the pressure of having to answer the questions. It was a surprise to me that in addition to the standard nuclear questions, the examination team spent so much time asking questions about how to deal with a loss of air conditioning. This had been a significant issue for them during the design phase, and I tucked that concern away in the back of my memory for possible future use. Lo and behold, a few years later, we lost three of four air conditioning units while we were at sea, and limped home with people able to stand the heat only long enough for 30 minute watches in the engineering spaces.

When we got into the power range testing program, one of the qualified Engineering Officers of the Watch (EOOW) came back to the ship from "Rye on the Rocks" one night, climbed up on the Wardroom table to demonstrate the dance he had been doing on the tables at the bar, fell off the table and broke his ankle. This made all the EOOW's work a little harder, because it was not okay to have an EOOW standing watch on crutches.

One day, Captain George Street, a Medal of Honor awardee from World War-II, had lunch in the Wardroom with us. It was a thrill to be with such an honored individual, whose feats of seamanship and fighting skill let him sink three Japanese ships in a nighttime encounter off the coast of Korea on *Tirante's* first war patrol in 1945. We cleared the dishes after the meal, and sat around the table with our coffee for a friendly discussion. He told us that they had done that after meals during World War II in his Wardroom, and then they would place a small submarine and a small Japanese target ship on the table and simulate various maneuvers that they could take to get themselves into firing position, since stalking a target took lots of time, cunning and patience when they could only go a few knots submerged. He said that when they started doing the simulations, he asked his Executive Officer for ideas first, then the Navigator, and on down the ranks to the lowest seniority person. This, he felt, didn't work very well because all of the experienced officers had been trained in a certain way, and they all reflected one kind of thinking. So one day, he started with the least senior officer and asked him for his ideas first. Inexperience, he found, could come up with some pretty silly thoughts, and just when he was about to abandon the idea, the new officer came up with some ideas that changed their thinking and introduced some totally new concepts. Captain Street's method has worked for me in business for many years.

Wayne Henry was in the class behind mine at the Academy, and he came on board in 1969. He was an outstanding baseball and softball player, and he was assigned to work for me while he was qualifying as Engineering Officer of the Watch. We worked it out that he could play on the Submarine Base Softball Team, and he played outstanding ball for them and still got his qualification work finished. I think he made an All Star team, which required playing some games away from the Base, but he still qualified EOOW on time. We've stayed close friends since those early days.

My years on *Nautilus* from May, 1968 through December, 1971 were long after the glory years - the time when those who went before established the reputation of the "First and Finest," and enjoyed worldwide renown for feats such as the voyage under the North Pole. Our years were a time of struggling to get good performance out of aging equipment that had been run hard for a long time. We had a great team of people that manned this ageing warrior, and it took quite an effort to get the ship to sea and perform well in that demanding environment. We did not carry the missiles that kept the Russians at bay, nor were we quiet enough to engage in "Blind Man's Bluff." But we worked our butts off to carry out the missions that were assigned to us, and, in my view it took a great group of dedicated shipmates to accomplish that assignment.

One example of the types of issues we dealt with was the main shaft reduction gears, which had been built for a destroyer, and operated as close to their maximum limits as any machine should do. In the early years, when the ship was proving the worth of nuclear power, this wasn't much of a problem, but as submarine technology developed, being quiet became more and more important, and our reduction gears made lots of noise at sea. As a result, we had many visits from some very, very smart people from the Naval Sea Command, Philadelphia Division who were the Navy's experts on reduction gears. Working with people like that and the great sailors on *Nautilus* was an excellent education in how to solve difficult equipment problems that has carried over into many different situations in the long years since.

It was the privilege of a lifetime to serve with the officers and men of USS *Nautilus*.

John Beakes, '68 – '71

1969 – Master Chief Parker's Retirement

Master Chief Parker was my first encounter with an E-9 [pay grade]. My first *Nautilus* job starting in May 1969 was Reactor Controls Officer. Master Chief Parker was a really smart guy, and I think we made a great team. I was well aware of his limitations, because he confided in me, but his many, many talents saved my bacon on several occasions.

When Master Chief Parker was absent one day during a busy time in port, I was concerned. He told me the next day, *"Mr. Henry, you needed me yesterday and I am sorry, but you DID NOT WANT ME ONBOARD."* I handled it an the Master Chief seemed to work even harder to make us successful. So, when Master Chief Parker invited me, and the entire boat, to his retirement party at 0600 (6 AM) in the Chief Petty Officer's club, I was all in. I don't know why, but the designated uniform was Service Dress Whites. The invitation said there would be lots of food at 0600. Long story short, the food never showed, but the booze did.

Somehow, I ended up back home in Navy Housing at 1100 (11 AM). I knocked on the door and really scared my wife because my wine-stained Whites looked like I had been shot! I passed out on the couch and did not report back to 571 until Officers' Call the next morning. After Call, the Executive Officer (XO), Lieutenant Commander Wally Schlauder asked me to stay behind. He said, *"Wayne, I was looking for you yesterday and needed you on board. What happened?"* I told him, *"XO, you DID NOT WANT ME ONBOARD yesterday."* He handled it and I probably worked even harder for him.

Wayne Henry, '69 – '72

1969 - SOFTBALL

I had played lots of baseball while growing up and through college. During the summer of 1969, *Nautilus* was in Electric Boat for SSTG replacement and lots of other stuff. When tryouts for SUBBASE FAST PITCH SOFTBALL was announced, I asked our Chief Engineer if I could tryout. Amazingly, he said YES. There could be several reasons including (1) He felt sure I would not make the team. Most of that team were folks whose primary collateral duty had been playing softball for years! (2) Lieutenant Commander Oliver was a real sports fan and had an opportunity to send one of his guys out to compete. (3) He just liked me.

Tommy Robinson

Here is an important footnote. The Navy had just invested a couple of years and a million dollars for me to operate 571's reactor. I was not yet qualified. Maybe most important, was a fact that if I made the team, I would need Official Orders to travel and a copy of all orders on nuclear-trained officers went to CODE 08 - THE MAN!

I won't bore folks with all details of my great play, but we won SUBLANT in Charleston, South Carolina. We then went to Earle, New Jersey for EAST COAST. This was monsoon season and it took three weeks to play a four day tourney. We finished second to Naval Air Station (NAS), but I had an outstanding tournament. When I finally reported back to 571, I checked in with our Executive Officer, Lieutenant Commander "Wally" Schlauder. He took my orders and his only comment was, *"Henry, YOUR BALL PLAYING DAYS ARE OVER!"*

The next day I got a phone call on the Mess Deck. It was the coach of NAS. He said, *"Lieutenant Henry, you had an outstanding tourney in Earle, so I want you to play First Base on my team to go to the next round in St Louis. We leave next week."* It was standard practice, that a winning coach from regional could pick players from losing teams to improve their chances in next round.

I said. *"Coach, I really appreciate your offer, but MY BALL PLAYING DAYS ARE OVER!"*

Wayne Henry, '69 – '72

7 - CDR David "Duke" S. Cockfield, USN *and* Crew

January 1970 – June 1972

1970 - XO FEELS SORRY FOR ME

We were short several officers in the Wardroom and had several folks not yet qualified. So, some of us were standing way too many watches. We would do Engineering Officer of the Watch, then Officer of the Deck four hours later. The 571 was in transit home and for some reason we were to do last day surfaced. I had been on mid watchh topside for about 30 minutes when our Executive Officer (XO), Lieutenant Commander "Wally" Schlauder called and told me he would be willing to stand the rest of my watch. We were expecting smooth sailing and 45 degrees temperature for next six hours. I expressed genuine appreciation for the XO's offer and turned over the watch.

Within 30 minutes, we hit a major squall. It was raining sideways and temperature took a serious nosedive. There was a huge scramble in the Wardroom as the XO sent someone down to get him maximum foul weather gear. I simply sat in Wardroom, eating mid-rats [snack] and made no offer to retake my watch. Thanks, XO!

Wayne Henry, '69 – '72

1970 - FORMAL DINNERS

While at sea, the Executive Officer (XO), Lieutenant Commander "Wally" Schlauder announced that one evening each week would be formal dinners in the Wardroom for all officers not on watch. Uniform to be service dress blue. The Chief Engineer, Lieutenant Commander Oliver informed the XO that he doubted any officer other than the XO had that uniform on board. Undeterred, the XO announced that the uniform for the special dinners would be long sleeved khaki shirts with necktie. At the first dinner, we all showed in uniform and it was a good looking group - until I looked closer at the Chief Engineer seated next to me. Then I observed that he was wearing a standard issue Navy black sock stretched to its limit and tucked into his shirt collar. That was our last formal dinner on board.

Writing about my time on SSN 571 makes me truly appreciative of all the great folks with whom I served.

Wayne Henry, '69 – '72

Tommy Robinson

1970 – The Owl Saga Continued

I wrote the proclamation that every crew member signed to repeal the orders given to the Engineer to get rid of the Owl. The Owl was hit as gear adrift by the Operational Readiness Safeguards Evaluation (ORSE) team. It was rather funny because I even convinced the Captain to sign the proclamation by promising that the Owl would always take a brief trip foreword of frame 45 during any future ORSE inspections. The last person to sign the proclamation was the Engineer, Mr. Fast. When he saw the Captain's signature, he was just beside himself because the Captain had ordered him to get rid of the Owl. He finally calmed down when I explained the travel plans for the Owl during future ORSE Inspections.

After the proclamation was completely signed, I figured that something additional had to be done to ensure the Owl's legacy would live on. That's when I got the idea for an owl patch. We had a crew's competition to design the patch. If my memory serves me, the winning design was submitted by an Interior Communications Technician who's name escapes me. I also made a "peace sign" that hung around the Owl's neck. It was made from a steam trap gasket and some sink stopper bead chain. It establish that the on going battle to rid *Nautilus* of the Owl had finally come to an end "PEACE DEC 70." That was the day when he was finally declared safe on board.

The first time he was removed from the boat is history – the collision with *Essex* – we sure didn't want any bad Ju Ju that might result in that kind of past experience. I still wonder what happened to the Owl. I toured *Nautilus* during her conversion at Mare Island Navy Shipyard for decommissioning and the Owl was gone. The yard personnel told me everything was removed from the boat and locked up to prevent collectors from taking parts off the boat. Is the Owl still in lockup at Mare Island?

John Dudas, '69 – '72

1970 - A Hot Run

In the Fall of 1970, October I believe, we were on a southern operation off Cuba and running in very warm waters. The Air Conditioning (AC) units were in bad shape. We had four 60 ton units, two in the Engine Room and two in Lower Level After Machinery. The Auxiliary gang, non-NUC Machinists Mates, maintained them. When we sailed we were running on 3 1/2 units since each motor ran two 30 ton compressors with separate heat exchangers. One by one they over heated and failed. Running in warm Caribbean waters with injection temps in the high 70's and 80's didn't help. The Engineering spaces on *Nautilus* normally were warm. Heat was generated by steam generators, reactor, four electrical turbine generators and two main engines with both LP & HP turbines. The normal temp was in the high 80's with AC. As soon as the AC died temps climbed fast, 95, 102, 110, 118 and up. It got warm forward of frame 45 too but they started in the 70's and they didn't have large equipments generating additional heat. Watch standers aft of fram 45 started passing out and the Electronics for rector control became a very large concern. If we were to SCRAM the reactor a recovery would have been doubtful due to the state of the Electronics in the high temps.

I was an Engineering Watch Supervisor/Engineering Officer of the Watch (EWS/EOOW) at this time so I could relieve anyone - and did. Very soon it became necessary to limit watch standers to only two in Maneuvering. Everyone else was moved forward of frame 45. Normally there would be 12 watch standers aft of frame 45 [NUC land]. One of the two in Maneuvering had to be a EWS or EOOW so I was on a 6 person rotation then a 4 person rotation. During the worst heat we were on about 10 minutes in Maneuvering then retreated to the the After Room for 10-30 minutes then up forward. We were in skivvy shorts and flip flops and the temp was 130-135. The Commanding Officer and Executive Officer came back to check on us once or twice. This bad heat lasted about 20 to 24 hours before we could get out of the gulf stream and into cooler waters.

We had to stay submerged for 48 hours and move slowly out of the operation area at three or four knots and remain quite. Then we could surface. Just after we left the operation area we shut down the Engine Room turbines and surfaced running on the diesels. We kept the reactor critical since we were concerned about the possibility of the nuclear instrumentation failing. With the boat on the surface and the diesels running for power and propulsion, we made very slow head way, again about four to five knots. This allowed the ship to be ventilated and start to reduce the temperatures.

This did not happen overnight and during all this time we were very vulnerable. Shortly after we surfaced a U.S. destroyer and submarine rescue vessel (ASR) with some our shipmates and other volunteers started to shadow us. The original idea was to transfer former *Nautilus* crew members from the ASR to *Nautilus,* however, the weather did not cooperate and the seas were too rough. Slowly the Engineering crew got a chance to go to the Bridge since we had the worst of it. I wrapped myself around a mast in the upper level of the sail and feel asleep for about an hour or so in the rain. The Officer of the Deck and Lookouts knew I was there and let me rest. At that time I was only one of four EWS/EOOWS available for duty. The Heat had wiped out two or three including Master Chief Parker.

Bruce Kinne, '68 – '71

1970 – Sleeping Topside

While at sea the chilled water system ruptured and we lost ALL air conditioning (AC) on the entire boat. The piping insulation in the Engine Room was almost non-existent, so the heat would come right through. It drove everyone in the Engine Room to the Stern Room with watch standers periodically taking a short tour through Maneuvering and the Engine Room just to check on things.

There were no watch standers in the Engine Room for the remainder of the trip to Norfolk. I even gave the rods a quick shim to maintain primary temperature on one of my walks and told the Reactor Operator what I had done. He later went in to see if the temperature had settled out and to make sure things were okay.

I hung three lube oil thermometers in the overhead just forward of Maneuvering near the main engines and the air temperature reached 170 degrees. A person had to hold their breath a lot when they walked though due to the extreme heat. That night we pulled into Norfolk and all but the duty section was put into the temporary barracks. The duty section slept topside for the next two nights.

It was not until the second day in port that the tender repair party could come down to commence repairing the ruptured chill water elbow that had given away. They had never seen anything so hot!

The bottoms of the nuclear instrumentation cabinets in the Reactor Compartment were full of oil and wax that had melted out of the mag amps and other electrical components in the cabinets. It was something to see, and it still worked!

There are more stories like that during my time on *Nautilus*. What an adventure. When up north in Arctic waters, the condenser heads would have three or four inches of ice on them and the lower level watch stander wore a sweater and blue working jacket while the upper level watch stander was sweating in his shirtsleeves.

John Dudas, '69 – '72

1970 - St. Croix U.S. Virgin Islands

As usual *Nautilus* was there for some sort of anti-submarine warfare training, that is to say, we were the target. Anyway, St. Croix had two major cities in the early 1970's, Fredricksted and Christiansted. Today old Fredricksted is Krausses Lagune Estates, a large refinery and oil storage facility. The pier we used to tie up to is now used for unloading containers. A new pier has been built to the east and it is used for unloading oil.

When we tied up there in the late 1960's it was a private pier owned by a lady. Upon our first arrival, the Executive Officer who was on the Bridge, shouted down to have the gee-dunk trucks pulled back away from the brow. One of the older Chiefs reminded him that the trucks were also hers and she could tell us to leave - tread softly here. The pier had power and good fresh water. The depth was over 65 feet and the water was crystal clear. Of course we didn't shut down the reactor. The boat went on daily operations for five or six days at a time. My watch section only got one day ashore because we only had three sections at that time. Unfortunately the other two days were back to back with little rest. By the time it was our turn for a day off, I had been up for 36 hours and had to be showered, shaved, in civilian clothes and off the boat by 0700 (7 AM) or I would go back to sea and work. So, like the rest of our watch section, we were off the boat by 0700. Everyone had different liberty agendas. Mine and a couple of other Machinist Mates was to quickly find a public beach with benches, shade and cool breezes. We all parked ourselves on the benches and slept for a few hours. After waking up we wondered into a small shopping area looking for a beer and something to eat. Eventually one place "opened early" for our small group after we made a donation. We also learned how to get to Christiansted where the tourists played among the restaurants and bars. So off we went by island bus in pursuit of cold beer and food. Christiansted was a tourist stop for smaller cruise ships and civilians with much more dollars than we had. Everything there was quite and plush. After a couple of beers and some lunch it was off to find a shady place to doze for a while. Around 1600 (4 PM) we drifted back to Fredricksted and frequented the bars until the boat returned around 1800 (6 PM). We might have stayed out until 2000 (8 PM) but by then it was time to get back to the boat and sleep because we had duty the next morning. Summary, saw a little, could have use more rest, almost not worth going ashore.

Bruce Kinne, '68 – '71

1970 – Spare Parts, or Not

I was the M-Division Supply Petty Officer and took care of all our mechanical supply needs. Normally this is easy since you just go to the Master Parts List (COSAL) for the boat, get the Federal Stock Number (FSN), then order the part from the Submarine Base New London. Our problem was we were a unique "one of a kind" and nothing was standard or easy, even if we had the FSN. Numerous times, I had to go back to the original manufacturer and ask, plead, or beg to have parts sent to to the boat and the bill to the Submarine Base Supply, New London. This often got me in hot water, but the Captain knew what I was doing and always covered for me.

One specific item that was very difficult to get were leather seal rings for hydraulic manifold valves that controlled the opening and closing of the main steam stops and turbine root valves. These valves were of 1942 design (fairly new) but by 1968, very hard to find since nuclear boats after the Skate Class were all standardized to S5W reactor plant. Well I finally tacked these seals down to a warehouse at Portsmouth Naval Shipyard that had old stuff warehoused for fleet diesel boats, 1941 to 1948. *Nautilus* had been in the yards there for over a year so most of the shops knew us well and knew how hard we worked to get spare parts. The enlisted supply system worked like this – Bruce calls Joe, who knows Frank over in Engineering, who in turn talked to Mike in the old fleet boat section and eventually we usually got what we needed. In return for their services we supplied a few pounds of coffee, or maybe a meal, to the right people.

Another time we needed parts for the emergency diesels. These were 268As, mostly found in LCM-8s [landing craft] and mine sweeps. We needed blowers, cylinder liners, and other parts so we raided the mothballed diesel boats, and actually had to cut locks to gain access. At one point we found that our engine casing was so badly eaten away by salt water that we had to rebuild it using DEVCON (Plastic Steel) using a NAVSEC approved procedure for "minor engine block repairs."

Refer to: MILITARY SPECIFICATION ENGINES, DIESEL MARINE, PROPULSION AND AUXIILIARY, MEDIUM SPEED MIL-E-23457B(SHIPS), 3 March 1976, SUPERSEDING MIL-E-23457A(SHIPS) 4 January 1965

I ended up calling the DEVCOM Company and getting about 25 Gallons of this stuff shipped directly to *Nautilus*. It was not a simple task and went like this:

1. Discovered that Submarine Base Supply cannot get large quantities because there is no FSN for 5 gallon buckets. Small tubes and one quart containers available, nothing larger.
2. Direct purchase not an option according to Submarine Base Supply.
3. Made direct contact using telephone [outside line] in Control Room:
4. *"...DEVCOM Corporation, how my I help you?" "This is Petty Officer Kinne from USS Nautilus (SSN-571). I need to speak to someone about procuring a large amount of DEVCOM..." "You'er WHO from WHERE?"*
5. Then I said, *"My name is Petty Officer Kinne from USS Nautilus (SSN-571) in New London, Connecticut and I need to speak with someone in your distribution or sales group about obtaining a large quantity of DEVCON."*
6. After a few minutes I spoke with an engineer who then put president of the company on the phone. I explained my dire situation and how I planned to use DEVCON for repairs in accordance with the references to the NAVSHIPS technical materials. They asked if 25 gallons (5 containers) would be enough. I said yes and thanked them for their help and of course told them to send the invoice to Submarine Base Supply.
7. Within two days the DEVCPM was delivered to the boat and repairs commenced. I believe it took us about five days before we were ready to test the diesel. It took that long because there was only one or two guys in M–Division capable of twisting around and getting into the Diesel sump to effect the block rebuild with the Devcon and then do some rough machining for the cylinder liner insertion.

Everything worked fine as a I recall, except for the phone call from the Submarine Base Supply Officer. Remember the Captain was semi-aware of what I was doing and of course covered for me; although I had to make myself scarce on the lower base for awhile. No Questions asked.

On another occasion we used an Emergency Patch Kit from the Damage Control (DC) kit to get the DEVCON to temporarily fix the mechanical coupling for the boat's drain pump. This was a true jury-rig. However, without the jury-rig the trim pump would have remained out of commission. We would have had a real problem with no way to pump water out of the boat.

Bruce Kinne, '68 – '71

1970 – Two Other Memorable Repairs

Charging Valve - the story goes like this. There is a remotely controlled valve that is opened and shut when you add primary grade water to the reactor. This valve is in the Reactor Compartment upper level starboard side just on the other side of the bulkhead from the two charging pumps in forward Auxiliary Machinery Space (AMS). This valve had to be open in order to add water to the primary loop and we were having a lot of problems with it. It was just worn out! So go get another one! Easy to say but this valve on *Nautilus* and the one at the S1W prototype in Idaho were the only known ones in existence. This took me a week or so to discover. Remember, no internet in 1968-70.

My first step was go to the COSAL and get the Stock Code, should be easy, however, the Navel Supply System did not carry it, OBSOLETE! Okay, let's find out who made it, should be easy, it has name plate information. Found it, the COMPANY had burned down and gonr out of business 1959. Find detail blueprints – Nope! I called IDAHO, got any - NOPE! Now what! Research some more and made phone calls to Portsmouth Naval Shipyard and to Electric Boat. I found out from some old-timers that after the first North Pole attempt that ended back in Hawaii that a lot of parts were needed for repairs. BINGO!

High pressure gauge glass for level indication consists of one piece of glass with clear mica inserts on the steam/water side inside two metal frames. The belleview washers when stacked properly with the centers of curvature facing each other act as tension springs and thus maintain the stress on the nut and bolt keeping a tight seal on the glass and mica.

Steely Eyed Killers of the Deep

For every bolt we had at least 40 washers and there were 20-24 bolts per 12 in glass. We had three over laps x 4 units so you figure. The best part was that each washer had to checked against a gauge to the correct curvature then coated with Neo-lube before stacking and assembly. More fun stuff!

Bruce Kinne, '68 – '71

1970 - Loss of Port Main Engine Throttle

This, I thought, was very interesting. We had two main engines, a HP/LP turbine combination on both sides of the Engine Room, each drive their own reduction gear, shaft and screw. While returning from one our trips, on approach to New London, the Maneuvering Watch was set and we lost control of the throttle rack for the port HP turbine at the same time. THIS IS BAD! We need both screws for maneuvering and docking in New London. As Engineering Watch Supervisor I had to sit and/or stand over the port engine throttle rack and open and close it by hand wheel attachment as the change in bells (speed) was passed to me over the sound powered phones from the throttle man in Maneuvering. This worked well even with the very high temperature in this area (right on top of the Port HP Turbine) until I started getting direction to increase speed by three turns (RPMS). I had no instrumentation there except steam chest inlet pressure, so a turn count order like that was impossible to judge and this was reflected in my reply, "... ^%j*& do you think I am doing out here, who the !#^(*& thought this up - you tell them that if they want three more turns on the port shaft to come on down and do it themselves..." Well we finally got into port and tied up to the pier after about four hours of manually controlling the port main engine by hand. This was just another of the wonderful one-time events on *Nautilus*.

Bruce Kinne, '68 - '71

1970 - Liberty - San Juan, Puerto Rico

Liberty in San Juan was a bit more interesting, because we actually tied up and got some time off to relax. Not a whole lot, but enough, and no daily operations. Of course we all went to Old San Juan to visit all the sleazy bars and strip clubs, meet street local personalities, and maybe some cops. My most notable memories are: the fishnet stockings; the stripper and the boa; and carrying John Craft back to the boat and dropping him on the tender's quarter deck. So here they are:

Fishnet stockings – Most us even back then knew what fishnet stockings were. What we did not know was how large the netting space could be until a memorable late afternoon in a very "fashionable" bar. A tall young lady, maybe 20 years old, walked into the club from a back entrance. She wore only a low cut fishnet stocking material body suit. The size of the diamond open areas had to be at least one half to one inch wide. Just unbelievable! Needless all sailor eyes moved in unison and all mouths dropped. She was buck naked underneath the body suit. There was almost a riot. The bartender did appreciate that the sailors stopped drinking but it was his decision to cut them off. The locals were trying to keep the sailors away from her, the police were called and they asked her to change clothes. She refused and they tried to arrest her. The police finally convinced all parties to quite down. She then left, changed into something less revealing, though not by much, and came back, much to our delight.

The stripper and the boa – We entered this particular club which had a good size stage and some skaggy strippers just going through the motions. No one in our group had too much to drink as yet, and it was still is light outside. This new stripper starts her act and takes a big snake out of a box and starts dancing with it. Her manager sitting in the front row was acting as a safety valve, however his attention is riveted on another stripper sitting next to him. We are not impressed with the dancer on stage or her snake and we continue to sip our beer. I glanced at the reflection in the mirror behind the bar and saw the stripper on stage starting to have trouble with the snake. We yelled at her manager in the front row who just waved us off. He's still busy with the other stripper. Meanwhile the lady is down on one knee and the shake is coiling around her trying to pin her other arm. We tossed some beer bottles at the manager and he starts coming for us then he realizes what is happening on the stage. He gets up on the stage and with the help of another stage hand is able to get the snake off of her and back into the box. We were told that power to the heat lamps that kept the box warm and the snake happy failed. Instead of dancing with a happy sleepy warm snake the stripper got a grumpy old cold snake. After that episode we left seeking bigger and better entertainment.

Carrying John Craft – Skoglund and I were walking back to the boat and we saw John Craft wandering about by himself. He was smashed and likely to get mugged in his condition, so we got him into a cab and rode back to the boat. *Nautilus* was moored two boats outboard of the tender *Fulton and* we had to cross over *Fulton* first. Because we were in civies [civilian clothes], we had to ask permission to cross over without saluting, but standing at attention showing our ID cards. This is hard to accomplish when you are also supporting a shipmate who passed out in a cab on the way back. So here Skoglund and I are carrying Craft up the gangway. We stopped, showed our ID's, and requested permission to cross over. The quarter deck Junior Officer of the Deck (JOOD) was a young Ensign and he just had to be an asshole, *"You men stand up straight and come to attention!" "Sir we have ..." "I said come to attention!"* So we dropped John on the Quarter Deck and snapped to attention. Then the JOOD starts yelling at us about dropping John. I started to say, *"Sir, you said ..."* and both the First Class and Third Class Petty Officers who were also on watch started to chuckle. This is not good. *"Pick up that drunk and get off my quarter Deck - Now!" "Yes sir!"* We hoisted John up and headed down a ladder and over to the first diesel boat. The Topside Watch had heard most of this eschange and just waved us over to the next boat and the next boat waved us over to *Nautilus* where we stuffed John down the Stern Room hatch and into his bunk.

Bruce Kinne, '68 – '71

1970 - Engineering Qualification

By September 1970 I was qualified EOOW/EWS/Engineering Duty Chief and standing six on six off when underway and two or three days on and one day off in port. This was a BIG DEAL for me since I was only a Machinist's Mate 2nd/class. The EOOW/EWS is normally a very senior enlisted NUC, either a First Class Petty Officer or Chief. However, we had a hard time getting people qualified. So here I was after only 5 years in the Navy and qualified EOOW/EWS.

Only me and Master Chief Parker were both qualified in those positions. The boat was getting First Class Petty Officers and Chiefs from other boats, but they were S5W (reactor) trained and for some reason seem to have trouble qualifying on the S1W in *Nautilus*. My final engineering qualification board was a number of one on one sessions with the Captain, Commander Cockfield (later Admiral) in his stateroom.

No sooner did I qualify and walk out of his cabin, aft most in the Wardroom and closest to the Control Room, there was a 1-MC announcement, *"Kinne report to Maneuvering."* I reported there to find that I have been penciled in on the watch bill and had to relieve Master Chief Parker. I did that and about ten minutes into the watch, a call comes over the 2-MC (Engineering Communications), *"EWS report to Maneuvering."* I report back and I am told by the Duty Engineer (EOOW) that he needs to go look at something in the Stern Room. So I relieve the EOOW and he relieves me as EWS. No sooner do I pass the word on the 2-MC that Kinne is now the EOOW than the reactor operator in Maneuvering, just two feet from me, calls out *"Reactor SCRAM!"* So, now it starts, TEST KINNE TIME. Well I handled myself very well, with the exception of telling two of the officers who crowded into Maneuvering to observe me to *"Shut the *&*^%$@#% up or get out of Maneuvering."*

After notifying Conn of the SCRAM and being ordered to answer all bells because we were submerged in an operations area, the Engineering crew conducted a quick investigation found the problem. The Engineer had opened the control rod hold supply breakers and conducted a FAST SCRAM RECOVERY. After the plant was returned to normal, and I finished my watch, the Captain and the Engineer, critiqued my performance and reminded me in no uncertain terms that while I conducted the recovery 100% correctly per procedure, that I could not tell officers to SHUT the $#&^%(&%^ UP. They also said that there was no doubt who was in charge in Maneuvering, however, my choice of words left something to be desired.

Bruce Kinne, '68 - '71

1971 – Search for Missing Gear

In 1971 we were pulled out of a North Atlantic Operation and sent at flank speed above the Arctic Circle. Our mission was to retrieve a missing piece of gear from a Boomer [missile submarine] before the Russians got it. I doubt the Russians were ever looking, but we found it after searching for three days on the surface above the circle.

There were numerous other interesting sightings; some WW-II mines, Japanese fishing balls, and an "iceberg" that turned out to be a snow covered mountain 70 miles away!

I was the Officer of the Deck at initial sighting and I was also the Weapons Officer so the Commanding Officer relieved me and sent me topside to supervise bringing the item on board. We recovered the missing item and stowed it in the Torpedo Room. Some days later, we took the recovered item to U.S. Navy facilities in Holy Loch, Scotland. I expected to be met by folks who would congratulate and debrief us. Well, nothing like that happened. I did not have the duty, but did not leave the boat, as I was awaiting a call regarding transfer of the recovered item.

About 1600 (4 PM), I called the Squadron Weapons Officer, a Lieutenant Commander. I introduced myself and told him that I was not sure he was yet cleared to know this, but I needed some help disposing of the "item." He was quite dismissive of the lowly Lieutenant on board *Nautilus*, but indicated he would get back to me. He did not. At 1600 the next day, I called him and told him, *"This is Lieutenant Henry again. You did not call me back, so here is what is going to happen. If you do not pick this item up by 0900 tomorrow morning, I will offload it onto your pier and you can figure out what to do with it."* I hung up, somewhat fearful of having chewed out a senior officer, but convinced I did the right thing.

I advised Chief Lincecum to rig for offloading torpedoes at 0700 (7 AM) the next morning. We were ready by 0730. About that time a 285 pound civilian drives a cherry picker down the pier. We hoisted the item to allow the cherry picker to grab it. The last I saw of the secret item, it was being driven down the pier in full sight of everyone.

The Forward Torpedo Room, and forward berthing in particular, had been completely disrupted while we had the item on board. We set about restoring the forward berthing spaces for the transit back to New London.

I hate to say this, but it would not surprise me if that item is still lying out back of some warehouse over there.

Wayne Henry, '69 – '72

1971 – Searching the North Atlantic

Here is my take about the search for a radio buoy. There are a lot of things floating around up in Arctic waters which caused a lot of false sightings. We put a rifleman on the Bridge to shoot the glass balls from broken fishing nets so we could search without seeing them again. We blew hundreds of them apart in the time we spent on the surface.

I think it was *Tringa* that was sent north to help us search. She had been in Portsmouth, England and arrived the same day that we found the buoy. She was rolling from yard arm to yard arm in the sea swells. We flooded down the forward deck of *Nautilus*, put a swimmer in the water and roped the buoy on board with the forward capstan then lowered it down into the Forward Torpedo Room. We took some salt water down the hatch while doing this evolution but we got it safely on board.

I was stationed on *Thomas Jefferson* before *Nautilus* and knew about the system that set the buoy free. A long while after the episode, I ran into some of my shipmates from the "TJ" and they told me what their investigation had uncovered. A bad sea pressure switch had corroded and the dissimilar materials that it was made from created a battery in the salt water. This caused enough current to set off the system and the exploding bolts holding the buoy. The bolts, in fact, exploded and sent it on its way. The buoy sent out a message "Submarine Sunk" and the "TJ" had to surface and radio that they were okay during their patrol. *Nautilus* was pulled off our NATO operation to go north to find the buoy which we did.

After we unloaded the item in Holly Loch we pulled into HMS Faslane, the British Submarine Base in Scotland, for some rest and relaxation. We missed the NATO operations that would have sent us to Bergen, Norway because of this episode, but Faslane was a good time anyway. But that's another story.

John Dudas, '69 – '72

1971 – HMS Faslane

Faslane was fun to say the least. We traded everything with the Brits and at 0600 (6 AM) the Topside Watch called below and ask me to come Topside to see the British sailor who had swapped me a full set of colours [flag] in exchange for my blue jacket. As a result he did not have colours to raise that morning and was on board *Nautilus* begging me to give back the colours until he could get more from his supply system. He was the Captain's man and would be in real trouble if they did not have any flags to raise that morning. Great little Submarine Base in Faslane.

John Dudas, '69 – '72

1971 - COMSUBLANT Lost at Sea

In 1971 we were directed to participate in an exercise off Norfolk with the brand new submarine *Sea Devil*. Commander Submarine Force Atlantic (COMSUBLANT), Admiral "Dennis" Wilkinson, first Commanding Officer of *Nautilus*, was riding *Sea Devil*. A story was circulating that the Admiral was riding *Sea Devil* because wanted to make sure he collected his sea pay. Nonetheless, we were at periscope depth when we transmitted *"COMEX"* (Commence Exercise). *Sea Devil* was supposed to announce *"COMEX, AYE"* and then proceed to avoid detection by *Nautilus* and several other surface and air craft for the next 24 hours.

I was the Officer of the Deck, and recall clearly that we did not hear *Sea Devil's* reply. So, after attempts to reach her were unsuccessful (remember she was hiding), we reported *"Possible SUB SUNK."* Twenty-four hours later, *Sea Devil* surfaced and said, *"We remained undetected."* The response, *"You don't know how many people were searching!"*

There have been several times over the years that others discovered that I served on *Nautilus* from '69-'72 and had questions. They wanted to know if I was on board when those dummies reported Admiral Wilkinson lost at sea. I told them the story, but to this day don't know that we could have done anything differently. Of course, *Sea Devil* maintained that they responded correctly, and likely they did. I guess if it happened today the National Security Agency (NSA) could clarify for us.

Wayne Henry, '69 - '72

8 - CDR Alex Anckonie, III, USN *and* Crew

June 1972 – December 1976

1972 – More on Air Conditioning

It was winter and we were doing some NATO games. The trip was approximately two weeks. After three days out we lost ALL Air Conditioning (AC). Some of the details are: Chill water temperature was 120 degrees; Many salt water leaks which resulted in a 99% humidity; Temperature in Upper Level Reactor Compartment (ULRC) was 180 F; Maximum number of people on watch in engineering spaces ~4 (normal 8-9); Most watches lasted less than 30 minutes and many passed out as they went back into after machinery.

Anyone going aft from up forward had to have phone communications because there was fear they might not make it. The low pressure blower could only be run for five or ten minutes in low due to high bearing temperatures and when they lit it off it rained in the ULRC.

All perishable food was ejected including everything in the chill and freeze boxes. The last thing left was a block of cheese and it melted on the stainless floor in the freeze box. The last two editable items that I remember were grapefruit juice (100 F) and some dry Mexican tamales.

When *"FINEX"* (finished exercise) was passed over the 1-MC the Commanding Officer sent out an SOS equivalent. An Auxiliary Submarine Rescue (ASR) was sent to us containing anyone who knew anything about *Nautilus*. The ASR broke a shaft in high seas and returned to port a day after us. We submerged and put on a flank bell. You could not make it any hotter due to the speed. We arrived at State Pier in New London in late night and it was snowing. Sailors poured out of all the hatches in their skivvies and no shirts. Family members thought we were crazy. We put many dehydrated sailors in the hospital that night on saline drips. It was at that moment that I knew I would never ship over for four more.

Maybe someone will tell the story about several trips to sea with no operable air compressors. Why did we do this? The squadron wanted us to do mid-shipmen cruises to encourage interest in the submarine service. I don't think we made any converts.

John Lewis ,'71 – '74

1972 – *Nautilus* High Jacking Event

Now this Big N event took place in the fall of 1972 and it became known among Squadron 10 Staff as the "*Nautilus* High Jacking Event." At the time I was on temporary additional duty (TAD) to Squadron 10 while waiting for a flight to Rota, Spain to meet up with *USS Jack* and report as the replacement for the Auxiliary gang Chief Petty Officer.

Nautilus was returning to New London from an operation just off the South Carolina coast. When she was off the New Jersey coast she radioed that she had lost all air conditioning (AC) and was on the surface with the majority of the crew suffering from heat exhaustion. This is where the "High Jacking Event" begins. The Squadron 10 Commander sent a message to all local commands asking for former *Nautilus* crew members to form a relief crew to be sent out to relieve the stressed crew members on *Nautilus* and bring the boat back to New London.

They managed to round up about 20 of us and loaded us onto USS *Skylark* (ASR-20). *Skylark's*, Commanding Officer (CO), at the time was another old former *Nautilus* crew member, Lieutenant Commander William Furnholm. We spent a little over a day transiting out to *Nautilus* only to be informed that the boat's CO felt that they could manage to get her home by rotating the crew from topside to below deck and would appreciate having the ASR escort them back, *"Just in case we need you guys."* After spending three days riding that ASR, and being served food, that words can not adequately describe, on metal trays, I made a decision to never accept an offer to transition from Chief Petty Officer to Limited Duty Officer. Us A-gangers would never be assigned to ride the boats again as an O-ganger (unless one had been anointed as a NUC should that possibility even exist).

Then another event took place before we arrived at State Pier that added to the adventure. We had just past Race Rock Light when *Skylark* came to *"All Stop."* She was boarded by a "real life" Leroy Jethro Gibbs and his Naval Criminal Investigative Service (NCIS) team and a couple of dogs. Apparently some of *Skylark's* crew were involved with "marketing unauthorized products" and "Gibbs" and company wanted to catch them on board with their products. This action took an additional 10 hours of cycling on station before docking at State Pier.

When we finally tied up the Squadron 10 Engineer met us on the pier and informed three of us Engineering types that we had been "volunteered" to get *Nautilus'* AC back in commission and running. The only one of our trio that I was really familiar with was John

"Mickey" McGovern. We started with the AC two units in the lower level machinery space. When we first went down the ladder memories flooded back of standing watches in the space affectionately known as "Twin Falls" due to the leaking shaft seals. The exotic stainless steel shaft seal covers with the drain lines were still there." We removed the condenser plugs for the zinc nodes and discovered there weren't any attached. Next we tried to insert a bore scope for a look around inside the condenser only to find that the area was completely over grown with eel grass and barnacles. It should be noted here that the boat had sat alongside the pier for six weeks with the AC units shut down and all the sea valves had been left open.

I asked "Mickey" how the hell are we going to get all that crap out of the condensers without taking them apart. He told the Squadron Engineer that he and I were going to conduct a couple of experiments to see if the crap inside the condensers could be removed without a complete and costly dis-assembly of the AC units and that he would let them know if the experiments worked or not. Then we left the boat and headed over to Maxies. Murph was also still open then. But before we left, "Mick" had me extract some of the eel grass and he put the stuff into a couple of glass dishes along with some barnacles that were attached to one of the plugs. He had another small bottle, about quart size, that contained a clear liquid with him. We took all this scientific stuff with us and proceeded to Maxies to conduct our scientific research. We ordered a couple of pitchers of beer and commenced the experiments. "Mick" opened the quart of the "Secret Formula" and poured it over the eel grass. We then sat there in deep concentration, sippin' beer, and watched what was happening in the glass jar. After two hours of close observation, and some more beer, we discovered that the secret formula was dissolving the eel grass and causing the barnacles to come loose from the plug, SUCCESS!

We packed up our experiment, finished the last beer, popped a few breath fresheners, returned to the boat and informed the Squadron Engineer and CO that we had found a way to remove all the eel grass from the condensers without taking them apart. When asked if he had written up a procedure for them to review before work began, "Mick" gave them a Bob Stroud response, *"Do you want these units back on line or do you want to waste time discussing it?"* They left him alone and we began the "treatment."

We shut the sea valves, removed the internals of the matrix valves, blanked the valve covers and filled the condensers with the "Secret

Formula." While the stuff was doing it's work we removed all the refrigerant and oil from the units. We took out more than three times the R-12 that was needed and enough oil to keep the main turbine lubricated. The "Secret Formula" was allowed to work overnight then we made an adapter on the matrix valve for a fire hose and opened up the discharge valve and commenced to flush the condensers. When the flushing was completed we bore scoped the condensers and observed that they were clear. The "Secret Formula" worked!

The units were reassembled one at a time and the correct amount of R-12 and oil put back in. We lit the unit off and made adjustments to the matrix valves then loaded the unit down for a final checkout and repeated the process on the other units. The two units in the engine room were ball busters but we got them running also.

I'm sure that some of you scientific types must have figured out by now what the "Secret Formula" really was - for everyone else, it was made by the Clorox Corporation. Yep! That's what it was, pure Bleach. It just underscores the fact that a person doesn't always need a engineering degree or PHD to solve problems. Just apply the simple basics that all submariners know, *"How the hell can I get this sucker back on line?"*

Barry "Dan" Danforth, '60 – '61

1973 – Red Devil Blower

We were on our way to Fort Lauderdale, Florida and *Nautilus* was on the surface. It was suffering hot down below particularly in the Engineering spaces. We only had a couple of the Air Conditioning (AC) units still working. In order to cool down the Engine Room we opened the hatch midway in the Engine Room and rigged a Red Devil blower elephant trunk up the hatch with the blower setting in the center passageway. The Engineman on watch was a fellow named Sprague. I was the Upper Level Reactor Compartment watch. The heat was so bad Sprague got sick and climbed up the hatch and heaved a bit. When he came back down he and I sat on a tool chest seat and just hung our heads. We only moved once an hour to get readings then returned to the bench. The Red Devil blower is a real noisy machine especially when running at a very high RPM. All of sudden we heard the blower grind almost to a stop then the RPM's started picking backup until it was at full speed again. At the same time feathers were being blown all over the Engine Room along with some blood and guts.

A seagull, or some other sea bird, apparently believed Sprague had put out lunch for him and he got too close to the intake. We nearly died laughing, and every time someone new came aboard, we repeated the story and the laughing started all over again. We believed we could see the seagull going down that trunk, flapping his wings trying to escape. By far it was the funniest experience I had in my four years on *Nautilus*.

John Lewis, '71 – '74

1974 – Appeasing Admiral Rickover

It was 1974 and we were in the midst of a long overhaul in the Electric Boat shipyard. *Nautilus* was totally engulfed in repair work, three shifts a day. We lived in a barge moored to the pier. Admiral Rickover visited the shipyard a couple of times during this period and since he couldn't stay on *Nautilus*, I suppose he thought it fitting to stay on her barge. He stayed in a room that had been specially prepared for him a day or so earlier. The admiral liked quiet so movies were suspended while he was aboard. He ordered the air conditioning system shut down in the evening because it was noisy. To complete the "rig for silence" routine, a barge watch was placed on the deck below officer's country to make sure all remained quiet. I was concluding my ten years of Navy service at this time and I couldn't believe the ridiculously special treatment this man commanded. I certainly knew of no other officer accorded this deference.

I was standing the "Rickover watch" one night, cursing under my breath, when I passed the base of the ladder connecting the second and third decks and looked up to see this scrawny little old man doing squats in the passageway, in his skivvy shorts. Having never seen an Admiral, any Admiral, let alone the "father of the nuclear navy," in his skivvies, I guess I paused a little too long observing the scene. He shouted down the ladder indignantly to me, *"Don't you have anything better to do sailor?"* Since then I've thought of countless really cool answers to that question. But that night I just bit my tongue and moved on.

Garry Garner, '72 – '75

Tommy Robinson

1975 – Hard Times/Fine Officers

I spent many a long watch with Mr. Riffer in Maneuvering. What a great officer, decent human being who had a tough job to do. In 1975 *Nautilus* was not the "pride of the fleet" that she had once been and I stated that when I spoke to the *Nautilus* reunion group in 2008. What kept me going was a keen sense of duty and the leadership of some really fine officers such as Mr. Riffer, Mr. Fast, Mr. Lisceno, Mr. Erickson, Mr Troxler, Mr. Taylor, and the list goes on.

Mr. Riffer gave me some sage advice when I transferred to NR-1. I remember to this day, he said, *"Stanosz, you are the best Electrician I have served with in the fleet, but you have got to learn to watch what you say."* It was a privilege to serve with those officers. AND, I was compelled to be outspoken on NR-1. It had to do with only a crew of 15.

Anyway, I have for five or six years been giving my version of the 1975 jam dive from the Engineering/NUC standpoint to officer candidates at Marquette University. No non-volunteers, more awe! Thanks, Mr. Riffer.

Greg Stanosz, '73 – '76

1975 - Hide 'n Sink

Not knowing exactly where you are at any given time is something you get used to being a Machinist's Mate. You spend most of your time in the Engine Room or auxiliary machinery space, isolated from the bigger picture. When you hear the announcement, *"Set the Maneuvering Watch,"* you're either leaving or coming into port. During a fleet exercise, when you hear: *"General Quarters, all hands man your battle stations,"* your ship has entered the arena, *"Let the games begin!"*

Far away from the periscopes' stand, Sonar and Control rooms; I was clueless as to the actual happenings of the simulated war game. My assigned battle station was way aft in the hydraulic pump room. The machinery was in great shape and ran perfectly. I just kept an eye and an ear on things. Each hour I would get permission to remove my headphones so I could jump down into Aux #2 and log the gauge readings on the air conditioning and atmosphere control equipment. Then I would zip back up and don the headphones again.

Steely Eyed Killers of the Deep

One piece of equipment, the signal ejector, in the hydraulic pump room did play an active role in the games. Basically, it's a miniature torpedo tube. Mounted roughly at a 30 degree angle off vertical. It's used to deploy counter-measure devices (CMD), or signal flares (green, yellow, or red smoke, with or without illumination). Operating the signal ejector was fairly straightforward. Open the breech, pull the pin on the flare or CMD, insert it in tube, close the breech, flood the tube with seawater, open the outer door (ball valve) and fire. Finally, shut the outer door. Never forget the first rule on a submarine: Keep seawater out of the people tank!

What some were calling uneven and unfair, considering the age of *Nautilus* and number of opponents, today's main event would prove to be quite entertaining, to say the least. A much younger tag-team versus an ageing veteran. This is a fight to the finish, ladies and gentlemen, a virtual death match.

Introducing the principles: In the red corner, from various ports along the east coast, decked out in their haze grey trunks with dark grey trim, I present you with "The Carrier Group" comprised of USS *Kennedy*, her attached air wing, and a couple of anti-submarine warfare (ASW) destroyers. Their opponent, sitting all alone in the deep blue corner, fighting out of Groton, Connecticut, wearing the matte black trunks, *"The First and Finest," "The Queen of the River,"* ladies and gentlemen, I'm honored to introduce to you, the underdog, USS *Nautilus*.

A standing round of applause, whistles, and cheers.

Ding! The beginning of Round One.

If I recall correctly, the first green signal flare sent up announced the beginning of the exercise. If we managed to evade the "enemy" for the duration of the "round," we'd fire off another one to reveal our location.

"Aux2, Conn. Load and fire one green smoke."

"Conn, Aux2. Load and fire one green smoke, aye."

"Conn, Aux2. One green smoke fired."

We headed for the depths, hiding in the different thermal layers in the Mediterranean Sea to dodge some jabs. If your opponent can't see you, the best he could do would be to land a lucky punch. We turned invisible.

Apparently, we won a few rounds. I launched so many green flares that day we would need to restock the pyrotechnics locker when we got back alongside the tender. I was about to notify "the powers that be" that the next one would be our last, when I heard:

"*Aux2, Conn. Load and fire one red smoke.*" Are they psychic up there, or what?

"*Conn, Aux2. Load and fire one red smoke, aye.*"

I was then told to transfer my headphone jack into 1JV receptacle for further instructions. What the heck is this all about?

"*Aux2 going from 2JV to 1JV, aye.*"

An officers in the Conn came on the line and told me that as soon as the next red flare left the signal ejector, to IMMEDIATELY reload and flood a third red smoke, but to wait for the order to fire. I was told not to bother communicating back that I had fired the second flare, or when the third one was loaded and flooded, just do it, and be ready to launch. The order to fire would be announced over the 1-MC speaker. Did I understand the order?

"*Aye, Sir. After firing this next flare, immediately load another red flare 'wet,' and wait to fire.*"

Hmmmm, this is a twist. Now I'm really curious about what's going on up there?

"*Load the second red flare.*"

A few moments later...

"*Flood the tube, and fire.*"

I did as instructed, and within seconds, had reloaded the signal ejector with the third red flare and flooded it with water. My right hand at the "ready" on the launch lever.

"Fire!"

That time, I may have shoved the lever with just a little more gusto, as if I was firing an actual torpedo at an enemy ship. Little did I know at the time...

"Secure from General Quarters. Return to normal watch rotation. Petty Officer Heesen, outstanding shooting on the aft tube!"

A smile crossed my face when I heard that one, but I still had no idea what was so "outstanding" about launching flares. I mean, it's just a flare - no big deal, right? Geez, they always keep us Engineering types in the dark.

After getting relieved off the watch, I headed to the Mess Deck for a fresh cup of coffee. One of the guys who was in the Conn during the exercise saw me and filled me in some of the details. It turns out that *Nautilus* had managed to sneak in, undetected by the ASW destroyers' sonar, and put three torpedoes into the "bird farm." We didn't actually fire any torpedoes, but he said the Fire Control system had the aircraft carrier "locked on" as a target long enough to make and record the "hits." So, that was the reason for changing colors, one red flare for each hit. Okay, now I understand. I asked him if he knew anything about the special launching instructions from one of the officers, and the "outstanding shooting" comment.

The reason for the unusual firing procedure just goes to show you what type of Skipper, Commander Alex Anckonie, was. John Wayne and Ernest Borgnine would have snapped to attention and saluted, or simply bowed and stepped aside. The Captain "had the Conn" during the last round. He watched the trajectory of the first flare through the periscope and maneuvered the submarine so the second flare would cross the bow of the carrier. And, then, after a slight pause, the piece de resistance, the coup de grâce, the final flare. It landed right, smack dab, on the flight deck of *USS Kennedy*! Heh, heh, heh. Talk about rubbin' it in their faces. Are we good, or what?

I can only imagine what the scene looked like when all the CO's got together with the Commodore to critique that exercise. Trash talk the

"*First and Finest*" and you'll be wearing those "scrambled eggs" on your face instead of on your hat visors.

Pretty slick aiming there, Cap'n.

Donald "Don" Heesen, '75 – '76

1976 - Missing Toilet Paper

On our first extended underway after the mid 1970's overhaul, the Chief of the Boat (COB) came to me, the Executive Officer (XO), with a problem. It seems all the toilet paper had gone missing. This was very perplexing since both the COB and I distinctly remembered the working party that had loaded and stowed enough toilet paper to last a six month deployment. Forget the fact that no one could wipe their behinds!

In spite of this, the stowage locations were almost empty. The COB had the Chiefs keep their ears to the deck plates, and soon learned that there was a rumor going around that we had no toilet paper, so everyone was confiscating whatever they could, and hiding it in their favorite hidey holes. Where the rumor started, nobody knew, but it had become fact in the minds of the crew. No amount of verbal pressure from the COB, trying to convince them otherwise, would cause them to return the toilet paper.

I told the COB to gather up every bit of toilet paper he could lay his hands on, including the non-pilfered supplies in the Chief's Quarters and Officer's Country. After the noon meal, we placed them all in the Crew's Mess, which made a fairly substantial stack, and then I held an XO's call for the off and off going sections. I spoke of the rumor, told them it was untrue, showed them the stacks of toilet paper, and asked them to return what had been confiscated so we could keep it all in its normal stowage and free up some of their limited personal space.

It worked! Within a few hours we had enough toilet paper to complete the deployment.

Frederic "Bill" Rohm, '74 – '78

1976 – Substituting Night for Day

I was serving as Executive Officer (XO) on *Nautilus* when we left the shipyard at Electric Boat after the final overhaul in 1976. One of our first underway took us to the vicinity of Guantanamo Bay in the Caribbean. This was our shakedown cruise where we were to provide basic services to a destroyer squadron that was preparing for deployment, and was also our time to prepare for some upcoming certification exams, the most pressing of which was a Operational Readiness Safeguards Examination (ORSE) we were scheduled for on our return to New London in about six weeks.

Bill Riffer, the Engineer, and I were talking over various options on how to get all our training in and came up the idea of switching night and day. The destroyers came out of port in the morning, and wanted some ping time while we ran basic patterns they provided us. They would then return to port for the night. Bill and I figured the un-augmented watch ought to be able to handle that, so everyone else would sleep all day, then we'd all get up at night and run drills and training. The Captain agreed and this worked great for the first few weeks. Then we were notified the Destroyer Squadron (DESRON) Commodore wanted to bring some of his staff aboard to observe and learn more about submarine operations.

I asked the Captain to switch day and night back for the day the DESRON Commodore was coming, but with a twinkle in his eye, he told us to stick with the plan. So about 0600 (6 AM), a small boat brought the Commodore and his staff aboard. After greeting them, we had a steak dinner in the Wardroom. After dinner, as the destroyers began to ping away, we turned out the lights and started the evening movie, then everyone but the watch hit the rack. We fed them mid-rats [midnight snack] at noon, and of course ALL the watch standers told the DESRON folks that sleeping all the time off watch was perfectly normal. At about 1600 (4 PM), the boat picked up the skimmers who were completely confused and tight jawed. After they were gone, we held reveille and began our "daily nightly" training routine.

I've often wondered what they really thought. I know the DESRON Commodore wrote our Commodore, and both Commodores wrote our Commanding Officer, but the Skipper never told me what was in those letters. He'd just grin when I'd bring it up, but I suspect we added to the legends about crazy submariners.

Frederic "Bill" Rohm, '74 – '78

1976 – Of Whales and Sonars

We sustained a hit while underway in the Mediterranean. It was a soft broadside bump by a whale. Must've caused a good size headache for a good sized whale. A dull thud was both heard and felt. A dry dock inspection in La Maddalena revealed the boat did get nudged on the starboard side, amidships. It was just a slight indentation. *Nautilus* ran so smoothly that anything "abnormal" was easily noticed, by me, anyway.

We sneaked out through the Straight of Gibraltar underneath one of those huge super tankers because a lot of Russian fishing trawlers were hanging around the area. We were headed out on some Top Secret mission. The sound of that tanker's propeller blades so close was another thing I don't think I'll ever forget and the loud "pinging" from multiple Russian destroyers when we arrived at our mission's destination. That'll do a number on you, big time! Psychologically, I think the Russians' active sonar was the greatest, "Oh, shit!" factor.

Donald "Don" Heesen, '75 – '76

1976 – Chess Champion

One of the enjoyable factors when I was on the Big N was also having the All Navy 1975/76 Chess Champion on board. He was a NUC Machinist's Mate 2nd/class. This dude would play six of us at the same time. Three on two adjacent tables in the Crews Mess. He would look at the first board, make instant assessment and move his piece, and move to the next board, and repeat. I never beat him. I don't think anyone did during that cruise. I did give him a few stale-mates, though, and a few times when he got to my board, he'd go to make his move and then, *"Whoa ... hmmmm,"* so at least I gave him pause.

He got into a stink with the Executive Officer and Captain. I believe he tossed an insubordinate-type of comment to the Engineer and got written up for it. Then they started screwing with him. When we arrived in Naples, Italy he got on the phone to one of his Navy chess buddies. Within two weeks he had orders transferring him to a desk job in Washington, DC. It appears that his chess buddy just happened to be a two-star Admiral. One needs to be careful with whom one screws with, eh? I thought it was frickin' great!

Steely Eyed Killers of the Deep

Gotta love it when an enlisted guy pulls one over on those O-gangers, especially when a Snipe [engineering rate] does it.

Donald "Don" Heesen, '75 - '76

9 – CDR Richard "Dick" A. Riddell *and* Decommissioning Crew

December 1976 – March 1980

1976 – Skimmer to Submariner

After two and a half years of steaming around the western Pacific I was ready to get stationed a little closer to home. I was eligible for transfer when we arrived back in Hawaii. Being on a destroyer that was home ported in Pearl Harbor had its perks, but it still was just an island five thousand miles from Massachusetts. So, as we were getting underway from, what would be my last visit to the Philippines, I submitted my request chit for transfer to the East Coast. The transfer didn't look promising. A few days later my Senior Chief informed me that since a lot of Vietnam sailors were not re-enlisting, all Engineering rates had been classified as "Critical Rates." He said, *"The only way a Machinist Mate, especially a 'hole-snipe,' could possibly get out of WESTPAC would be to volunteer for submarine duty."*

Hmmm ..."I need to think about that one for a minute, Chief."

Let's see, I've been through a typhoon with twenty-five to thirty foot seas, survived the "old school" Shellback [equator crossing] initiation, slept in a berthing compartment directly below a five-inch deck gun on a destroyer that was no stranger to the gun-line of Vietnam, have gone days without sleep, and without stepping foot topside due to the seemingly, never ending Battle Stations and routine Engineroom watches, Very familiar with the term "water hours" [restricted water use], dangled from a helicopter in a "horse collar," high-lined in a Bos'ns Chair from one destroyer to another, and certified NAUI scuba diver. Yeah, I figured I could handle the living and working conditions on a submarine and the submarine school is in New London, right down the street from Boston. Sign me up!

"Okay, Senior Chief, you can let the Chain of Command know that I'm volunteering for submarines."

Well, there must have been a heckuva shortage of non-NUC Machinist Mates in the submarine world. I had orders and travel pay in hand within 48 hours after docking. Though I would miss Hawaii and the gorgeous girls of the Far East another new adventure is about to unfold.

I'm fairly certain that more than a few of you reading this had similar reactions when, upon graduation from Submarine School, I opened the envelope containing my orders and saw: USS *Nautilus* (SSN-571). Wow! What the...! Are you kidding me? THE *Nautilus*? I had to read it twice to make sure my eyes weren't playing tricks on me. Unbelievable! Who would've thought their first assignment in the submarine service would be on such a notable piece of Naval history? I felt honored to say the least. Yeah, yeah! Okay, on with the tale...

Not long after reporting aboard we got underway for the Mediterranean. Say "Goodbye" to Groton, Connecticut and fresh air for a while, boys. It's time to go and play Hide 'n Seek with the pros. There was an interesting cross-section of crew members; some of us newbies right out of schools, the brainiacs (including the All Navy Chess Champion) back in the Reactor Zone, and veteran diesel and nuke boat sailors, just a lot of super intelligent sailors. Also on board was a handful of Midshipmen, assigned temporary additional duty (TAD) for their qualification cruise. They would be leaving the boat in a week or two. I already had enough stuff to focus on without concerning myself with them, or so I thought.

Rule:	Keep the seawater out of the people tank!
Question:	How deep can she go?
Answer:	All the way to the bottom!

I was told that since *Nautilus* was celebrating her 21st birthday, the potential for failure of the structural integrity of pressure hull and fittings due to metal fatigue, restricted our operational depth to 800 feet.

I was assigned to Chief Ray "Chimp" Sanborn's A-gang and I was breaking in on watch back in AUX 2 and hydraulics. Peer, a very salty, Machinist Mate 1st/class was assigned to indoctrinate me on the workings of the atmosphere control, air conditioning, and hydraulic equipment. Break-in Watch routine went something like this; take a set of readings on all the operating units, go over the operating procedures for one or two of the systems a couple of times, then grab a cup of coffee and shoot the breeze for a few minutes. Repeat every hour while on watch until the new guy shows he can handle it solo.

It's about 0230 (2:30 AM), on the third or fourth day underway, and except for those of us on watch, most of the crew were asleep. The boat was riding smoothly around 600 feet below the surface, cruising along at a pretty good clip. I was getting a handle on all the machinery; one or two more supervised watches and I figured I'd be good to go. The 0200 (2 AM) readings were already logged, and Peer and I were down in Aux 2 so we could talk without disturbing the guys snoozing. All of a sudden, the submarine went into a hard dive angle.

"Damn, I wish they'd quit screwin' around up there in Control!"

Steely Eyed Killers of the Deep

Then I saw Peer's coffee mug slide right off the workbench and smash on the deck plates. It happened so suddenly that neither of us could have reacted in time to save it. Coffee and broken ceramic shards christened the immaculately clean deck plates and bilge sections. Uh-oh, he's gonna be pissed. I think I remember him telling me that his wife had custom ordered the stein from the Navy Exchange to commemorate his advancement to First Class. My gaze shifted from the mess on the deck to the expression on Peer's face. *Oh, $#!@.* A blank look on his face and he's white as ghost. This doesn't look good!

"They aren't screwing around. Something's wrong and it's our gear that's messing up. Get up to the hydraulic room. NOW!

Oh, isn't this just freakin' lovely! My first trip on a submarine and one of the saltiest sailors I've ever met looks like he just met, face to face, with the Grim Reaper! Damn! What the hell did I get myself into?

Since I was closest to the ladder I was on it in a flash. Then came the announcement no submariner ever wants to hear:

Aahoogah! Aahoogah! *"Jammed dive. Jammed dive. This is not a drill. I repeat, this is NOT a drill. Jammed dive."* Aahoogah!

I opened the hatch and scrambled up the ladder as best I could. Not a small task since the ladder on the aft bulkhead was no longer vertical. The boat was at about a 43 degree down angle. Gravity was pulling me off as I was trying to gain purchase of the rungs, so I hoisted myself up through the scuttle. Peer was right behind me.

When I got up in the berthing area, I saw a few guys already out of their racks trying to get into their coveralls while hanging on with one hand. Some managed the feat, some tumbled. I opened the Hydraulic Room's door and stepped aside. I knew enough to get out of the way and let experience handle this emergency. I'd follow his lead and do as he requested.

We went into the pump room and did a quick survey of the space. A few technical manuals had toppled over the restraining bar designed to hold them securely in place on the bookshelf, and there was some fluid was on the deck by the forward bulkhead. As Peer was assessing the hydraulic plant, I grabbed a few rags, wiped up the spill, and stowed the manuals in a cabinet. Okay, what next?

Tell me what you want, Peer, and I'm on it."

"Pump outlet and system pressures are good. The pump's running fine. Valves are lined up correctly. The rudder's working, but there's no pressure on the stern plane's gauge. Let's fire up the other pump and swap 'em out anyway, just to be sure."

"Okay."

Note: When the sub was underway, to help ensure equal wear on both hydraulic pumps, they were routinely swapped out in accordance with the Planned Maintenance System (PMS).

Pump # 2 was running at the time, so we started pump #1, brought it on line, and shut down #2. The system pressure gauge again showed that both pumps were operating properly, yet the needle on the stern plane ram gauge still sat on zero, and we were still in a dive.

"There's nothing else to do here. The problem's gotta be up in Control. Let's go! Move it!"

We were out the door in a flash, running, sliding, and slamming forward on the down hill slope. We flew. We were moving so fast that time almost seemed to stand still. Those DeLaval pumps always got up to speed instantly, thank goodness. At this point, I don't think a full minute had elapsed since his mug broke. Even having to open, close, and secure those heavy watertight bulkhead hatches along the way, I think we set a record for the fastest hydraulics to Control Room dash.

I heard the Captain announce, *"All engines, back full! Fishtail the rudder!"*

The submarine was still going down as we arrived in the Control Room. The Stern Planes Angle Indicator showed the planes had "dropped to their stops." Without waiting for the Captain's command, the Diving Officer, another crusty ol' salt, Torpedoman's Mate 1st/class John "Mack" McPhilmy, ordered the Manifold Watch, *"Weis, get some air into that forward group. We gotta bring her nose up!*

He grabbed the valve handle and quickly cranked open a couple of valves in the manifold. Weis replied, *"Air into the forward ballast tanks, aye, Mack."*

McPhilmy told Peer that it looks like the stern planes' control valve got stuck in the "Vent" position. After shifting the Control Valve Actuator through Normal, Emergency, and Hand with no change. Peer took a look at the slide valve under the helm seat, and informed "Mack" that it would have to be taken apart to fix the problem. There was nothing we could do until then. Helplessness is not a good feeling.

When the Captain ordered the cover placed on the depth gauges I looked up and saw the digits rolling. We were already below 800 feet, and still going. I watched the "8" roll over to "9" as the cover got put in place. This was not looking good, at all!

Well, after a few more tense moments the submarine slowed, and the bow finally started to rise. Phew! You could feel the tension in the boat lighten immediately. Not completely, mind you, but I think everyone knew we were no longer heading to the bottom. Then, some of that tension returned. It kept rising until we hit about a 45 degree up angle. Whatever loose gear that had been propelled forward and not picked up during the dive, now went aft along with some new items. A chaotic mess to clean up, for sure. But, at the time, all that really mattered was that we were on our way to the surface.

Yeah, I'm thinking, "*Whoohoo! Hallelujah! #@?#!^&-"A"-Ditty-Bag!*"

After the submarine settled "on the roof" Peer unscrewed the cap bolts, removed the upper half of the control valve, repositioned the slide piston, and reassembled it. The system returned to NORMAL and away we go.

Okay, so what the heck caused the incident in the first place? Well, remember those Midshipmen, on board for their qualification cruise? They had to do something while we were underway, nobody rides for free except Admirals, eh? You don't want to let them loose in the Reactor Compartment, or Engine Room. You just want to give them a simple job where someone "salty" can keep a close eye on them. No problem, they were assigned to watches usually reserved for the new Seaman and Fireman strikers, Planes and Helm Stations. Piece of cake! The college boys can steer and move a yoke back and forth, right? Take directions, and watch a few gauges and angle indicators, right? Not too difficult, right? Besides, the Diving Officer is directly behind them, within reach if anyone needs a little wake-up slap on the back of their head. Pay attention and do as you're told, exactly as you're told, and you'll probably avoid an embarrassing headache.

For those who are not aware, here's a little information about the designed layout of the hydraulic system that controls the planes and rudder. Pipes are installed along both the port and starboard sides of the sub. If the submarine sustains damage on one side, the path of the hydraulic fluid can be shifted to the pipes running along the opposite side of the boat. Redundancy is rampant in a submarine. There are three modes of operating the planes and rudder; Normal, Emergency, and Hand. Yes, there's actually a hand-crank situated in the rear of the backrest of the bow planes, stern planes, and rudder's station chairs that operates a small hydraulic pump. To change modes, the Helmsman or Planesman would simply grab the control valve's operating lever take it out of the slot labeled NORMAL, move it to the next slot, VENT to momentarily relieve the thousands of pounds of hydraulic fluid pressure in the valve, then out of VENT and into the EMERGENCY slot. Cycle the yoke in and out, or the helm right and left to ensure the planes or rudder respond accordingly. Not too difficult to understand or accomplish.

Time for a little on-the-job training (OJT) for the Midshipmen. No books, just listen and watch as the Diving Officer explains and simulates the procedure. Well, when it came time to actually shift modes, things didn't go smoothly for the Midshipman setting in the stern plane's chair. Just as he slid the actuating lever into EMERGENCY, he didn't think he paused long enough in the VENT position, so he quickly shifted the lever back to VENT and then slid it into EMERGENCY again. OOPS! He should have just left it in EMERGENCY. The slide piston inside the control valve got "hydraulically locked" in VENT. The rudder and stern planes are hollow steel, teardrop shaped wings. The hollow voids are filled with synthetic concrete to prevent collapsing under the pressures of the sea when the submarine is submerged. They are large and they are heavy. With no hydraulic fluid to hold or control them they "dropped to their stops." Full dive, full bell, and lousy brakes.

For the next couple of days, hardly a word was spoken unless it had something to do with the operation of the submarine. There was no joking around or the usual quick-witted banter. On the third day after the casualty everything went back to normal.

My thanks to Tommy Robinson for putting me in touch with John "Mack" McPhilmy. When I telephoned him we BS'd like it was yesterday. I reminded him how we were glad he didn't bother waiting for the order to put some air into that forward group of ballast tanks. He saved our butts. He told me, *"I was getting my ass on the surface and anyone else who wanted to go with me was welcome!"* Ha, Ha, Ha, Same ol' Mack

Thanks, again, Mack! It's good to be alive to tell the tale.

Donald "Don" Heesen, '75 - '76

1976 – Stern Plane Jam Casualty

Don Heesen's story of the casualty needs just a couple of clarifications. I am qualified to provide these because I was the Officer of the Deck during the casualty.

Angles: A little bit more than he remembers. We hit 47 degrees on the down angle and on the return to the surface we exceeded the range of the inclinometer but measured about 60 degrees using the line left by the coffee in the pots after we got to the surface.

The casualty was not caused by operator error but was caused by a stripped rubber dental coupling in the stern plane feedback servo. When it stripped the system got a full rise error signal which caused the planes to go to full dive.

I did use emergency blow of the forward group. I remember well the Diving Officer questioning did I want *"Emergency Blow?"* which earned him a very sharp unprofessional response but he got the picture and hit the switch. We did not cover the depth gauges. Who had time to do that? The reason for the sharp up angle was once the Stern Planesman got into emergency mode and got the planes back to full rise, he put his feet on the control panel and refused to let go until we surfaced. He was a Seaman by the way, not a Midshipman. Speaking of which I did talk to all three Midshipman after the event and all three assured me they were NOT going to volunteer for submarine duty when commissioned.

However, Heesen's general picture of an exciting few seconds is very accurate.

William "Bill" Riffer, '74 – '77

1976 - Drills vs. Casualties

I have a bit of a different take on this story which conforms to the one our brand new Commanding Officer at the time, Dick Riddell, told in a speech a few years back, and I will defer to him to provide the text. Briefly, he had ask me to set up a stern planes jam drill for that time frame. After we recovered from the afore mentioned event, he called me into his Stateroom and asked in saltier terms than I will use here, why in heaven's name I was conducting a drill without his permission to start. I explained to him this was not the yet to be scheduled drill, but was in fact a well handled casualty, and that sometimes we ran drills on *Nautilus*, and sometimes *Nautilus* ran drills on us!

William "Bill" Rohm, '74 – '76

1978 – The Baptism

Reprinted with permission of The Day, New London, Connecticut.

Jennifer Papineau was five weeks old when she became the first and only baby to be baptized on *Nautilus*. Her father Lieutenant Commander Paul Papineau was the last Engineer. The ship's brass bell was removed from the sail and the hole on top sealed with heavy grease. The bell was flipped over and holy water added to the "christening font." Jennifer was bundled in blankets to protect her from the snow, held over the bell and baptized on December 3, 1978. Her full name and the date were engraved on the bell.

Jennifer Grogan, The Day

1977 - Sailing Boat Story

For those of you have listened to many of my stories over the years I was thinking about this one that probably most of you have not heard, even Lisa my wife.

While I was in the Navy on USS *Nautilus* about 1977 we made what we called a Med Run or voyage to the Mediterranean for Naval operations. We traveled to the island of Isola Maddalena off the coast of Sardegna and our ship docked against a submarine tender. Sardegna is a slower paced traditional Italian lifestyle island off the western coast of Italy. For recreation the sailors went on an LCM-6 Mike Boat (see ref 1) to an island nearby called Isola Caprera that had a Club Med and the sailors were given a free day at the resort where we could feast and use the facilities at will.

So I took my first-ever sailing boat lesson on a Flying Junior (called an FJ) at the Club from a French speaking instructor. I figured that even though I don't know French I could figure out what he was saying, I mean how hard could it be. This is a small one mast, two sail, fiberglass

Steely Eyed Killers of the Deep

sailboat about 13 feet long that has Styrofoam packed into the sides so that it can't sink. If you have ever been in Boston in the summer you can see them out on the bay with their white sails skittering all over with novices trying to get their sea legs. After checking out a boat I teamed up with a fellow sailor that knew something more than I did about sailing and shoved off from the dock at Caprera on a beautiful sunny day over crystal clear Mediterranean water intending to stay close to the beach and make a few loops around to see the sunbathers then dock up long before sunset. However the midday wind was not in our favor and was blowing west taking us from the west side of the island toward Maddalena about 5 miles away.

Tacking (see ref 2), a special sailing skill that helps you move in a direction other than just where the wind wants to push you, was going to be part of my 2nd lesson in French the next day, I think it was the next day since he told me in French. I don't know how much time you have spent on the water but most people will say that one mile doesn't look like much distance but it is a long way and five miles seems like more than five times that distance, believe me.

Gilligan's Island theme song

Just sit right back and you'll hear a tale,
a tale of a fateful trip
that started from this tropic port
aboard this tiny ship.

The mate was a mighty sailing man,
the Skipper brave and sure.
Five passengers set sail that day
for a three hour tour, a three hour tour.

Suddenly, the boat tipped over and off we went into the drink and I'm not sure we even had life jackets or anything more than our smiles. We took our shoes off and tied the laces together and put them around our neck's and then with the boat lying sideways in the water we grabbed the gunwale and hoisted the boat upright and each got on a side to steady her raising the mainsail again while the water washed across the boat. At a distance everything looks fine. The mast is up you can see two heads in the boat, the sail was billowing and the boat was moving, the only problem was the gunwales were at the waterline and we were the only two that knew it.

Since we were highly trained submarine sailors we were not prepared to be underway on wind power being blown out to see during this all-expenses-paid outing and without a radio or signal flare or any other device to call for help. We were afraid that we were going to sail into the sunset and have to grab flying fish for food and wrap messages around the feet of seagulls in hopes they would perch on the window sill of a great writer who would then pen a book about our story (see ref 3) that would live on long after our remains had settled at the bottom of Davy Jones Locker.

Fortunately without oar or rudder the westward wind pushed us toward the rock pounded surf of the desolate arid shores of Isola Maddalena. Did I say fortunately? Perhaps if we survived the impending ship wreck we could meet some beautiful native girls like Mister Christian did in "Mutiny on the Bounty" and have Disney World build us a big tree house like that of the "Swiss Family Robinson" and be rulers of a new civilization. Unfortunately as we were approaching the island we could see through the crystal clear water patches of beautiful white sand against darkened areas that had things in it like sea urchins. These are cute little small globular animals, which are close kin to sand dollars, that constitute the class Echinoidea. They have small spines on them that break off in your feet when you step on them unless you have shoes on that currently were not able to be transferred from our necks back to our feet.

"The Charge of the Light Brigade"

Half a league, half a league,
half a league onward,
all in the valley of Death
rode the six hundred.
'Forward, the Light Brigade!
Charge for the guns!' he said:
Into the valley of Death
rode the six hundred.

So imagine our elation and fear all at once as the fates tossed us like a fish that flops from side to side when it's thrown on the beach. Nevertheless, there was no turning back or alternatives and so from time to time one could hear across the water, shouts of pain (see ref 4) as a foot impaled itself on an urchin as we tried to leapfrog from one white patch to the next as our less than sturdy vessel silently made its way toward the pounding surf, looking very much like a submarine with it's periscope up and it's tubes flooded, preparing to launch its "fish" against the islands bulwarks.

We hit the beach running, or at least hopping, avoiding the lime rock and trash and bottles that had washed up from the prevailing winds from Italy. We made land looking like Tom Hanks in "Castaway," get the picture? While lying on the beach picking the spines out of our feet, watching the sun beginning to head over the island, we looked around for any convenient native girls and hoped someone at the dock would miss us and come looking, but not TOO quickly. Before long a powerboat from the dock approached and we were told that we looked like we were doing fine and so no one was concerned until we seemed to disappear then he headed out. I guess our clever trick to manage the boat could have also been our undoing.

After a quick glance up and down the beach we departed, sans the native girls, and headed back to Club Med with an unbeatable sea story to share with our shipmates over beers and burgers.

Since then, few things as adventuresome as that have happened to me. I suppose it's because I haven't been in places like that and also because I'm more cautious as I get older and avoid or at least prepare for hazards better. But for me the best things in life are the heart pounding sweating near misses since they make for great stories and make others wonder just how much of its real.

References:
1. Vietnam era landing craft with the gate that drops in the front so the troops could run up the beach, that's what we had to get around.
2. Tacking, you know what tacking is, I don't need to explain it, it's embarrassing, I should have had the 2nd lesson even if it was in French or Swahili.
3. See you have to do something stupid and then die doing it in order to be famous. I was hoping to do something great and ride in a ticker tape parade in New York City but it never happened.
4. Sound waves travel differently depending on the temperature of the surface of the ground over which they are passing and this is called refraction. With cooler temperatures sound can travel great distances over water by something called a temperature inver-

sion. A temperature inversion is when the temperature is coolest right next to the ground and warmer as you increase in height above the ground. Since the temperature increases with height, the speed of sound also increases with height. This means that for a sound wave travelling close to the ground, the part of the wave closest to the ground is traveling the slowest, and the part of the wave farthest above the ground is traveling the fastest. As a result, the wave changes direction and bends downwards. Temperature inversions most often happen at night after the sun goes down when the ground (or water in a lake) cools off quickly, while the air above the ground remains warm. This downward refraction of sound is why you can hear the conversations of campers across the lake, when otherwise you whould not be able to hear them. Remember they can probably hear you too!

Richard Molinski, '77 – '80

1979 – Song Time

La, La, La, La, Doobie, Dah, Dah, Dah!

Ode to Reactor Principles. Sung to the tune of *"Everything you wanted, but didn't get for Christmas, is now on sale at Sears!"*

All this stuff about the curries, leaves me with the blurries,

'bout every thing that Fermi ever tried.

Playing with the protons and hiding from the photons,

it's no wonder that the curries finally died!

Well, they heated up some radium, in the basement of a stadium

and waited for the steam whistle to blow.

While they watched the neutrons shoot, they heard the whistle, "toot, toot, toot!" Had visions of rolling in the dough!

Hymie said, *"That's the best I've seen, I'll use it in a submarine!"*

And off he went to Congress with a vision.

"Now you all know the Navy, is the Nation's bread and gravy,

and I just want a little bit of fission!"

Steely Eyed Killers of the Deep

Well, Congress, they all disagreed, about the things the Navy needs,

till Hymie took off his shoe and beat the table!

"Put your shoe back on, you little rat (and you know they all agreed on that!)
"I wonder if your foot might be unstable!"

Well Hymie finally got his way, and we all got our start that day,

they built a submarine, the *Nautilus*.

Sailed around, without refueling, saying *"Hey, these guys need some schooling, and that day was the start of all of this!"*

Now with your boat and all your buddies, you sit here with your studies.

How did they talk you into sighing on?

Yes, now you sit and wonder, why didn't Fermi blunder?

I wouldn't have to read this stupid song!

Excerpt from page 171 of the "Turnover Book"

Richard Molinski, '76 - '80

1979 – Dear Mom

I'm just sitting here in the pit with nothing to do but gaze out over the beauty of the main seawater bay bilge. Yeah, it is beautiful. Kinda makes me think of the old two seater back home out in the backyard! Oh Yeah, there are other things to do on watch here. Yesterday I spent my time counting the Auxiliary Electrician's freckles.

But it's not to say that I'm not having fun here. There's so much to see on a submarine. Why only this morning I took a tour through the laundry room. It was truly amazing!

Well, I was met with a rather large disappointment here; contrary to what I told you, there are no doughnuts in the Engine Room!

Your unsung only low hung son, Chuck (?)

Excerpt from page 172 of the "Turnover Book"

Richard Molinski, '76 – '80

Tommy Robinson

1980 – Overcoming Adversity

I reported to *Nautilus* in January 1979 in New London and immediately went to work straightening out service records and doing other administrative functions. I also noticed the crew members. What great group of people. Probably the most important event for me was when the Chief Petty Officers on *Nautilus* selected me to receive the last Bronze Plaque as Sailor of the Year for my work on *Nautilus*. It was just so exciting for me that I was speechless.

Shortly after being assigned to *Nautilus* I went legally blind in my left eye. Doctors said I would lose the other eye later. In May 1980, after decommissioning *Nautilus*, I was assigned to the Pentagon for duty. While there I used the Bethesda Naval Hospital. Navy Doctors used laser treatment to save my right eye until I got just over twenty years of Active Duty. I was then forced into retirement and went legally blind in the right eye too.

I am very pleased that I got the assignment to *Nautilus*. I had a very enjoyable tour of duty and met some really great people. Now that I am retired there is nothing better than the camaraderie that can be enjoyed by every ex-serviceman.

Robert Tyndall, '79 – '80

10 – Flotsam & Jetsam Miscellaneous Submarine Stuff

Snorkeling the North Atlantic

Snorkelling for extended periods in the North Atlantic and Straits of Denmark, between Iceland and Greenland, in the winter (and it's always winter up there, even in summer) is like those grim pictures of the Dark Middle Ages, where people are getting stuck with spears, burned with flames, and eaten by demons. When the snorkel head valve shuts, fog comes up from the Torpedo Room bilges, all the tin cans go "crinkle, crinkle," and when the head valve opens, the fog crawls back into the bilges and the cans again go "crinkle, crinkle."

If you are on the surface and standing Lookout (I don't know why there are Lookouts. You can't the bow of the boat through the fog) the radar is off and all you have is the ECM and sonar. You go on watch, up to the Bridge, and quickly "lock" yourself in, before a big wet green one comes over Bridge and soaks you for the next four hours. When you get off watch you go back to the Engine Room, pull off all your wet stuff and put it on top of the engines. Then you peel a dry set off the engines, knock off some of the salt and put them on, go get some chow, go find a bunk and it seems in a few minutes you start the whole cycle over again.

When you are in the Crews Mess, you put a slice of bread under the plate so it will stay within reach when the boat takes huge rolls. We had four batteries instead of the usual two, so the Crews Mess was smaller and you didn't have so far to reach. The reefers took up part of what would have been the full size mess. Sonar was in the Torpedo Room and one of the batteries was in the Pump Room. Potatoes were in one shower and fruit in the other. Potatoes were also stored up in the After Battery deck hatch when we put the depth charge doubler (lower) hatch up. It weighed about six million pounds. Food cans and bricks were the walking surface. I'm sure one of our missions was to pave the ocean bottom with bricks. I expect that Russian divers, if they have any, can have good footing and not stir up mud when hooking cables to a wrecked boat. This would have been a secondary objective as the primary reason was to build up a pathway with the bricks so the Germans would have an alternate route to Moscow with the next armored thrust.

Laundry? Wasn't any! You put your dirty stuff in a bunk bag and then, at various times, did comparative screening of your skivvies in order to reclaim the cleanest of the dirty. The only reason we never got a plague started was because it was too damn cold for the germs. When we did make it back to New London and got on the train to New York City, most of the people kept a good distance from us. I don't know why. It didn't seem to bother the people in Scotland. The locker club at the YMCA, smelled just like Hogan's Alley. These new "Nintendo" sailors don't know what they missed.

George Clancy, '58 – '63

It's great that you are able to recall these sub-human adventures! Since I glow in the dark only from serving in *Nautilus* I can only imagine the outright discomfort that you look back on so graphically. I guess if the subject moves you, then you can paint pictures with words. I can see the flour in the air, on the fish, everywhere with a scattering of coffee and corn mixed in, hear the coffee pot wheez'n and farting, and guys pulling on their earlobes. From our vantage point TODAY this is straight out of the Three Stooges. No wonder Morgan said, *"In a pigs ass"* on a turnaround in the North Atlantic.

John "JC" Yuill, '57 – '60

I think that was the trip when Phillips held the fuel racks in, so the engines wouldn't keep shutting down while snorkelling in heavy weather. We kept getting high vacuum shut downs when the head valve went under. I guess the Engine Rooms got tired of shutting down and restarting every four minutes. We dunked the head valve once again and either Brown or Phillips held the fuel racks in. The diesels don't much care if it's outside air or inside air that they are eating. A Fairbanks-Morse eats a shit load of air, and with two running, even more. I think they shut down by reason of no more air. A lot of cans of flour and all that shit we stuffed outboard of the torpedoes ruptured. Anything cooking in the galley, flashed to mush and resembled pea soup. The coffee urn did some spectacular eruptions. Any stuffed sinuses at once released their burden of snot. Morgan was inaudible, no doubt as a result of the rarefied air in the ship. I noticed that the exploding cans of food was getting harder to hear but that may been in part due to people screaming and writhing in pain due to ear drum sensations. I don't think they did that a second time. Anyone that slept through it when we equalized had an ear stuck to the flash cover like a shit bowl plunger stuck on a smooth flat surface.

George Clancy, '58 – '63

Submarine Homecomings – Then & Now

Tommy comments, *"Now days when a submarine arrives dockside from patrol and tosses lines over to the pier the sail is usually decorated with a big Hawaiian style lei. The boat is greeted by a military band playing rousing music, with all local brass present, and of course, families on the pier. There are mom's and children holding signs 'Welcome Home Dad,' girlfriends waiting to hug their sailors, an occasional guy waiting to kiss his husband and/or a girl anxious to embrace her wife".*

Gary says, *"It brings tears to my eyes."*

George questions, *"No single Johns? No Main Induction Mary, Moonbeam, Anna Banana, Hungry Helen, Three Way Eula or Harry's wife coming for his laundry?*

Barry wraps up our brief conversation, *"Back in the Squadron Ten days pulling into State Pier was quite different. The wives and kids were waiting inside the gate while the Bank Street 'movie stars' and other 'well known' locals were waiting just outside the gate. Sometimes it could become a rather tense situation when the wife and movie star were 'welcoming home' the same steely eyed killer of the deep.'"*

Tommy "Robby" Robinson, '63 – '67

George Clancy, '58—'63

Gary Brown, '59 – '62

Barry "Dan" Danforth, '60 – '61

Blow and Go

Blow and Go! That's what the submarine escape technique was described as, and it was in use during my submarine training in the 1950s. A description follows a little later.

But first, a little background and history of submarine escape equipment and use. This is by no means an attempt to be a seminal treatise, but rather a general overview of the subject.

When the idea of men in submersibles was first conceived, not much thought was given to their escape in an emergency sinking. Most of the primitive energy was given to putting a man or men inside a submersible ship to carry out some usually covert act. As a sad consequence many brave souls perished in any number of these contraptions.

The primary first design that was later used for submarine escape was originally intended to save miners trapped in accidents. It was later used to as a good way to swim under water undetected as there are no bubbles exhaled. Finally, it was conceived as a submarine escape device.

The device was a re-breather in which the wearer exhaled into a bag filled with something like soda lime which absorbed or "scrubbed" the Carbon Dioxide (CO_2) from his breath. Oxygen (O_2) from a small compressed bottle was then bled into the air leaving the bag and into the wearer's lungs. This lasted as long as the O_2 was available. It was a simple and ingenious invention. But simple as it was, it held many drawbacks as a submarine escape device. The first problem, with the primitive design, was the limited depth at which the re-breather was useful, only one atmosphere or 33 feet. Below that depth the wearer suffered from O_2 poisoning.

In 1853, Professor T. Schwann designed such a device in Belgium and 1878 saw the design of another such re-breather by Henry Fleuss, also for use by miners.

By 1900, the British Davis Escape Set (DES) was first produced in quantity. In the years between 1903 and 1907, Professor Jaubert invented Oxylithe, a form of sodium peroxide as the scrubbing agent in the device.

In 1909, British Royal Navy Captain S.S. Hall and Dr. O. Rees improved the design. It was accepted by the Royal Navy for shallow water diving but not for submarine escape until a later date.

During the 1920s, Charles "Swede" Momsen of the U.S. Navy developed his version of an escape device known as the Momsen Lung which became part of the U.S. Navy's primary submarine escape tools. He was also instrumental in the concept and design of a submarine rescue chamber. Because of political wrangling and interference by superior officers, the project was handed off to Momsen's associate named McCann. The chamber eventually ended up being named the McCann Rescue Chamber.

With this device, the disabled submarine would release an emergency buoy from the submarine's deck and it would float to the surface, streaming a messenger cable which was then attached to a bale on the sub's hatch. The rescue chamber would winch itself down to the submarine's deck and over the submarine's hatch using the messenger cable. It would then seal itself to the deck of the submarine and open the deck hatch where as many as six men could then leave the boat, enter the chamber and be hauled back to the surface. This operation would be repeated as many times as necessary in order to rescue the submarine's crew.

The McCann Rescue Chamber was carried for many years on the deck's of submarine rescue vessels (ASR). The Deep Sea Rescue Vessel (DSRV), a self contained rescue submarine capable of operating in extreme depths, replaced the Chamber during the Cold War period. The McCann Rescue Chamber has since been retired. It was used only once in the daring and suspenseful rescue of 33 men from the sunken submarine, USS *Squalus* (SS-192) after she sank on May 23, 1939 off Portsmouth, New Hampshire. The *Squalus* story is best chronicled in the book, "The Terrible Hours" by Peter Maas.

Over the years from 1916 to 1927 there were a number of submarines sunk, from which only a handful of men made successful escapes; submarine HMSS E-41 sunk in 30 feet of water. Stoker Petty Officer Brown became the first person in the Royal Navy to escape a sunken submarine with no device. He was the only survivor. This incident was followed by the loss of HMSS K-13 in 38 feet of water. Twenty-nine sailors died in the after compartment. Two officers attempted escape from the conning tower. One died, the other survived.

In 1927, USS *S-4* (SS-109) was lost with all 38 hands but the boat was later raised, reconditioned and re-commissioned. As such it participated in a number of controlled submarine escape experiments, some to a depth of 206 feet, using the improved Momsen Lung. These tests, though successful, were felt questionable. True success was thought to be elusive for a real world escape from a sunken submarine in cold, dark water, despite escape training. However, it was the only game in town.

In 1929, the British designed the Davis Submarine Escape Apparatus (DSEA), also a type of re-breather, which was judged to be superior to other contraptions and was adapted by the Royal Navy. DSEAs were placed on all Royal Navy submarines by end of 1929; one for every crew member. However, the British lost HMSS *Poseidon* on June 9, 1931 in 120 feet of water and only eight men successfully escaped. The crew was divided among compartments and not all devices were available to the number of men present so the ratio was upped to 130% of crew on board. This tragedy was followed by the loss on January 3, 1939 of HMSS *Thetis* and only four men successfully escaped. In 1941, HMSS

Umpire sunk and twenty one men escaped. Six subsequently drowned in the turbulent and freezing seas.

During WW-II, one of the most famously decorated U.S. submarines, USS *Tang* (SS-306), skippered by the subsequent Medal of Honor recipient, Richard "Dick" O'Kane, was lost in a freak night surface battle with Japanese forces on October 24, 1944. Her very last "fish" made a circular surface run and struck her on the port side abreast the After Torpedo Room. Those on the Bridge were blown free and *Tang* quickly settled by the stern into the 50 plus feet of sea the Formosa Strait. Those men in the Forward Engine Room, secured by a watertight doors from the last three flooded compartments in the stern of the boat, moved forward to the After Battery and then to the Control Room. It was also flooding through a sprung bridge hatch after a night of heavy depth charging by the Japanese. The men then moved into the Forward Torpedo Room where they prepared to make their escape through the escape trunk. About thirty men made it to this escape position. Of the thirteen men who escaped, five were able to hang on to the previously released Emergency Buoy. Three others reached the surface but were unable to breathe and/or drowned and drifted off. The other five men were never seen again after leaving the escape trunk.

Of the officers and men who were on the Bridge, only three were able to swim throughout the night. They were picked up the next day with the few other survivors by a Japanese Destroyer escort. They were cruelly and brutally beaten and subsequently imprisoned in one of Japan's worst prisoner of war (POW) camps, the infamous Ofuna Camp. All nine men survived the war in this camp and were the only Americans to have ever escaped on their own from a sunken submarine and lived. All but those on the Bridge used the Momsen Lung.

In the 1960s, a new device named the Steinke Hood after its inventor, Lieutenant Harris Steinke, entered the U.S. Navy as the primary escape device. It was essentially, an inflatable life Jacket with a hood that completely en-closed the wearer's head trapping a bubble of breathing air and it was adopted by the U.S. Navy for submarine escape. This device was standard throughout the Cold War period.

Meanwhile, in Great Britain, 64 crewmen and 18 contractors in HMSS *Truculent* sank in 50 feet of water after a surface collision on January 12, 1950. Only ten men were recovered after many had attempted the escape using a re-breather device. The Royal Navy quickly returned to the prior development of a total insulated exposure escape suit designed by Captain Phillip Ruck-Keen. His result came to be designated as the Submarine Escape Immersion Equipment (SEIE), culminating in the present MK-10. This is a whole body suit and one-man life raft combined that allows an escaped submariner protection against hypothermia and has been tested from a submarine to the depth of 600 feet at a safe rising rate of approximately 6 to 10 feet a second. This new system has now replaced the Steinke Hood as a means of escaping from a sunken submarine by the U.S. Navy.

The Steinke Hoods adoption into the U.S. Navy was viewed more as a psychological tool keeping in mind the extreme depth of waters in which modern submarines operated. However, the SEIE does allow the submariner much more in the way of a feasible means of escape down to at least 600 feet.

Now, as promised, a brief description of what I had to do while in submarine school back in 1957. The simulated submarine escape using the "Free Assent Method" or "Blow and Go" as it was affectionately called.

The escape tower at the U.S. Submarine Base in Groton, Connecticut, was torn down after a fire in the 1960s. It stood 100 feet high, a vertical tank of water about 10 or 12 ft. in diameter, with three locks or escape chambers at different levels. The shallowest chamber was at 18 feet from the surface, the second at a depth of 50 feet, and the bottom chamber was 100feet deep. The chamber resembled a Torpedo Room escape trunk. The 18 and 50 foot levels were reached by means of an elevator which ran near the side of the tank.

After a pressure test in an air chamber to see if the prospective submariner was psychologically suitable for such service, we students were taken to the 18 foot level where we entered the chamber with an instructor. There were two hatches, one to enter the chamber from the outside and the other leading into the tank of water. The instructor flooded the chamber about chin high and the water was over the top of the tank hatch, all while adding compressed air to equalize the pressure inside and outside of the chamber. Once that was done the instructor could safely open the tank door.

We were fitted with the standard life jacket and one at a time were told to take a deep breath and duck through the hatch into the tank, assume the position of arched back, hands by your side, where another instructor (he had air available to him) would hold you, checking your posture, then signal you to start exhaling as hard as you could. Once he was satisfied that you were 'blowing' for all you were worth, he'd release you to start your rapid assent to the surface where we popped out of the water like a breaching whale.

There were other instructors in the tank on your way up to insure, during your assent, that you kept forcibly exhaling. Should one not do so, he was grabbed by the instructor and pulled back down to the escape chamber to prevent air embolism. Fortunately I had no problem with all of this as I had "eaten, drank, and slept" skin diving since an early age and had studied the physics of compressed air diving and their consequences.

A short lesson might be in order here in to explain this, seemingly unnatural phenomenon. When one breathes in compressed air at whatever depth he may be at, lets say 100 feet, the air in his lungs has the capacity of about three times what he would have on the surface because it is compressed. As the person ascends, the water pressure decreases and the air in the person's lungs expands. If the person didn't exhale forcibly, the expanding air would rupture the lungs, quickly resulting in death. That's why it is impossible to run out of air. The trick is to exhale the expanding air quicker than the water pressure decreases, hence the nick name, 'Blow and Go."

After completing the 18 foot escape, we were taken to the 50 foot level and the exercise was repeated. I didn't make the assent from 100 feet as that was optional and I thought two assents were good enough for one day.

I hope anyone who reads this will gain some insight into what all potential U.S. submariners had to deal with to become a submariner, eventually completing training on a submarine allowing one to thereafter wear the treasured dolphin pin signifying, "Qualified in Submarines." I've now been qualified in submarines for over 50 years and it is one of my proudest achievements. It has also entitled me to membership in the Holland Club which signifies that event.

John "JC" Yuill, '57 – '60

The Air Expulsion Head

HEAD – Toilet compartment aboard a vessel; originally a small lower deck forward with the most privacy, well defined on vessels such as *Santa Maria, Mayflower*, etc.

This definition is as described in "Royce's Sailing Illustrated" and the U.S. Navy's "Bluejacket's Manual."

We all have a need for devices such as these, be it fancy or plain. When we were tiny tots, we all either went "pee-pee, wee-wee, piddle, or poop." Now that we are sophisticated adults and we take a "piss, whiz, leak, dump, or crap." Some go "see a man about a dog" - a phrase who's meaning has forever eluded me. If one is properly polite and politically correct, one has a bowel movement (BM). In this electronically enlightened age we say we are going to "download" our most recent meal. Of course, the most proper and respectable elite among us probably "relieve themselves in the facility."

As youngsters in school, when nature called, we were required to raise our hands and extend either one or two fingers to indicate the task at hand. Why the world a teacher would want this information is way beyond me, but the technique usually worked to get out of class at least once a period.

The venue for all this activity is likewise fondly known by a myriad of names. We go to the "John" to the detriment, or amusement, of all so named. We also go to the "rest-room" where I strongly doubt there is very much restorative rest to be had. We have the lavatory, (Latin – Lavare, to wash), and the toilet, (French – toile, a room with a bowl-shaped fixture for defecation or urination). This term is not to be confused with another French word, toilette, which is the process of grooming oneself. Unfortunately, some of us visit the toilet without using the lavatory. Often, we are said to be "on the throne" in none other than "the throne-room." Of course, some also disappear for hours in the "library" while those in Great Britain go to the "loo." There are endless names for these facilities, but you get the point. As Shakespeare once said, "A rose by any other name ..."

While at Submarine School, part of the training involved learning the operation of the boat's sanitary system. The "school boat" I studied was the USS *Becuna* (SS-319). She was a class: *Balao*, variant: *Perch*, laid down April 29, 1943, launched January 30, 1944, and commissioned May 27, 1944. She made five war patrols during WW-II and is credited with sinking four ships with a total tonnage of 18,600 tons, a respectable war record. By the time I studied her, she had undergone many modifications, being thereafter designated as a 'Guppy 1A', but much of her interior layout remained as she was built, including the heads.

Tommy Robinson

Upon graduation from Submarine School on March 27, 1957, class 141, I was assigned to the USS *Nautilus* (SSN-571), the world's first nuclear vessel. Most of what I'd learned in Submarine School suddenly went out #1 torpedo tube. Permit me to jump ahead for a moment to describe, for comparisons sake, the sanitary systems aboard *Nautilus*.

They basically worked like this: The bowl is made of stainless steel with a large, rotating plug valve in the bottom. Think of a solid cylinder with a long slot cut through the side. When the slot is open to the bowl by rotating the cylinder, the waste flows through it to a sanitary tank below. Rotating the lever the other way closes the valve. This valve was known as the "flapper valve." A small amount of water, through another system, is used to put a water seal on the plug before and after use. Below the flapper valve is a large gate, or stop valve which seals off the bowl from the sanitary tank. To empty a sanitary tank, done only by qualified watch standers, one would shut the flapper valve, stop valve, and check the inboard vent on the sanitary tank, shut. Now the tanks were ready to be emptied by air, or blown dry.

Blowing sanitary tanks is usually done once a day and at a fairly shallow depth to minimize the amount of compressed air needed to overcome sea pressure outside the boat and to minimize the venting time after emptying is completed. Once all systems are correctly lined up the order *"Blow Sanitary Tanks"* is given from the Control Room. After the tanks are emptied they are full of compressed air and must be vented. This is the not so great part since, being at sea and submerged, the foul air in the tank must be vented inside the boat. It's sort of like being locked inside a wooden, "three-holer" out-house after depositing a week's worth of corn-beef and cabbage. The venting is done through large activated charcoal filters to minimize the smell. Of course, no filter on this earth could be efficient enough to eliminate the entire stench that wafts throughout the boat until the ventilation system can absorb it. Pretty simple, huh?

Now we will examine the Air Expulsion Head. On the "Fleet type" submarines that served so magnificently during WW-II, the primary way to flush the heads was to apply air pressure directly to each "unit" after use, blowing the waste from a small receiver tank overboard. This, on the face of it, may not seem so difficult, but to actually perform this complicated task, one practically had to have a Ph.D. in Engineering and Physics, plus a through knowledge of the sub's "plumbing" system. Any variance from the procedure, or the slightest lapse in total concentration could result in a face full of whatever one just put into the bowl.

Steely Eyed Killers of the Deep

The other consequence was that one could flood the boat through the toilet. I don't know which would have been worse.

The accompanying instructions of one such head could never begin to illustrate just how complex, mind-blowing and inherently evil this device was. The following instructions were copied from the after head in the USS *Guardfish* (SS-217), a *Gato* class fleet boat, and should enlighten you if not make you forever grateful for the toilet in your home:

Before "Deposit."
1. See that bowl flapper valve "A" is shut, that gate valve "C" in the discharge line is open, and that valve "D" in the water supply line is open.
2. Open valve "E" next to the bowl to admit necessary water to bowl. Close valves "D' and "E."

After "Deposit."
1. Pull lever "A." Release lever "A."
2. Open valve "G" in the air supply line.
3. "Rock" valve "F" lever outboard to charge measuring tank to 10 PSI above sea pressure.
4. Open valve "B" and "rock" air valve "F" inboard to blow waste overboard. Close valves "B" "C" and "G." An alternative to "blowing" waste overboard with compressed air was to "pump" it overboard. The instructions were the same except that instead of opening the air valve, there was a pump handle nearby which required arms like Pop-Eye the Sailor Man to operate.

So it probably was the most diabolical submarine devise ever conceived, likely, by Satan himself, designed to flush human waste into the big "green locker." I was forever thankful that *Nautilus* didn't have one of those constipation-inducing, waste disposal contraptions as part of her design. Now, if you'll pardon me, I have to go use the head.

John "JC" Yuill, '57 – '60

The North Pole – Fifty Years Later

"I may never do anything else in my life that anybody outside my own family cares about. But I have done one thing that gives me a place in history."

Tommy Robinson

I was reading a book about the 1928-1930 Byrd expedition to Antarctica when suddenly, these words quoted by an unknown member of that expedition, jumped off the page at me. I stared in wonder as they seemed to levitate off the page. It was if someone had plucked those very sentiments from my brain. I was transfixed. I read and re-read the sentence over and over again, wondering how anyone could have experienced those exact same emotions as I.

The book, "With Byrd at the Bottom of the World," written by Norman D. Vaughan with Cecil B. Murphey, recounts the adventures of the very young Vaughan who, by skills acquired in training sled dogs in New Hampshire, obtained a position on that expedition, where Byrd would become the first person to fly to the South Pole. It turned out that Vaughan was a key player in the success of that long and perilous expedition, although at the time, he felt that he was just part of the team doing anything he could and feeling privileged just to be along on such an adventure.

His duties were to train the almost 100 sled dogs and plan and coordinate all the logistics involved in use of the dogs. The plan was threefold. The first part was to transport by dog sled from the two supply ships, six hundred and fifty tons of supplies and building materials, including three airplanes, needed to construct Little America, the ice base from which the expedition would begin.

The second part was to strike out from Little America and lay a cache of supplies along a southern route to the Queen Maud Mountains, about halfway to the South Pole. Once there, he was to be part of a geological party to explore east and west for evidence of historical and geological importance.

The third part of the plan was to be a sort of life guard station to rescue Byrd should his plane be forced down at or near the pole. That Byrd expedition would later turn out to be the end of the era of primitive exploration with the use of expendable dogs. The final chapter in that form of Arctic and Antarctic exploratory history would be forever closed. Newer forms of exploration and new technology would soon follow and, as fate would have it, I was to be a part of it.

Vaughan, waited some sixty some-odd years to write his account noting that, *"Being twenty-five and not as mature as some of the others, I didn't appreciate at the time the lasting personal significance of membership in the Byrd expedition. I had not begun to understand that in the years ahead, no matter what else I did; I would point back to the months in the Antarctic as my finest."*

Steely Eyed Killers of the Deep

These are my very same personal reflections of when, at age 20, on August 3, 1958, I was part of USS *Nautilus'* transit under the North Pole; another first in history.

As I now look back fifty years on my role as a tender and naive crew member in *Nautilus,* I realize that I was not alone in having those same emotions so well expressed by Norman Vaughan. I'm now sure that, to a man, anyone who has ever been blessed with such an experience would, no doubt, feel those very same thoughts.

John "JC" Yuill, '57 – '60

PANOPO

They were a special bunch, the ones called "PANOPO,"
from the Pacific to Atlantic, under Arctic ice they go.

It was in "fifty-eight," volunteers for submarine all,
'twas a magnificent feat, the Naval historians recall.

Commissioned in 1954 – *Nautilus* was Rickover's dream,
same day Mamie Eisenhower broke champagne on her beam.

First Skipper Wilkinson and his cocky Plank Owner crew,
established many records as most submarine sailors do.

Our first nuclear submarine crew on *Nautilus* SSN-571,
never even once uttered the words, *"It can't be done."*

While submergence and speed records crumbled and fell,
the sturdy *Nautilus* and famous crew performed so well.

Unencumbered by human personal thoughts of glory,
they became "seaworthy pioneers" in the nuclear story.

Although historically known for the famous polar trip,
Nautilus is now Connecticut's "authorized" state ship.

Tommy Robinson

In two thousand and four, fifty years after it all began;
she stands as a National Naval Monument honored by man.

Americans should be proud of *Nautilus* and her crews;
be forever overwhelmed at what submariners go through.

They are out there today, deep down, out of sight,
standing on alert, itching and ready for a fight.

Pioneered by *Nautilus* and crew fifty years ago,
salute the submarine force. My, what a debt we owe!

Tom Nix - Friend of Jack "Mother" Baird

Submarine History 101

This tale is required reading for A-gangers

The tail of how we A-gangers came into being is as old as J.P. Holland's first submarine. It has been rumored that David Bushnell's *Turtle* was manned by a revolutionary war outhouse builder who was adept at making chicken salad out of chicken shit. The continental Navy brass had this new fangled thing-a-ma-jig that was supposed to deliberately sink itself, travel under the water, attach a bomb to an enemy vessels hull, then bag ass out of the area and return to the surface.

No one really knew how to make it work - enter the outhouse builder who's name was Aux Lary Man. Now Aux Lary Man made the damn thing work but the weapons designer's at BuOrd didn't take into account that the Limey's covered their ship's hulls below the water line with copper, thus he experienced the first broach ever recorded by a submarine Diving Officer. Although he didn't blow up the Limey vessel he scared the living crap out of them, causing them to haul ass out of New York Harbor. When he returned to shore he grabbed a 1770s version of a crescent wrench, the weapon of choice for most A-gangers, and went looking for the Weaponeers who designed the system.

Aux Lary Man headed down to one of his favorite taverns, Ernies on the Thames, for a few pints and to see his true love Bea Tru Toyou, a former Wave Smithy. They married and in between sea duty and a couple of tours of recruiting duty they had a offspring Eng N. Man. The son grew up, joined the Navy, and was in the precom crews for *Alligator* and *Hunley*. Fortunately he never made any patrols and went on to serve on *Holland*. The Commanding Officer (CO) of *Holland* had served with Eng N. Man's father when he was a young Ensign and credited the elder Man for keeping his boats running. He wasn't great with names and always called the senior Man, "Auxillaryman." Rather than try and correct the CO the younger Man assumed the name Auxillaryman and to this day all descendents of this legendary Naval Hero have proudly kept the name Auxiliaryman. And to quote an old Naval saying, "This is a No Shitter."

Barry "Dan" Danforth, '60 – '61

A SAILOR'S LIFE

People on the outside think, a sailor's life is swell,
but I'll tell you something folk's, a sailor's life is hell.

I've stood endless hours just waiting for my mail,
and I've stood a million watches and been on every special detail.

I've scrubbed a million bulkheads and chipped ten miles of paint,
a meaner place this side of Hell, I'll swear to God there ain't.

I've shined a million miles of brass and scrubbed my dirty duds,
I've strung a million hammocks, and peeled a million spuds.

I've cruised a hundred thousand miles and never a decent port,
I've spent many nights in dirty jails for trying to be a sport.

And when the final taps do sound and I have done my share,
I'll take my final shore leave right up those golden stairs.

Tommy Robinson

T'is then St. Peter will greet me and loudly he will yell,
"Take your seat in Heaven Sailor. You've served your time in Hell."

Barney Wixom, 58-61

The Horse & Cow

I have only been to the Horse and Cow (H&C) once, having never seen the Pacific until many years after leaving the Navy, and that was only a year or two ago, but I wanted their patch for my SubVet's vest because of their fame as a submariner's bar.

My SubVet's group, from Yakama, Washington had toured USS *Nevada* at Submarine Base Bangor, Washington and afterwards everybody went to the H&C for refreshments. I had my 12 year old grandson, Trip, along, and we were carpooling, so had no choice but to go too. The *Nevada* Chief of the Boat's wife had said it was a family place during the daytime, so I thought there was a possibility I could take Trip inside.

The sign on the door said no one under 21, so he and I got the keys from our driver and went back to sit in the car in the parking lot. Pretty soon another *Nevada* wife came out, and said we should go in. I said I didn't want to get anyone in trouble, so she called someone on her cell phone, who said to bring him in, that it would be okay if Trip stayed in the outdoor garden.

Well, I'm still convinced that it would not have been okay with the liquor control people, but nonetheless, my 12 year old grandson had lunch at the H&C and I got their patch!

Gary Brown, '59 – '62

The 2006 Nautilus reunion's "Channel Fever Night" was held at the Bremerton, Washington Horse and Cow (H&C). It was sold in 2011 by owner, Mike Looby, who opened up a new H&C in Guam for the forward deployed fast attacks. Mike recently stated in the local newspaper that he intends to reopen a new H&C in down town Bremerton in late 2013. I'll be one of his first customers.

Tommy "Robby" Robinson, '63 – '67

ADMIRAL WILKINSON FIRST COMMANDER of INPO

I went to work in the nuclear business for Duke Power in 1972 after leaving *Nautilus*. Duke's CEO, Bill Lee, was the grandson of one of Duke's founders and the second most impressive nuclear professional I ever knew. Maybe it is a stretch to say that I "knew" Admiral Rickover, but I did do the interview and he called late one Sunday afternoon while I was Officer of the Deck at Pier 12 wanting to know why the Commanding Officer (CO) was not on board! The CO was on board 10 minutes later. Thank goodness for uniform races.

In 1979, Lee invested considerable time and talent at Three Mile Island (TMI) after the problem up there. He had a major goal to assure other NUCs, including Duke's units were not shut down in over reaction to TMI. He was successful in that goal, and he made a commitment to the Atomic Energy Commission (AEC/NRC) that the nuclear industry would stand-up a world class organization to provide improved standards, controls, audits and oversight. Bill Lee served as interim head of the Institute of Nuclear Power Operations (INPO) and launched a massive executive search for a Chief Executive Officer (CEO).

In 1980, I got a call in my office and the caller announced, *"Wayne, this is Bill Lee. Guess who we got to head up INPO? We got Denny Wilkinson!"* I told Bill I am not sure who that is. He said, *"Wayne, you were in the nuclear Navy, right?"* I told him I was, but the only Wilkinson I knew was the first CO of my boat and I later knew him as VADM Eugene P. Wilkinson, COMSUBLANT. He then revealed, of course, that he knew that. He was so excited about getting the Admiral that he wanted to share the news with someone who may have known him. And, he wanted to share the story that they had two executive searches going at the same time. Interestingly, a fellow named Wilkinson surfaced to the top of both lists. One had an Admiral on top named Eugene P. and the other had a civilian on top named Denny. Of course, the Admiral's nickname was "Dennis."

Rest Of The Story - A couple of years later I got a 0700 (7 AM) call from Bill Lee's Executive Secretary. She asked if I knew where Bill was. I told Phyllis in a very respectful manner that I did not know, but how could she not know. I will admit to having been a little concerned. She called me much later that day after the mystery was solved. When Bill Lee closed the deal with the Admiral and signed the INPO contract, he had one final request - a ride on a nuclear sub. Admiral Wilkinson said he could not promise results but would do all he could. Wilkinson had called Lee on a Sunday evening telling him if he could be in Key West at ZERO DARK THIRTY the next day, the debt would be paid. And, so it was.

A couple of years later Bill Lee told me about his ride on an *Ohio* class boat. I never saw him more excited than he was in telling that story. In fact, I told him he best dial it back a bit, as some of his information probably was not cleared to discuss!

Wayne Henry, ' 69- '72

For those of you, who like me, have spent many Christmas' at sea.

The Night Before Christmas – Submarine Style

'Twas the night before Christmas, and what no-one could see,
the men with the dolphins were under the sea.
Most of the crew was flat on their backs,
snoring and dreaming all snug in their racks.

Those men on watch were making their rounds,
some manning the planes or listening for sounds.
Back in Maneuvering or down in the room,
they all hoped the oncoming watch would appear soon.

I'd finished some PM's whose time was now due,
and hoped for some sleep, even an hour or two.
Against better judgement I took a short stroll,
and found myself wandering into Control.

The Nav had the Conn, the CWO was in place,
the COB had the Dive and a scowl on his face.
The helm and the planes were relaxed but aware,
the QM and ET were discussing a dare.

To comply with the orders the Nav told the Dive,
to bring the boat up with minimum rise.
The orders were given and soon they were there,
at periscope depth with a scope in the air.

Steely Eyed Killers of the Deep

The QM confirmed our position with care,
the broadcast was copied, and we brought in some air.
The Nav on the scope let out a small cry,
he shook his head twice and rubbed at his eyes.

He looked once again to find what it was,
that interrupted his sweep and caused him to pause.
Try as he might there was nothing to see,
so down went the scope and us into the deep.

I ask what it was that caused his dismay,
he sheepishly said, *"I'm embarrassed to say."*
It could have been Northern Lights or a cloud,
or a meteorite, he wondered aloud.

But to tell you the truth I guess I must say,
whatever it was it looked like a sleigh.
And though it passed quickly and never was clear,
I almost believe it was pulled by reindeer.

We laughed and teased him and I got up to go,
when our moment was broken by, *"Conn, Radio."*
They told us a message was just coming in,
we looked at the depth gauge and started to grin.

"Radio, Conn." "I feel safe to say,
your attempt at a joke is too long delayed.
If it had been sooner it might have been neat,
but I doubt we're receiving at four-hundred feet."

"Conn, Radio." "You can come down and see,
we're not playing games to any degree."
I headed aft with nothing better to do,
surprised by the fact it was still coming through.

It stopped and was sent to Control to be read,
the Nav read it slowly and scratched at his head.

Tommy Robinson

Then again he began, but this time aloud,
to those that now waited, a curious crowd.

*"To you Denizens of the Deep and men of the sea,
who risk your life daily so other stay free.
I rarely have seen you on this, my big night,
for far too often you are hidden from sight."*

*"But purely by luck I saw you tonight,
as your scope coaxed the plankton to glow in the night.
And lucky for me, I've finally won,
the chance to say thanks for all you have done."*

*"I know that you miss you families at home,
and sometimes you feel as if you're all alone.
But trust what I say and I'll do what's right,
I'll take something special to your families tonight."*

*"It might not be much, I know that is true,
to thank you for all the things that you do.
But I'll do what I can, while you do what's right,
Merry Christmas to all, and to all a goodnight."*

Author Unknown

Tommy "Robby" Robinson, '63 - '67

11 - Eulogies and Tributes

*"There is not one of the ocean's monsters
could trouble the last sleep of the crew
of the Nautilus, of those friends riveted to
each other in death as in life."*

Jules Verne, "20,000 Leagues under the Sea"

*"There is a port of no return, where ships
may ride at anchor for a little space.
And then, some starless night, the cable slips,
leaving an eddy at the mooring place — Gulls
veer no longer. Sailor, rest your oar.
No tangled wreckage will be washed ashore"*

Leslie Nelson Jennings, "Lost Harbor"

Steely Eyed Killers of the Deep

My Eulogy for "Doggie"

Quartermaster Senior Chief Lyle B. Rayl, USN, Ret.
April 18, 1922 – April 13, 1995

I was just a snot-nosed kid of 18 on April 8, 1957 when I reported on board *Nautilus* from Submarine School. I began my Navy life in port as part of the Seaman gang, chipping paint, handling lines, and generally trying to stay out of harms way. When underway, I stood planes and helm watches for a time but became fascinated with the duties of the Navigational Department. I was allowed to "strike" for the rate of Quartermaster and was placed under the ever watchful eye of one Lyle B. "Doggie" Rayl, then a Quartermaster 1st/class.

The ensuing years under "Doggie's" thumb shaped my life more than he or I would know at the time. I tried very hard, learned some things well, and failed miserably at others, signaling for one.

I'm sure I tried his patience to the breaking point at times but all he would usually do is shake his head as if to wipe a cobweb from his brain. If he thought that I wasn't moving fast enough he'd bellow, *"Yuill, get HOT!"* That usually did the trick.

"Doggie" was probably the most stoic person I've ever known, but he was not without a sense of humor. Many a time when I'd have the duty in port, he'd come out of the "Goat Locker" [Chief's Quarters] with his "dress canvas bent on," [uniform] turn to me as he was screwing on his hat and say, *"Yuill, I'm going on the beach. You're in CHARGE."* In charge of WHAT? I was the only one in the Navigation Department left on board. If he said it once, he said it a hundred times, and always I thought, with a twinkle in his eye.

I quickly began to realize just how fortunate I was during the transpolar cruise of 1958, to be his striker and be associated with the likes of him. Lieutenant "Shep" Jenks, Quartermaster 1st/class Ron Kloch, and Quartermaster 2nd/class Rick Williamson, made up the rest of the Navigational Department.

I was in awe of the man who had survived the attack on Pearl Harbor and had swum to safety on Ford Island from the devastated battleship USS *California*. He also signaled the famous message, *"Underway on Nuclear power"* by flashing light when *Nautilus* first got underway on January 17, 1955.

I was out of the Navy some twenty years or so when I finally realized just how much of a positive influence "Doggie" had made on my life. One of the great comforts in my life is that I wrote to him and told him how much I appreciated all that he had done for me.

Now "Doggie" has gone on "eternal patrol" and more than ever I feel privileged to have known him as a shipmate, a teacher, and a friend. If I close my eyes and listen real hard I can still hear him one last time saying, *"Yuill – I'm going on the beach. You're in charge!"* Rest your oar "Doggie" and God Speed – Your Striker,

John "JC" Yuill, '57 – '60

A Tribute to "Pappy"

Torpedoman Master Chief Leory Ingles, USN, Ret.
July 31, 1916 - April 12, 2001

Torpedoman Master Chief Leroy Ingles was a big, friendly man who called the sailors "my kids." They called him "Pappy" Ingles. As Chief of the Boat (COB) he assisted the Executive Officer and had the most authority of any enlisted man on board.

"He was father confessor to all the kids," said Vice Admiral Ken Carr, who served on USS *Nautilus* as a young Lieutenant and went on to command all the submarines in the Atlantic Fleet before becoming Chairman of the Nuclear Regulatory Commission.

In 1954, "Pappy" Ingles was personally selected as COB for USS *Nautilus* by Admiral Hyman Rickover, who led the program to develop submarines powered by nuclear reactors.

"Pappy" Ingles was on USS *Nautilus* on January 21, 1954, when first lady, Mamie Eisenhower, broke a bottle of Champagne across the bow, and USS *Nautilus* slid into the Thames River at Groton, Connecticut. Eight months later, USS *Nautilus* became the first nuclear-powered ship in the Navy. On January 17, 1955, "Pappy" Ingles was at his station when USS *Nautilus'* first Commanding Officer, Commander Eugene "Dennis" Wilkinson, ordered all lines cast off and flashed the historic message, *"Underway on Nuclear Power."*

USS *Nautilus'* shakedown cruise to Puerto Rice set many records, proclaiming the dawn of a revolutionary means of warfare in which missile carrying submarines could prowl in the ocean depths for months. That first voyage was 10 times as long as a submarine had previously travelled submerged without using a snorkel, and it was the first time a submerged submarine had reached such a high speed, 16 Knots. It was also the longest a submarine had remained underwater.

In 1934, when Leroy tried to enlist in the Navy at age 18 the recruiter turned him down, telling him he had a crooked back. He went down the hall to the Army recruiter who arranged an immediate physical. *"I've never seen a better specimen than you,"* the recruiter said. *"You're in the Army."* He served in the Army for three years then applied to the Navy again. By this time the Navy was looking for more sailors and accepted him, supposedly crooked back and all.

Leroy's first assignment was on the aircraft carrier USS *Saratoga*. His next duty was on USS *Sturgeon,* his first submarine. During World War II, he was assigned another submarine USS *Paddle* and made 13 war patrols.

After the war, he was assigned to a succession of submarines and was promoted to Chief Warrant Officer. After two years, he decided he would rather be an enlisted man and asked to be demoted to Chief Petty Officer.

In 1954 he applied to be COB on the first atomic submarine USS *Nautilus.* He was thrilled when he learned that Admiral Rickover would interview him. Rickover, a famously difficult interviewer, personally examined all officers, anybody who would be involved with the nuclear reactor and candidates for COB. Pappy's interview ended with the Admiral ordering him to get *"the Hell out"* of his office. A few days later, "Pappy's" phone rang. The caller was Rickover, who said, *"Let me be the first to congratulate you."*

"Pappy" served on USS *Nautilus* for about three years before being transferred to other submarines, including USS *Theodore Roosevelt*. In 1958, when the Navy created two new enlisted pay grades, Senior Chief and Master Chief, "Pappy" was promoted from Chief to Master Chief, making him the Navy's first Master Chief Torpedoman.

"Pappy" retired after serving his country for 30 years, 27 of those in the Navy.

Paraphrased from NYT obituary by Douglas Martin

Tommy Robinson

My Eulogy for "Dutch"

Torpedoman Chief Lynus J. Larch. USN, Ret.
January 27, 1922 – March 8, 2005

Just what is a Chief Of the Boat, or COB as he is known? Upon graduating from submarine school, I thought I knew what one was. He was by assignment, the most senior enlisted man aboard a submarine. As the senior Chief Petty Officer, it was his job to act as a liaison between the enlisted crew and the Wardroom, being especially the Executive Officer's right-hand man. We were taught in school that, among other things, he was responsible for the assignment of duties to the non-rated men, the overall observation of various ship departments, a booster of moral, and was the first line of discipline for minor offenses. He was the "go to guy" for just about anything having to do with the every day routine of the boat.

"Dutch" Larch was the COB when I reported to *Nautilus* on April 8, 1957. He assigned me a "'rack" in the lower starboard bunk room in the Torpedo Room, and placed me in the ever competent hands of A.J. "Gunner" Callahan, the head of the Deck gang, and he quietly oversaw my progress from landlubber to qualified submarine sailor.

As I slowly felt my way through the maze and ways of becoming a submariner, I began to see more clearly who "Dutch" Larch, as COB, really was. He was the perfect example of leadership as I viewed it. I just knew that he had already done all the things he asked of any of us. He asked, suggested, cajoled, and yes, sometimes ordered one to do things, but always from a point of leadership. For my part, he was mostly in my background, a presence felt rather than seen.

Among his many traits was his good sense of humor, which he greatly exercised. He could be heard at most any time of day or night from either the "Goat Locker" (Chief's Quarters), the Crews Mess, Topside, or any other compartment he might happen to be in, either dispensing or receiving some particle of wit. Often, it was at the expense of some crew member, usually a new and inexperienced one. As a "newbie," and later as an accepted member of the crew, I was sometimes the object of that humor and always felt it funny and well intentioned. Most importantly, he was never mean-spirited in his humor. I soon learned that it was one of his best tools to make a point of getting things done. When "Dutch" was afoot, could laughter be far behind?

As COB, he exuded confidence and inspired it in others. He aspired to excellence in all his undertakings and transferred that zeal to those around him. He was a guiding influence for us new sailors and a trusted source of experience for the old hands. He was like one of those western stage coach driver of old who instinctively knew when to urge the "team" on and when to "rein them in." He could "read" people well and was the personification of good leadership. He was a big and lasting influence throughout my life, both on *Nautilus* and later as a civilian.

But he was much, much more. He was a loving husband and father who provided for his family in every way. He was a generous and kind hearted man. He was a good friend to those who were fortunate to be considered so. He was a great shipmate and set a fine example to all and for me personally, was my Chief of the Boat. I will forever miss and never forget him. Rest you oar "Dutch" and God speed.

John "JC" Yuill, '57 – '60

My Eulogy for "Mister Nautilus"

Fire Control Technician Senior Chief John J. Krawczyk, USN, Ret.
August 16, 1923 – October 17, 2006

"Just one more!" Those words ring in my memory every time someone takes my photograph. They were probably spoken by John J. Krawczyk, about a million times over the years while he was attempting to photograph just one person or one hundred. It was always a tradition and a great source of amusement among his "subjects," and most likely an endless aggravation to John, to heckle and encourage him during one of his many prolonged "sittings." Being the eternal perfectionist and professional, he was never satisfied with any photo he ever took. The next one would always be better, and it usually was.

The routine would always begin at some *Nautilus* gathering, be it a Christmas party at Paula's in Groton, a group shot in the crews mess, topside, or any one of the numerous reunions over the years. John would pass the word that he was about to take "the" photograph, then carefully set up his equipment while the gathering crowd assembled. Invariably, the set-up would take more than three minutes, a lifetime in the mindset of the crew, whose attention span equaled that of a two year old, who would then begin to good-naturedly rib and generally harass poor John to the point of distraction. John never batted an eye, but like Santa Claus in "The Night Before Christmas," "He went straight to his work." He could not and would not be hurried. The set-up had to be just right or he wasn't going to "shoot." Of course, the longer he took the more vocal the crowd got. By the time he was ready, he had a better chance of "shooting" that proverbial bunch of two year old kids than the assemblage of supposed human adults that were his subjects. It was like "herding cats" to watch him order and cajole folks into the perfect position. Finally and at last, he would snap the shutter, only to utter those famous three words, *"Just one more!"* Thus began a series of "just one more" photos' that sometimes counted up to ten or more.

To be fair, I'm not sure who enjoyed the routine more, those being photographed or the photographer. John always endured the heckling and ribbing with the utmost patience and good humor. That was John in a nutshell, good-natured and patient. It was a comic routine worthy of Saturday Night Live, and all who ever underwent the ordeal loved it.

John wasn't just loved for his outstanding photographic skills. He was so much a part of *Nautilus* that one would be hard pressed to separate the two. Consequently, he was known as "Mr. Nautilus." He was excellent in his rate as a Fire Control Technician and while underway, standing my Quartermaster watches in the attack Center, I recall the many hours he would spend at the Mark 101 Fire Control Console, hovering over it like it was a new-born baby, tweaking "this" or fussing with "that"' until, like his photography, it was as near to being perfect as humanly possible.

He was very seldom seen without one or two Hasselblads around his neck, ready for the next interesting "shot." John probably documented *Nautilus* in photographs more than any other ship in history, taking literally thousands of pictures over his and the boats career. He was always affable, and cheerful, and the consummate gentleman – the perfect shipmate whether ashore or at sea.

His kind is few and far between and those of us who knew him personally will forever remember him as a wonderful man and treasure that friendship. Here's to you John, "Just one more."

John "JC"Yuill, '57 - '60

Steely Eyed Killers of the Deep

My Eulogy for the Skipper

Commander William R. Anderson, USN, Ret.
July 17, 1921 – February 25, 2007

"For the United States and the United States Navy, the North Pole." Those words were spoken by Commander Anderson, Skipper of the nuclear submarine *Nautilus* (SSN-571), upon passing under the North Pole on August 3, 1958 at 11:15 PM, EDT. Electrifying words indeed, spoken by a quiet man who had guided *Nautilus* for the past two years on exploratory voyages under the Arctic icecap, culminating in this, the third and first successful attempt to gain the North Pole by ship. It was, perhaps, the pinnacle of his Naval career, but one would never know it by his relaxed and smiling demeanor as he joined his crew in the Crews Mess for a celebration.

Anderson was born in Bakerville, Tennessee, graduated high school from Columbia Military Academy, and entered the United States Naval Academy in 1939. During his time at the academy, he nurtured his interest in submarines and upon graduation in 1942, was assigned to submarine duty. He survived eleven war patrols in three different boats, *Tarpon* SS-175, *Narwhal* SS-167, and *Trutta* SS-421. Those war time experiences, plus later duty in *Sarda* SS-488, *Tang* SS-563, and in his first command, *Wahoo SS-565*, no doubt reinforced his ability to resolve any situation quickly and decisively.

There was not a soul in *Nautilus* who did not look up to him and respect the Skipper for his leadership abilities. For me, a very young sailor, he was even more, a father figure. While underway and standing Quartermaster watches in the Attack Center, I had the great good fortune to observe the Skipper "close up and personal," as the sports commentators like to say. He was, above all, always courteous, respectful, soft spoken, and decisive in his command style. One never doubted that he was not only in charge, but knew exactly what he was doing. He gathered "flies with honey rather than vinegar." If he ever had any doubts or anxious moments about leading one hundred-plus men under the Arctic ice, they were never evident to those around him. I would have followed him anywhere.

The Skipper was one of the most genuinely humble men I've ever known. To him, it seemed as if *Nautilus* should received any honors or acknowledgments of exemplary operations, it was due solely to the actions of the crew. While the ships crew, both wardroom and enlisted, do act as a team, I don't think it ever dawned on him that in our eyes, it was, perhaps, the other way around, that it was he who enabled us to perform well through his actions and leadership.

Though serving as the Captain of *Nautilus* may have been his ultimate Navy achievement, his accomplishments and service to our country did not end there. After leaving the Navy, he was elected to the United States Congress as a Representative from his home state of Tennessee. Afterward, he owned and operated a computer company. He also authored two books, "Nautilus 90 North" and "The Ice Diaries." Both tell the story of *Nautilus*' voyages under the ice.

He was a caring husband, a loving father, and will surely leave his imprint on his entire family, a legacy anyone would envy.

So, as he has received his final orders and shipped out on eternal patrol, he will not be forgotten, but rather remembered by all who knew him as a man we would like to emulate.

John "JC" Yuill, '57 – '60

My Eulogy for Ron

Quartermaster Senior Chief Ronald L. Kloch, USN, Ret.
March 24, 1930 - January 29, 2008

Ron was one of those guys you just can't forget. I've been fortunate in that I am able to remember almost all of my shipmates I served with in *Nautilus*. I suppose it's only natural that I'd remember the ones with which I was more closely associated. Such is the case with Ron. I got to know him while I was a very young "snot-nosed kid," chipping paint Topside in port, and standing helm and planes watches underway. I certainly was aware of his presence while I was lollygagging about in the Crew's Mess or in the Attack Center when I was off watch. He was one of the boat's "characters."

After the 1957 trip under the ice I decided I would like to "strike" (apprentice) for the rate of Quartermaster, so I made my wishes known to "Dutch" Larch, the Chief of the Boat. He sent me to "Doggie" Rayl, then a Quartermaster 1st/class, who headed the Navigation gang. He looked me up and down and handed me over to Ron Kloch, also a Quartermaster 1st/class, to make a Quartermaster of me. I now know what a challenge that was. I was an unsure and timid lad, partly because I was so much in awe of the shipmates around me, and also, amazed that at such a young and tender age, I was actually serving in and driving around the world's first nuclear submarine. Ron could see that right enough, but he also recognized some potential in me, for he was relentless in his duties to "shape-me-up" in the ways of Navigation.

His nimble mind never ceased to amaze me. He could do these incredible math problems in his head faster than I could get the numbers out to him. When he was on watch, he would lean over the chart desk, head cocked to one side with an ever present cigarette in the corner of his mouth with a steady wafting curl of smoke up into his eyes. He would spin the Hooey, a special protractor with a long arm projecting from it, around like a Samurai sword, laying out our position across the chart. He had this great ability to look ahead and anticipate things shown on the chart that I certainly couldn't see. He would often, if not always, be a step ahead of the Navigator in anticipating the next course or bell (speed) change. That is the mark of any good and skilled Quartermaster. Ron could take bearings at #1 periscope faster than I could write them down.

He was relentless in overseeing my duties such as making corrections to the charts from Notice to Mariners or Coast and Geodetic publications. That was probably one of the most boring and tedious jobs I've ever had. However, he instilled in me the importance of having those charts as correct as possible, a lesson driven home during all our subsequent trips, culminating in the trip under the ice in 1958.

I had four great influences during my time as a Quartermaster striker in *Nautilus:* Lieutenant "Shep" Jenks, the Navigator; "Doggie" Rayl, soon to be Chief Rayl; Quartermaster 1st/class Ron Kloch; and Quartermaster 2nd/class Rick Williamson. The day-to-day teaching efforts fell to Ron and Rick and I must have progressed to their satisfaction because before long, I was standing routine underway Quartermaster watches on my own.

In some areas I was not always a fast study. In the "black art" of signaling, one of the duties of a submarine Quartermaster, I was a miserable and utter failure. Ron had, as part of his surface Navy training, become a skilled Signalman, and as such, did everything he could to teach me Morse Code used for the flashing signal light, but to no avail. He saved my bacon many-a-night in New London when having the duty, required me to respond to the nightly signal drill [flashing light] from the submarine tender, USS *Fulton* (AS-11). Ron would delay his liberty just long enough to dash up the Bridge and answer the flashing light drill message from the *Fulton,* thus probably saving me, "Doggy," or perhaps, even the Skipper, a nasty note from the tender concerning *Nautilus'* lack of participation. I will be forever in his debt for that help.

Such events never seemed to faze Ron. He always seemed happy and in a good mood. Indeed, his favorite saying was, "Life is good." He not only tolerated me, but made me feel a vital and contributing member of *Nautilus,* always striving to show me something new in the ways of navigation. He made me want to be a good and responsible shipmate, and I earnestly strove not to let him and the department down.

Of course, he was not above making serious sport of me during my many barfing bouts into my trusty #10 can while seasick on the surface. The most memorable time was upon leaving New York City after our historic trip under the North Pole, when I miscalculated our diving time and took the 8 to 12 watch, relieving Ron, only to learn that we would not be diving till after midnight when my watch would end. I had not taken my Dramamine, and because of a tropical storm blowing off the east coast, knew I was in for a very rough time of it. Sure enough, it wasn't long before the color drained from my face; tan to grey to green, thus becoming totally useless at the chart table. Poor Ron had to assume my watch at the chart desk after standing four hours of his own.

Memories do grow fonder with time; at least mine do, and as I recall those long ago days, I choose to remember all those good things that happened to me and the shipmates that made them. Foremost among them would be Ron Kloch. I can see him now, delighting, and or groaning, at my attempts to grasp the many facets of his teaching. He never gave up on me. He was a true friend and shipmate and I shall be forever grateful to him. I know I'm a better person today for having been his "striker."

John "JC" Yuill, '57 – '60

A Tribute for Ray

*Machinist's Mate Master Chief Raymond H. Sanborn, USN, Ret.
January 25, 1937 - May 9, 2010*

I never called him "Chimp." I called him Ray. He was a salty shipmate who helped me qualify. He signed me off on the Control Room, including the Radio Room, Electronic Countermeasures Bay, and the Periscope Center, Trim and Drain Systems, and the High Pressure Air System. His signature was simply "Sanborn" and he always signed in red ink. I last saw him in 2004 and he was not in good health.

Several years ago I attended a Memorial Day event at Submarine Memorial West in Seal Beach, California where I met Rear Admiral Jeffrey Metzel. He was the only other *Nautilus* crew member there. I did not serve under him and we had never met before. We talked for almost an hour about shipmates we knew. I mentioned that Ray had recently passed away. His reply: *"'Chimp' was the best damn Auxiliaryman in the entire U.S. Navy."*

I met another Admiral about seven years ago when I was in Reagan International Airport awaiting a connecting flight. I was wearing a blue blazer with miniature silver dolphins on my lapel. Inside the terminal, I sat down across from a man wearing a blue blazer with gold dolphins on his lapel. He was Vice Admiral Patrick Hannifin, who was the technical adviser for the movie U-571. We moved to the bar and spent almost an hour talking about cabbages, kings and submarines. Jamie Deuel had been his Executive Officer on *Lafayette,* I believe. Here I, who left the Navy as an Seaman, was drinking expensive single malt scotch on the dime of a three star. Only in the U.S. Bubblehead Navy can that occur.

David Ross, '59 – '61

My Eulogy for "Mother"

Commissaryman 1st/class Jack L. Baird, USN, Ret.
December 26, 1925 – July 13, 2010

"Mother" Baird, that's what we Mess Cooks called him. Rather than the super smothering, cheek-pinching type of mother, he was more like a mother hen, ever watching over his brood, clucking and pecking at us to keep us in line. Let me say right away that mess cooking, especially underway, was the hardest job I've ever done at any time, anywhere in my entire life. It was back breaking work, up before dawn to long after dusk. We Mess Cooks were spud pealing, salad making, dish washing, deck swabbing, coffee making, meal serving, bus boy, slaves.

Jack was head of the commissary in *Nautilus* and as such had a lot of responsibilities; keeping track of food inventory, over-seeing the other

Cooks, keeping a "weather eye" on us Mess Cooks. When at sea during the mid-watch he baked the most delicious breads and pastries one could ever put in one's mouth.

He appeared rather gruff and short of patience when I first came on board *Nautilus* in April 1957 and I saw him in action in the galley. To be absolutely truthful, knowing that I would soon be mess cooking for him filled me with some amount of dread and foreboding. However, I quickly learned that he only demanded the attention and respect that his meals deserved when feeding some of the finest submarine sailors ever to sail under the sea, especially in such a fine boat as *Nautilus*, "The First and Finest." I soon learned to anticipate the needs of the cooks and always tried to be a step ahead of their needs if I could. This proved to be the key to his approval, not that he ever said anything, but sometimes, it's what's not said that has more meaning than praise. I got the message.

Jack had been a submariner for some time before coming to *Nautilus*, and as such, was very much a prime example of what a submariner should be. I soon observed that he indeed had a great sense of humor exhibited by a big grin and hearty laugh. He didn't seem so scary to me then.

Over these many years, I ran into Jack at several *Nautilus* reunions and he always greeted me with a hardy, *"Hello Yuill, still got your little MG car?"* Of course the man was the sum of many parts outside of the Navy, many of which I never got to see. He was a husband, father, and brother. I'm sorry I never had the chance to eat at his Nautilus Restaurant in Niantic, but I still have the July 1989 issue of "Yankee Magazine" with an article about his cooking on the Mobile Oil tugs. He also held a distinction that he and only nine other men could ever claim. He was both a Plank Owner in *Nautilus* and a PANOPO, having been one of the 116 men to first sail under the North Pole on August 3, 1958. He was undoubtedly many things to many people, but to me he'll always just be "Mother" Baird. Sailor, rest your oar.

John "JC" Yuill, '57 - '60

Of the many Eternal Patrol notifications that I have received, this one hits the hardest. As an 18 year old Seaman Apprentice, I mess cooked for Jack Baird on *Nautilus* back in 1955. He was great to me and to all on board *Nautilus*. What a wonderful person. Jack had a reputation for being tough, he was sometimes called "Black Jack" Baird, but the truth is, he had a heart as big as life. He was truly a compassionate and caring person under that gruff exterior. I had the extreme pleasure of being shipmates with Jack through my six years on *Nautilus*.

Jack Baird, along with "Doggie" Rayl and George Fields were the three seasoned sailors on *Nautilus* who truly guided and mentored me through my early years on *Nautilus*. Great guys, great sailors and terrific individuals, they will all be missed. I know that if we had the ability to look into heaven today, we would see "Doggie" and George welcoming Jack on board for their forever cruise on Eternal Patrol. They just don't make sailors like those any more. God bless them all. I miss them.

William "Bill" Gaines, '55 – '61

A Tribute to Captain Zech
Vice Admiral Lando W. Zech, Jr., USN, Ret.
July 29, 1923 – May 16, 2011

I reported aboard *Nautilus* in September 1960 and left in June 1962. All but a few months of that time Lando Zech was my Captain. Captain Zech went out of his way to help me set the course of my life to come.

Nautilus was my first duty and I came aboard as a Fireman and left as a Electrician's Mate 2nd/class. Toward the end of my tour I did my best to find a way to become an officer. I did not have a degree and the chance of that happening was slim. Yeoman Mullins discovered that the Navy was looking for future pilots in the enlisted ranks, as was done in WW-II. Unfortunately *Nautilus* was scheduled to be at sea on the only day I could take the Navy-wide exam. I asked the Executive Officer for help and Captain Zech called me up to the Wardroom. He asked me why I wanted to be a pilot rather than stay in submarines. I said that I wanted a commission and did not have a degree and the pilot program would lead to a commission when I received my wings.

Some time past and I heard nothing of my request. We left New London for a short cruise the day before the test date and I resigned myself to the task of trying to find another avenue to move my career forward. The next day, while at sea, I was called to the Wardroom. Captain Zech introduced me to a Commander who was sitting next to him. He explained that the Commander was the Commanding Officer (CO) of the testing facility at Floyd Bennett and had brought a package for me. Captain Zech tossed the package to Lieutenant Don Shelton, my Division Officer, and said, *"Set Hauck up in my stateroom and get this done."* It was the Navy-wide exam!

Captain Zech had called the CO of the testing facility and asked if he would like to go for a ride on the "World's most famous ship?" The Commander, of course, was thrilled and accepted. Captain Zech asked him to bring along one of the exam packages.

I left *Nautilus* in June 1962, received my commission and wings in March 1964 and flew the F-8 Crusader, a single-seat fighter. I left the Navy as a Lieutenant in late 1967 and became a commercial airline pilot. I flew as a Captain for National Airlines, Pan Am, and retired from Delta Airlines. I married the daughter of an Eastern Airlines Captain and we have five wonderful kids and seven grandchildren. I never would have had the rewarding career I have enjoyed nor met the wonderful woman that I share my life with if Captain Zech had not gone out of his way for one of his crew members.

I'm sure he touched many other lives and made them better for it. I simply wish to let those that loved him know of one more. May God bless all those he loved and loved him, with peace and gratitude.

Sigrid "Rab" Hauck, '60 - '62

A Tribute to Don Hall

Rear Admiral Donald P. Hall, USN, Ret.
December 6, 1927 – January 25, 2011

I had the pleasure of serving with Don Hall on *Nautilus* and again on SubLant Staff where he was Chief of Staff. Don, along with Admiral R.L.J. Long, were the first to congratulate me on my selection to take command of USS *Gudgeon* (SS-567). I always suspected that Don had an input into my selection for that command. We had a very positive professional relationship both on *Nautilus* and at SubLant where I was serving as force scheduling officer.

Good guy, a great naval officer, but tough. He took professionalism seriously, and if you worked for him, you had better take it seriously also. I liked Don very much.

William "Bill" Gaines, '55 – '61

A Tribute to the "Bull Nuke"

Engineman Master Chief J.C. Kerr, USN, Ret.
April 25, 1921 – May 23, 2012

J.C. was well known as the "Bull Nuke" and he was a Plank Owner on *Nautilus*. He did not have a first or middle name, just initials. That is how he is listed on the commissioning list, "J" "C" Kerr. He left *Nautilus* on December 14, 1955. He was in the very first Westinghouse class with three officers and five other enlisted of the commissioning crew.

Alfred "Al" Charette, '57 – '61

J.C. Kerr was legendary in *Nautilus'* commissioning crew. I clearly remember his calm demeanor, rare common sense, exceptional ability to fix almost any mechanical casualty, ready smile and crew-cut hair. I had not completed any nuclear power training when I reported aboard as a Lieutenant, Junior Grade, and Chief Kerr patiently helped me understand equipment and trace systems in the Engineering spaces that were part of qualifying in the ship. His leadership was recognized by all aboard. They truly broke the mold when he came along.

David "Dave" Boyd, '54 – '58

My Eulogy for "Jack"

Lieutenant Commander John B. Kurrus, USN, Ret.
May 8, 1931 – December 11, 2012

A smile, a BIG smile. That's how I think of, and will always remember "Jack." He was older than me by seven years, but always treated me with friendly attention while showing me various systems during my qualification in *Nautilus*. He also had this big laugh to go along with his smile. He was one of the most pleasant crew mates I remember. He was never out of sorts or short with anyone. He was helpful to a fault to all who knew him, which gathered to him, many longtime friends both in the Navy and out.

Among his many contributions to the "Big N" during his time aboard was during August 1957 when, after an aborted attempt to gain the North Pole from the Atlantic, the boat attempted a hovering surface in a polynya, a clearing in the ice. However, the periscopes struck ice instead, bending them back like straws and crushing the top of the sail. After finding a safe and open polynya, the boat surfaced and attempts to straighten number #1 scope was made. It was straightened but not without cracking the barrel of the scope.

"Jack" and Dick Bearden who were both qualified stainless steel welders were summoned to attempt repairs. Welding stainless steel using the Heli-Arc method under any circumstance is tricky but especially so in a cold windy environment. After erecting a tent to shield the work area from the wind they set about to accomplish the repair. It was tedious work under those conditions and each weld pass had to be dye checked for leaks. The welds repeatedly failed which required grinding them down and applying another pass. This went on for many hours until finally, the crack was sealed and the scope refilled with nitrogen so it could be used.

He and Dick were given commendations for this difficult work under terrible conditions. I was a Lookout watch during many of those hours and can attest to the diligence they both put in to that repair. He and Dick, along with the many others that worked on that repair made a huge impression on me, a young, green sailor.

He served with distinction through his navy career of 21 years, serving in four diesel submarines, *Cod* (SS-224), *Croaker* (SS-246), *Tench* (SS-417), and *Sea Robin* (SS-407), as well as two nuclear subs, *Nautilus* (SSN-571) and *George Washington* (SSBN-598). He also served on two submarine tenders, *Proteus* (AS-19) and *Fulton* (AS-11).

After his military service, he was employed for five years at United Nuclear as a quality control manager. He then moved to the Merchant Marine, training for his license as Chief Engineer, and along with several former *Nautilus* sailors spent another 16 years at sea in C.F. Industries bulk carrier, M/V *Jamie A. Baxter*.

All these years since, at our many reunions, he always greeted me with that same big smile and gracious manner. He and I have remained friends, conversing often over the phone, and finally, one last time at the 2012 *Nautilus* reunion, where he though in failing health, appeared one last time. Though it was difficult for him to talk, he managed that signature smile for all his shipmates who were, to a man, happy to see him.

Now he's gone on eternal patrol, but anyone who knew him, afloat or ashore, will always remember him, his smile, and his gentle ways. Steam on, "Jack," steam on.

John "JC" Yuill, '57 – '60

A Tribute to "Big Al"

Commander Alfred A. Charette, Jr., USN, Ret.
August 19, 1932 – May 31, 2013

Big Al – The Seaman's Pal
Sleep well my friend and shipmate.

When a shipmate passes on?
When a smiling face is gone?
Someone who was always there,
through thick and thin.
Who laughed at you when you fell,
while he was pulling you to your feet.
The one that gave you
a rough time on your quals.
When you got your dolphins,
he slapped you on the back,
and said, *"I'm buying next time at Bells."*
The guy that stayed behind to help,
then loaned you his last clean jumper,
so you could hit the beach together.
The mate that you staggered back with,
the one who always guarded your back.
On board he relieved you early for some much needed rest,
and brought you coffee just the way you liked.
When passing through your compartment,
he sometimes called you ugly and stupid,
and laughed at your stupid mistakes.
Then sat and listened while you told him your problems,
and helped you through the rough spots.
If he stayed in while you were out,
he checked on your family to see if they were okay,
and went and got a new battery for your car.

Tommy Robinson

The one that stood his ground with you,
when the smoke got thick, or the water got deep.
He is still a shipmate, after all these years.
What do you say?
The same thing he would say.
Standing on the shore at night, looking out on a moonlit sea.
"Rest your oar, Mate! For we will sail together again one day."

Christopher "Chris" Pauli, '59 – '62

My Eulogy for "Al"

Commander Alfred A. Charette, Jr., USN, Ret.
August 19, 1932 - May 31, 2013

I first knew Al when he and I came aboard *Nautilus* in 1957. I was a lowly Seaman and he was a Sonarman 2nd/class. He quickly advanced to Sonarman 1st/class and later Chief. He was one of many shipmates I served with that really took an interest in me. He was always helpful in my quest to become qualified in submarines. After striking for Quartermaster, I shared my watch space in the Attack Center near the Sonar shack. During quiet times while steaming submerged, I would spend time in his shack listening to all manner of clicking, clacking, and squeaking of various sea life while we "bored holes" in the ocean.

I most enjoyed those times because he was so knowledgeable and was eager to share anything of interest regarding Sonar and its uses. We shared many adventures together in the Attack Center while on watch and many good laughs off watch as well. Al seemed to be always happy and up-beat and never failed to answer a question or just share a chat in the Crews Mess. Al delighted in the use of puns in his wide ranging sense of humor. I suppose he is best remembered for a now famous recitation he performed at every *Nautilus* reunion about a Swedish school kid named, Archibald Assholeson. Al spelled his name phonically; 'A' is for, etc. He never failed to get a laugh, time after time.

After I left the boat in September, 1960, I only touched base with him during the reunions of the Nautilus Alumni Association. It was during those times that I really got to know his lovely wife, Marilyn and meet their children. I was especially honored to attend Al and Marilyn's 50th wedding anniversary.

Over the years he and others still located in the New London/Groton areas, were largely responsible for the many reunions held there. I was privileged to share on a few of those committees and I got a taste of some the responsibilities and effort he put into planning those events. He was the "spark plug" in generating those grand times.

He became *Nautilus*' historian and spent countless hours at the Submarine Museum near the front gate to the Submarine Base in Groton. It seemed that every time someone needed to know something regarding *Nautilus*, they were steered toward Al who never failed to give them the straight dope in his interesting and entertaining style. Consequently, he was interviewed many times by numerous organizations on video and for printed articles about *Nautilus* and her exploits during his tenure. He was one of the primary spokespersons for that great historic ship and the submarine Navy. He was my editor, fact, and spell-checker for my many *Nautilus* memoirs, and for that I will be eternally grateful.

He completed his Naval career as a Commander having served in various positions of leadership and command. The one word that describes him best to my mind is, "Leader."

He had that wonderful ability to lead people under his influence; a most admirable trait.

He will be sorely missed by not only his family, those who knew and served with him in the Navy, but also countless others in his community to which he contributed so much.

John "JC" Yuill, '57 – '60

A Tribute to Admiral Wilkinson

Vice Admiral Eugene "Dennis" P. Wilkinson, USN, Ret.
August 10, 1918 – July 11, 2013

The passing of Admiral Wilkinson is sad news for all who knew and served with him. He is a great loss to the country, the Navy and the submarine force. For those of us who served with Admiral Wilkinson on *Nautilus,* we had the pleasure of sailing with the Navy's finest. I am honored to have served with Admiral Wilkinson and have many fond memories of my years on *Nautilus* under his command and from the years following my time on *Nautilus*. I'm honored to have then Commander E.P. Wilkinson's signature on my enlisted submarine qualification card dated 3 January 1957. He also honored me with his presence at my change of command when I assumed command of USS *Gudgeon* (SS-576) in July 1975 and again at my change of command when I assumed command of Amphibious Squadron Three in 1986. Admiral Wilkinson never forgot those who had served with him. I'm sure that all of those who served with Admiral Wilkinson on *Nautilus* have their special memories. I certainly have mine.

I remember his Rum Soaked Crook cigars and his love for movies, which he would watch regardless of how bad they were or how many times he had seen them in the past. I was a movie operator and I remember sitting through movies when attendance was only the Admiral, the night Cook "Black Jack" Baird and me. I do remember at times, the Admiral would make Les Kelley sit through the movie with him. A "Bad Day at Black Rock" was one of his favorites.

I also remember the trip back from Key West when, because the only submarine statistic *Nautilus* didn't lead SUBLANT in was number of dives. We set forth to play porpoise and made continuous dives and surfaces throughout the trip north. There are so many great things I remember from that tour of duty on *Nautilus*.

Admiral Wilkinson's enjoyment in carrying out his duties as Commanding Officer (CO) of *Nautilus* and the obvious pleasure he received in leading a submarine crew, instilled in me, then a 19 year old [enlisted] sailor, and overwhelming desire to someday become a submarine CO. For all who served on *Nautilus* with the Admiral, I'm sure he left a lasting and positive impression. Of all the things I will remember from my association with Admiral Wilkinson, I will most remember his concern for his crew. He never forgot his crew.

William "Bill" Gaines, '55 - '61

12 - Nautilus Time Line

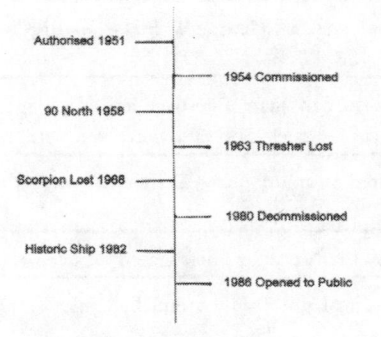

Authorised 1951
1954 Commissioned
90 North 1958
1963 Thresher Lost
Scorpion Lost 1968
1980 Decommissioned
Historic Ship 1982
1986 Opened to Public

This time line has been generated without the use of a deck log. The entries are from various sources, including newspaper articles, books, and the memories of crew members. It is not intended to be totally accurate but rather to be used as a bench mark reference for the sea stories.

07/01/1951	Congress authorized construction of the first atomic submarine.
12/12/1951	Navy Department announced she would be the 6th ship to be named *Nautilus*.
06/14/1952	Keel laid at Electric Boat, Groton, CT. President Harry S. Truman burns his initials "HST" into the keel.
12/24/1953	Commander Eugene "Dennis" P. Wilkinson selected as Prospective Commanding Officer (PCO).
01/21/1954	USS *Nautilus* (SSN-571) launched. First Lady Mamie D. Eisenhower was the sponsor.
07/01/1954	Commander Dennis Wilkinson assigned as Officer in Charge (OIC). Started sea and submarine pay.
09/30/1954	*Nautilus* commissioned. Commander Eugene "Dennis" P. Wilkinson assumed command as first CO. Voice call sign = Aggravate. Morse Code call sign = NWCL.

12/20/1954	First nuclear plant operation. Electronics Technician 1st/class Edward M. "Mike" Lovejoy, first qualified Reactor Operator (RO).
01/03/1955	First full power operation. Electronics Technician 1st Class Edward M. "Mike' Lovejoy was the RO.
01/17/1955	1100 EST first underway. *"Underway on Nuclear Power"* was transmitted by flashing light.
04/22/1955	Preliminary acceptance by the Navy.
00/00/1955	Torpedoman's Mate 1st/class George W. Fields was the first person to qualify in SSN's.
05/10/1955	Shakedown cruise to San Juan, Puerto Rico. High speed submerged run damaged deck. Several recordswere set.
00/00/1955	July – August visited Bermuda, Key West, and many other east coast ports.
05/11/1956	Final acceptance by the Navy for unrestricted service.
02/04/1957	Logged 60,000 nautical miles which equalled Jules Verne's 20,000 leagues.
04/08/1957	First reactor core re-fueling at Electric Boat
04/11/1957	Shakedown to Bermuda.
05/15/1957	Atlantic to Pacific via the Panama Canal. First west coast tour to show the boat and operate with units of the Pacific fleet.
06/00/1957	Commander William "Bill" R. Anderson helicopter's from Mare Island, CA to Nautilus, located about 40 miles at sea off San Francisco, CA, en route to Seattle, WA.
06/18/1957	Change of Command in Seattle, WA. Commander William "Bill" R. Anderson becomes the second Commanding Officer.
06/19/1957	Portland, OR visit.
06/24/1957	San Francisco, CA visit.
06/00/1957	Long Beach, CA visit.
06/29/1957	San Diego, CA visit.

Steely Eyed Killers of the Deep

07/14/1957	Pacific to Atlantic via the Panama Canal.
07/21/1957	Entered Electric Boat to be outfitted for Arctic operations.
08/19/1957	Underway for first Arctic probe, Atlantic.
09/04/1957	First submarine furthest North under the Atlantic ice cap – 87 deg N.
08/00/1957	Mediterranean run. Visited British and French ports.
10/28/1957	Returned to New London, CT for upkeep and coastal operations till spring.
04/25/1958	Departed New London, CT for the Pacific. Second west coast tour and "Operation Sunshine."
05/12/1958	San Diego, CA visit.
05/00/1958	Long Beach, CA visit.
05/17/1958	San Francisco, CA visit.
05/00/1958	Entered Naval Shipyard Mare Island, CA to replace burned Engineroom lagging, install a emergency breathing system (EBS), and attempt a condenser steam leak repair.
06/02/1958	Torpedoman's Mate 1st/class Theodore "Ski" Szarzynski died on board of a cerebral hemorrhage as *Nautilus* entered Puget Sound.
06/03/1957	At Everett, WA *Nautilus* purchased 140 Quarts of Barr's Leak (AKA Stop Leak) in local stores which fixed the condenser steam leak problem.
06/03/1958	Commander William "Bill" R. Anderson and Dr. Waldo Lyon conducted top secret air recon of the Bering Strait and the Cukchi Sea.
06/09/1958	Underway from Seattle, WA for first Arctic probe from the Pacific Ocean and the first attempt to execute top secret "Operation Sunshine."
06/19/1958	Turned back in the Chukchi Sea due to deep ice.
06/28/1958	Arrived Pearl Harbor, HI for visit.
07/23/1958	Underway from Pearl Harbor, HI for second Arctic probe from the Pacific Ocean and the second attempt to execute "Operation Sunshine."

07/29/1958	Transited the Bering Straight.
08/01/1958	Submerged in the Barrow Sea Valley.
08/03/1958	11:15PM EDST first to reach and pass under the North Pole submerged. The Commanding Officer announced *"For the U.S.A. and U.S. Navy - the North Pole."*
08/05/1958	Emerged from the ice pack and surfaced off Greenland and transmitted top secret message, *"NAUTILUS 90 NORTH."*
08/07/1958	Arrived at a rendezvous point with the helicopter off Iceland. Commander William "Bill" R. Anderson flew from Iceland to Washington, D.C. to meet with President Dwight D. Eisenhower.
08/12/1958	Arrived Portland, England for a visit.
08/27/1958	Arrived New York, NY and welcomed with a ticker tape parade.
05/28/1959	Entered Portsmouth Naval Shipyard for first complete overhaul and second core refueling.
06/22/1959	Change of Command. Commander Lando Zech, Jr., becomes third Commanding Officer.
08/15/1960	Overhaul complete. Refresher training. Experienced hurricane Donna.
10/24/1960	Mediterranean run. Visited Rota, Spain; Valletta, Malta; La Spezia, Italy.
04/20/1962	Change of Command. Commander Jeffrey "Jeff" C. Metzel, Jr., becomes fourth Commanding Officer.
00/00/1962	Participated in Cuban blockade.
04/10/1963	*Thresher* lost with three former Nautilus crew members.
08/00/1963	Mediterranean Run. Visited various ports.
10/00/1963	Returned to New London, CT.
10/12/1963	Change of Command. Commander Francis "Frank" C. Fogarty becomes fifth Commanding Officer.
11/22/1963	Hamilton, Bermuda visit. President John F. Kennedy assassinated. Crew recalled to boat and underway.

Steely Eyed Killers of the Deep

01/17/1964	Entered Portsmouth Naval Shipyard for second overhaul and Subsafe package installation - 27 months.
05/02/1966	Returned to New London, CT. Overhaul complete.
00/00/1966	Departed for Northern Run.
00/00/1966	Logged 300,000 nautical mile in the Spring.
11/10/1966	*Essex/Nautilus* collision at sea. Returned to Electric Boat for repairs to damaged sail.
02/15/1967	Returned to New London, CT. Repairs complete.
04/03/1967	Change of Command. Commander Norman "Earl" E. Griggs becomes sixth Commanding Officer.
08/15/1967	Entered Portsmouth Naval Shipyard for third overhaul and third core refueling.
05/23/1968	*Scorpion* lost with four former Nautilus crew members.
12/12/1968	Returned to New London, CT. Overhaul complete.
02/00/1969	Shakedown cruise to Roosevelt Roads, Puerto Rico visit. Machinist Mate 2nd/class Dennis N. Grant lost overboard.
01/31/1970	Change of Command. Commander David "Duke" S. Cockfield becomes seventh Commanding Officer.
10/00/1970	Antisubmarine Warfare exercise Squeezplay VI. Evaluated the new AN/SQS-26 sonar system.
06/24/1972	Change of Command. Commander Alex Anckonie, III becomes eight Commanding Officer.
08/15/1972	Entered Electric Boat for two year overhaul. MACS antenna array installed.
12/23/1974	Completed sea trials.
07/06/1975	Mediterranean run. La Spezia and Naples, Italy visits.
00/001975	Northern Run. Damaged periscope.
00/00/1975	Holy Lock, Scotland for periscope repair.
12/20/1975	New London, CT and home.
00/00/1976	Spring and a long series of West Indies cruises.
00/00/1976	Stern Plane jam casualty.

12/19/1976	Change of Command. Commander Richard "Dick" A. Ridell becomes ninth and decommissioning Commanding Officer.
04/00/1977	Mediterranean Run. Lison, Sousse, La Maddalena, Taranto and Naples visits.
09/00/1977	New London, CT and home.
03/00/1978	Bermuda visit.
12/03/1978	Jennifer Papineau Baptism
12/00/1978	Logged 500,000 nautical miles.
04/09/1979	Departed New London, CT for west coast on her final voyage.
00/00/1979	Guantanamo Bay and Cartagena visits.
00/00/1979	Atlantic to Pacific via the Panama Canal.
05/29/1979	Last day at sea on nuclear power. Arrived Mare Island Naval Shipyard.
03/03/1980	Decommissioning and reactor removed.
05/20/1982	Designated as a National Historical landmark by Secretary of Interior James Watt - Historic Ship (H.S. *Nautilus*).
05/23/1983	Designated as Connecticut's State Ship by Governor William A. O'Neill. Promoted by school teacher John Watts and his government studies class from Ellington High School, Ellington, CT.
00/00/1985	Departed Mare Island Navy Shipyard under tow. Officer in Charge, Commander John S. Almon.
00/00/1985	Pacific to Atlantic via the Panama Canal in tow.
07/06/1985	Homecoming. Arrived Groton, CT by tow.
04/20/1986	H.S. *Nautilus* opened to the public.